BIRNBAUM'S

Disneyland RESORT

THE OFFICIAL VACATION GUIDE

2020

Wendy Lefkon EDITORIAL DIRECTOR

Jill Safro EDITOR

Jennie Hess CONTRIBUTING EDITOR

H. Clark Wakabayashi DESIGNER

Alexandra Mayes Birnbaum CONSULTING EDITOR

Stephen Birnbaum FOUNDING EDITOR

DISNEP
EDITIONS

LOS ANGELES • NEW YORK

For Steve, who merely made all this possible.

ISBN 978-1-368-02754-0
FAC-038091-19214
First Edition, September 2019
10 9 8 7 6 5 4 3 2 1

Printed in the United States of America

Other 2020 Birnbaum's Official Disney Guides:
Walt Disney World
Walt Disney World For Kids

CONTENTS

To spotlight shops, attractions, shows, and restaurants making their debut, some listings are marked with the icon shown here. Look for it throughout the book. Here are a few highlights for 2020:

A WORD FROM THE EDITOR

Walt Disney, the man who pioneered the realm of family entertainment, was at once an artist, entrepreneur, and creative visionary. He was also a dad. And, like many of the folks who visit Disneyland each year, Walt treasured the time he spent with his kids. In fact, while his two daughters were growing up, Walt accompanied them to carnivals, zoos, and local amusement parks. It was something of a Saturday tradition for the Disney family. During these outings he'd often make the same observation: The youngsters were happily entertained, but the adults didn't have much to do. It didn't seem right that he'd be stuck sitting on a bench while the kids had all the fun. To his way of thinking, a park should appeal to the sense of wonder and exploration in guests of all ages. His bold vision became a reality on July 17, 1955, when Disneyland opened in Anaheim, California.

Now, more than six decades after welcoming its first visitors, Walt's original park is as beloved as ever—and it continues to grow. Disneyland Park has an exciting new adventure zone—Star Wars: Galaxy's Edge! This dynamic realm boasts two bona fide "E-Ticket" attractions. The first puts visitors at the controls of the *Millennium Falcon* spaceship, while the second finds intrepid travelers smack in the middle of a thrilling battle between the First Order and the Resistance. Hang on! Of course, Disneyland continues to delight guests of all ages with cherished classics such as It's a Small World, Pirates of the Caribbean, Peter Pan's Flight, the Haunted Mansion, and Fantasmic!—the park's nighttime extravaganza. Across the esplanade from Disneyland, Disney California Adventure is firing on all cylinders. Attractions such as Soarin' Around the World, Guardians of the Galaxy—Mission: BREAKOUT!, and Radiator Springs Racers helped put this place on the map, but they're just the tip of the iceberg. Guests are treated to an array of attractions and entertainment bearing that distinctive Disney Parks stamp. Among them are Mickey's PhilharMagic, Toy Story Midway Mania!, *Inside Out* Emotional Whirlwind, and Jessie's Critter Carousel.

When Steve Birnbaum launched this guide, he made it clear what was expected of anyone who worked on it. The book would be meticulously revised each year, leaving no attraction untested, no meal untasted, no hotel untried. First-hand experiences like these, accumulated over the years, make this book the most authoritative guide to the Disneyland Resort. Our expertise, however, was not achieved by being escorted through back doors of attractions. Instead, we've waited in lines with everyone else, always hoping to have a Disney experience like any other guest.

Of course, there's more to the Disneyland Resort than the theme parks. There's also a dining, shopping, and entertainment district known as Downtown Disney, and three Disney hotels. It all adds up to a total that is truly greater than the sum of its parts. And, though it has more than a half century of history under its belt, this is just the beginning—as per its founder's wishes: "Disneyland will never be completed. It will continue to grow as long as there is imagination left in the world."

TAKE OUR ADVICE

In creating this book, we have considered every possible aspect of your trip, from planning it to plotting day-by-day activities. We realize that even the most meticulous vacation planner needs detailed, accurate, and objective information to prepare a successful itinerary. To achieve that goal, we encourage the submission of factual information and insight from Disneyland staffers—but the decision to use such information is entirely at the discretion of the editor.

We have also packaged handy bits of advice in the form of "Hot Tips" throughout the book. These helpful hints come directly from the copious notes we have taken during our countless trips to the Disneyland Resort and the surrounding Anaheim area. We've also used our "Birnbaum's Best" stamp of approval wherever we deemed it appropriate, highlighting our favorite attractions and restaurants—the crowd-pleasers we feel stand head, shoulders, and ears above the rest.

You, the reader, benefit from the combination of our decades of experience and access to inside information from the Disneyland staff—that makes this guide unique. We like to think it's indispensable, but you be the judge of that 134 pages from now.

CREDIT WHERE CREDIT IS DUE

Enormous thanks to the teams of dedicated, detail-conscious Disneyland Resort Cast Members from Guest Communications, the Disney Resort Reservation Center, Food & Beverage, Merchandise, Resort Operations, Attractions Operations, Disney Vacation Club, Marketing, and Disney Parks Synergy for helping us ensure the factual accuracy of *Birnbaum's Official Guide to Disneyland 2020*.

Kudos to Michelle Olveira for her outstanding fact-checking, and to copy editor extraordinaire Diane Hodges. We'd also like to tip our hats to Jessica Ward, Jerry Gonzalez, Kathy Crummey, Jennifer Eastwood, Monica Vasquez, Marybeth Tregarthen, Kinden Sevorwell, Devon Munroe, Karen McClintock, Alyce Diamandis, Chris Ostrander, Valerie Lee, and Christina Fontana for their editorial support and production panache.

Of course, no list of acknowledgments would be complete without mentioning our founding editor, Steve Birnbaum, whose spirit, wisdom, and humor still infuse these pages, as well as Alexandra Mayes Birnbaum, who continues to be a guiding light—to say nothing of a careful reader of every word.

THE LAST WORD

Finally, it's important to remember that every worthwhile travel guide is a living enterprise; the book you hold in your hands is our best effort at explaining how to enjoy the Disneyland Resort at the moment, but its text is not etched in stone. Disneyland is always changing and growing, and in each annual edition we refine and expand our material to better serve your needs. Just before the grand opening of Disneyland, Walt Disney remarked that the main attraction was still missing—people. That's where you come in.

Have a wonderful time!

— Jill Safro, Editor

Don't Forget to Write!

No contribution is of greater value to us in preparing the next edition of this book than your comments on its usefulness and your own experiences at the Disneyland Resort. Drop us a postcard or send a note to the address on the right. Thank you!

Jill Safro
Birnbaum's Disneyland 2020
Disney Editions
125 West End Avenue, 3rd Floor
New York, NY 10023

GETTING READY TO GO

"It was all started by a mouse." —Walt Disney

*T*O ALL WHO COME TO THIS HAPPY PLACE: *WELCOME. DISNEYLAND IS YOUR LAND.* So said Walt Disney on July 17, 1955. Fast-forward 65 years, and the "happiest place on earth" is as welcoming as ever, hosting millions of visitors from around the globe year in and year out. The 500-acre Disneyland Resort has evolved a bit over time, but Walt Disney's original theme park, Disneyland, is still at its heart. Besides this magical kingdom, guests will discover Disney California Adventure theme park; the Downtown Disney District; a trio of on-property hotels: Disney's Grand Californian Hotel & Spa, Disney's Paradise Pier Hotel, and the Disneyland Hotel; and dozens of decidedly Disney dining and shopping destinations. Of course, you'll want to do and see it all, but where should you start? When should you go? And then there are the all-important questions of how to get there and where to stay. Maybe you want to extend your vacation—perhaps you'll include a visit to (or a stay at) the beach or one of the other nearby attractions.

That's a lot to think about. But don't worry: By the time you've read this chapter, you will have the information you need to make smart decisions. So read on, and remember—a little advance planning can go a very long way.

When to Go

When you weigh the best times to visit the Disneyland Resort, the most obvious possibilities often seem to be weekends, Christmas, Easter, and summer vacation—particularly if there are children in the family. But there are a few good reasons to avoid these periods—the major one being that almost everybody else wants to go then, too. (While the pedestrian traffic at Disney California Adventure {D.C.A.} is occasionally lighter than it is over at Disneyland Park, D.C.A. is a lot busier than it used to be.)

If you can only visit during one of these busy times and worry that the crowds might spoil your fun, there are some tactics for making optimum use of every minute and avoiding the longest of lines—notably, go to the park early to get a jump on the day (and on the crowds), use the free Fastpass system whenever possible, and remember that Disney keeps the parks open later during busy seasons. Note that "early entry" (aka "Extra Magic Hour" or "Magic Morning") is offered on select days to guests staying at Disneyland hotels, Walt Disney Travel Company guests, and day guests with a pre-purchased 3-day (or more) Park Hopper.

On the other hand, choosing to visit when the Disney parks are least crowded may mean that you miss some of the most entertaining special events—a treasured fireworks show or parade might not be listed on the entertainment schedule, and certain attractions may be closed for annual refurbishment.

A lovely time to visit Disneyland—when it's not too crowded but everything is still open—is the period after Thanksgiving until about a week before Christmas, when the Christmas parade takes place and carolers add festive music to the mix. Other good times to visit are the periods after summer—September through early October—and after New Year's Day.

When Not to Go: If crowds make you queasy, keep in mind that Saturday is traditionally the busiest day of the week year-round. In summer, Sunday, Monday, and Friday are the next busiest. If you decide to visit Disneyland Park during a weekend, opt for Sunday (it gets less busy as the day wears on). And remember that the week before Christmas through New Year's Day, Easter week, and the period from early July through Labor Day are packed.

CROWD PATTERNS

LEAST CROWDED

Second week in January to Presidents' week

Two weeks after Easter Sunday to Memorial Day week

End of Labor Day week to Columbus Day

End of Thanksgiving weekend to mid-December

AVERAGE CROWDS

Period just after Presidents' week until about two weeks before Easter Sunday

Sundays in spring, autumn, and winter, except holiday weekends

Memorial Day week to beginning of summer vacation

Week after Labor Day weekend

Columbus Day to day before Thanksgiving

MOST CROWDED

Any Saturday, year-round

Sundays throughout the summer and during holiday weekends

Presidents' week

Weeks before through weeks after Easter Sunday

Beginning of summer through Labor Day weekend

Thanksgiving weekend (Thursday through Sunday)

Week before Christmas through first week of January

Keeping Disney Hours

Operating hours tend to fluctuate based on the date and season. For updates, call 714-781-4636, visit *www.disneyland.com*, or use the (free) Disneyland Resort app. Details may change.

DISNEYLAND PARK: This park is typically open from about 10 A.M. to 8 P.M. Monday–Thursday, 9 A.M. to 10 P.M. on Friday and Sunday, and 8 A.M. to 11 P.M. on Saturday. Hours are often extended in the summer and during holiday seasons. Extra Magic Hour is offered on Tuesday, Thursday, and Saturday. This allows guests of Disneyland Resort hotels to enter the park one hour early. Those bearing multi-day park passes that include "Magic Mornings" (it is stated on the ticket itself) may enter the park one hour early on Tuesday, Thursday, and Saturday mornings. Details are subject to change.

DISNEY CALIFORNIA ADVENTURE: The theme park generally opens at 9 or 10 A.M. and closes at about 9 or 10 P.M. on weekdays, sometimes later on weekends and during the summer. Disneyland Resort hotel guests may enter the park one hour early on Extra Magic Hour days: Sunday, Monday, Wednesday, and Friday.

DOWNTOWN DISNEY: Many spots in Disneyland Resort's shopping, dining, and entertainment district open when the parks do, but some may open as early as 7 A.M. and most close at about 10 P.M. Sunday through Thursday (later on Friday and Saturday nights and during peak times).

TRANSPORTATION: The monorail begins making its 2.5-mile loop about the time Disneyland opens (including early-entry Magic Mornings) and runs until about 15 minutes before the park closes. Trams transporting guests between parking lots and the parks begin picking up guests about an hour before the first park opens, and continue transporting guests back to parking areas until about an hour or so after the last park closes. If you miss the last tram, ask a Cast Member about alternate transportation to the Mickey and Friends parking structure (usually in the form of a van).

DISNEYLAND WEATHER

If dry, sunny weather is your ideal, Anaheim may seem like a dream come true. Rainy days are few and far between and generally occur between the months of November and April, which is also the coolest time of year. During this season, Santa Ana winds sometimes produce short periods of dry, warm desert weather and sparkling-clear skies that unveil distant mountains usually hidden by smog. In summer, thin, low morning clouds make it prudent to plan expeditions to the beach for the afternoon, when the haze burns off and the mercury rises. Mornings and nights are generally cool. The average daytime year-round temperature is about 73 degrees.

	Temperature AVERAGE		Rainfall AVERAGE
	HIGH	LOW	(INCHES)
JANUARY	71	48	2.86
FEBRUARY	71	48	3.07
MARCH	73	51	1.90
APRIL	76	53	0.80
MAY	78	57	0.28
JUNE	81	61	0.10
JULY	87	65	0.03
AUGUST	89	65	0.01
SEPTEMBER	87	63	0.25
OCTOBER	82	58	0.72
NOVEMBER	76	52	1.38
DECEMBER	70	47	2.02

Holidays & Special Events

Disneyland Resort hosts special events all year long. For specifics, use the Disneyland mobile app, visit *www.disneyland.com*, or call 714-781-7290. Here are a few highlights to consider:

JANUARY–FEBRUARY

Three Kings Day—Día de los Reyes: Celebrate the 12th day of Christmas and the Latin American traditions associated with the Epiphany as part of Disneyland Resort's Festival of Holidays.

Lunar New Year: Disney California Adventure park welcomes the Lunar New Year with time-honored traditions and multi-cultural festivities. Guests may follow a young lantern's quest to reunite with his family and celebrate good fortune in Hurry Home—a special version of World of Color. Mulan may host a parade.

Valentine's Day: Sweethearts will swoon over the romantic backdrop that Disneyland Park provides on this love-struck holiday.

MARCH–MAY

Disney California Adventure Food and Wine Festival: Enjoy savory sips and nibbles at this popular annual event featuring culinary demonstrations, spirit seminars, appearances by well-known chefs, and more. Cheers!

Easter: The parks remain open late the week before and the week after Easter (this is a very busy time to visit). One of the parks hosts an *Egg-stravaganza*—a scavenger hunt for giant eggs—in the weeks leading up to the holiday. (Maps are offered for a fee.)

JUNE–AUGUST

All-American College Band: Disney's All-American College Band performs for nine weeks during summer (usually beginning in mid-June), Tuesday through Sunday. Performances take place throughout the park.

Fourth of July: This is one of the busiest days of the year—and one to avoid if you're easily overwhelmed by crowds. The more-patriotic-than-usual day features exceptionally festive fireworks at Disneyland Park.

EARLY SEPTEMBER–OCTOBER

Halloween Festivities: At Disneyland Park, Halloween Time lets guests celebrate in many not-so-scary ways. In addition to the fall color decor, the Disneyland Band and Dapper Dans celebrate with seasonal tunes. The Haunted Mansion attraction's holiday transformation gives this spot a *Tim Burton's The Nightmare Before Christmas* motif. Main Street, U.S.A., features hundreds of hand-carved jack-o'-lanterns. And Disney characters celebrate the holiday by donning their spookiest Halloween costumes. (For policies regarding costumes, visit *www.disneyland.com*.) Disney California Adventure park gets into the Halloween spirit with the new Oogie Boogie Bash—A Disney Halloween Party. Expect spooky touches such as a Halloween-themed World of Color, a "Villainous" dance party, and a stage show with the one and only Mickey Mouse.

NOVEMBER–DECEMBER

Thanksgiving Weekend: The four days of this holiday weekend are filled with musical entertainment and the early installments of Disneyland's A Christmas Fantasy Parade and It's a Small World Holiday, and the holiday transformations of Cars Land and Buena Vista Street, all of which kick off in mid-November. The parks usually observe extended hours.

Holiday Festivities: By early November, Disneyland's Main Street is festooned with greenery and poinsettias, while more than a million lights create a wonderland that glistens from the Town Square Christmas Tree to Sleeping Beauty's Winter Castle. On two festive evenings in December, a massive choir walks down Main Street in a Candlelight Ceremony. It features a live orchestra and guest narrator who reads the story of the Nativity. There's also a holiday-themed fireworks show, "Believe . . . In Holiday Magic." It's presented throughout the holiday season. It is not to be missed.

It's a Small World is transformed into a world of holiday magic. A Christmas Fantasy Parade also takes place. Haunted Mansion Holiday extends through holiday season. Disney California Adventure has the Festival of Holidays, a holiday version of World of Color, and Viva Navidad!, an energetic street party hosted by the Three Caballeros.

The Disneyland Resort celebrates Kwaanza, Hanukkah, Diwali, and New Year's Eve in festive fashion, too. Happy holidays!

MAGICAL MILESTONES

Walt Disney once said, "Disneyland will never be completed. It will continue to grow as long as there is imagination left in the world." Truer words were never spoken. Here's a sampling of major milestones and important dates in Disney history.

1901
Walter Elias Disney is born on December 5 in Chicago, Illinois. He spends part of his childhood in Marceline, Missouri.

1922
Walt and collaborator Ub Iwerks start Laugh-O-Gram Films, an animation studio located in Kansas City, Missouri. (The business lasts one year.)

1923
Walt and his brother Roy open the Disney Bros. Studio in Hollywood, California.

1928

The Disney studio introduces the world to the immortal Mickey Mouse with *Steamboat Willie*, the world's first cartoon with a synchronized soundtrack. (Walt Disney himself provides the voice for Mickey.)

1932
Flowers and Trees wins the Disney Studio its first Academy Award.

1937

Disney releases *Snow White and the Seven Dwarfs*, the world's first feature-length animated movie.

1940
Great works of classical music meet Disney animation with the release of *Fantasia*.

1955
Disneyland opens its doors in Anaheim, while television's original *Mickey Mouse Club* begins a four-year run.

1967

Disneyland debuts Pirates of the Caribbean—one of the most popular and beloved attractions of all time.

1971
Walt Disney World opens in Florida.

1989
Disney animation experiences a renaissance of sorts with the release of the Studio's 28th animated feature film, *The Little Mermaid*.

2001
For the first time since its opening, the Disneyland Resort gets a new theme park: Disney California Adventure.

2003
The Many Adventures of Winnie the Pooh makes its debut in Critter Country inside Disneyland Park.

2004
Turtle Talk with Crush opens at Disney California Adventure park. Like, totally awesome, dude.

2006
Captain Jack Sparrow joins the merry marauders in Pirates of the Caribbean.

2008
Toy Story Midway Mania! opens at Disney California Adventure.

2011
The Little Mermaid—Ariel's Undersea Adventure makes a splashy debut.

2012
Cars Land races onto the scene with new fan favorites, including Radiator Springs Racers and Mater's Junkyard Jamboree.

2019
The Force awakens at Disneyland Park in an exciting new land called Star Wars: Galaxy's Edge. There, guests can fly in Han Solo's ship at *Millennium Falcon: Smugglers Run*, ride out an epic battle between the First Order and the Resistance, customize a lightsaber, and wet their whistles at Oga's Cantina.

WEDDINGS & CELEBRATIONS

The Disneyland Resort's customized Fairy Tale Weddings program lets brides and grooms create an affair to remember in the parks or at one of the Disneyland Resort hotels—either indoors or out. Couples may go the traditional route or plan a themed event with invitations, decorations, souvenirs, napkins, and thank-you notes emblazoned with their favorite Disney character couples, including Cinderella and her Prince, and Mickey and Minnie Mouse.

One spot for tying the knot is the rose garden gazebo at the Disneyland Hotel, in a picturesque garden setting where the bride or couple may arrive in Cinderella's crystal coach. Another choice is the courtyard area at Disney's Grand Californian. A fantasy reception may follow (in any of these hotels), at which the fanfare of trumpets greets the happy couple. Mickey Mouse and Minnie Mouse may arrive to help the newlyweds with the cake-cutting moment.

A Disney wedding coordinator assists with the arrangements for the wedding and reception—everything, that is, except providing a guest's very own Prince or Princess Charming.

The bridal salon (at the Disneyland Resort Center, between the Disneyland Hotel and Paradise Pier Hotel) helps guests through the planning and preparation stages, and even through those pre-ceremony jitters.

For more information about creating a happy occasion in a happy location, contact the Disneyland Fairy Tale weddings department, which coordinates events at all three hotels and in Disneyland: 714-956-6527. For more information about Disneyland honeymoons, contact Disneyland Resort Travel Sales at 800-854-3104.

Quinceañeras

Along with the popular wedding program, the Disneyland Resort also offers customized Quinceañera celebrations for young women who are coming of age. These popular family-oriented milestone events invite the birthday girl to become a "princess for a day" and step into the fairy-tale realms of *Cinderella* or *Beauty and the Beast*. Held in a large ballroom, the celebrations feature dinner, dancing, and time-honored Quinceañera traditions. For details, call 714-520-7079, or visit *disneyland. disney.go.com/events-tours/quinceaneras/*.

Planning Ahead

Collect as much information as you can about the attractions you're interested in from the sources listed below (and this book, of course). Then consider all the possibilities before making definite travel plans.

INFORMATION

For up-to-the-minute information about special events and performance times, the latest ticket prices, theme park operating hours, rides under refurbishment, and other Disneyland Resort specifics, use the Disneyland app and/or contact:

Disneyland Resort Guest Relations; Box 3232, Anaheim, CA 92803; 714-781-4565; *www.disneyland.com*.

If you are staying at one of the Disneyland Resort hotels (see the *Accommodations* chapter), contact Guest Services at the hotel for help in planning your visit to both the parks and the surrounding area.

www.disneyland.com

For additional Disneyland Resort information, visit *www.disneyland.com*, the official Disneyland Resort website. It can help you plan your vacation, learn about the three Disneyland Resort hotels, book travel packages, and order theme park tickets, plus check park hours and show schedules. You can also book your Disneyland Resort vacation through *www.disneytravel.com*.

Disney MaxPass

Fastpass is Disney's complimentary service that lets guests spend less time waiting in line for popular theme park attractions (see page 58). But for a daily fee, MaxPass allows guests to book Fastpass assignments via mobile device. Here's how: First, download the free Disneyland app. Select all members of your party who wish to use MaxPass. Link all tickets or passes. Select a park and book your Fastpass assignments!

MaxPass service includes unlimited Disney PhotoPass downloads (see page 85). Most annual Passholders may add MaxPass to a valid AP for $100 a year or $15 per day. The Disney MaxPass feature is an included benefit with Disney Premier Passport. Details are subject to change in 2020.

Inside the Disneyland Resort: Cast Members (the friendly folks who work at Disneyland) can answer questions. Information stations in Disneyland Park include City Hall in Town Square and the Information Board near Central Plaza, at the far end of Main Street. In Disney California Adventure, the Chamber of Commerce is on the east side of the Entry Plaza and the Information Board is at the far end of Buena Vista Street, adjacent to the Red Car Trolley stop. At any Disneyland Resort hotel, visit the lobby for assistance.

For other Anaheim area information, contact these bureaus of tourism:

Anaheim/Orange County Visitor & Convention Bureau; Call 714-765-2800 during business hours to reach a representative, or go to *www.visitanaheim.org*. You can visit them in the Convention Center at 800 W. Katella Ave., Anaheim, CA 92802.

Long Beach Area Convention & Visitors Bureau; 301 E. Ocean Blvd., Suite 1900, Long Beach, CA 90802; *www.visitlongbeach.com*, 562-436-3645 or 800-452-7829.

Los Angeles Convention & Visitors Bureau; There are four walk-in Visitor Information Centers in Los Angeles: Union Station, 800 N. Alameda St., Los Angeles, CA 90012; 6801 Hollywood Blvd., Hollywood, CA 90028; 900 Wilshire Blvd., Los Angeles, CA 90017; and San Pedro Los Angeles Waterfront, 390 W. 7th St., San Pedro, CA 90731; *http://www.visitlosangeles.com*.

RESERVATIONS

Given the popularity of the Disneyland Resort, advance planning is essential. To get your choice of accommodations, especially for visits during the busy spring and summer seasons, make lodging reservations as far in advance as possible—at least six months ahead, if you can, since area hotels fill up rather quickly during these months. For visits at other times of the year, check with Visit Anaheim, the Anaheim/Orange County Visitor & Convention Bureau (714-765-2800), to see if any conventions are scheduled when you want to travel. Some of these events can crowd facilities enough to warrant altering your travel plans.

TRAVEL PACKAGES

The biggest advantage to purchasing a travel package is that it almost always saves you money over what you would pay separately for the individual elements of your vacation, or it offers special options not available if you simply buy a ticket at the ticket booth. This is especially true the longer you stay. And there is the convenience of having all the details arranged in advance by someone else.

Finding the best package for yourself means deciding what sort of vacation you want and studying what's available. Don't choose a package that includes elements that don't interest you—remember, you're paying for them. And if it's Disney theming and "extras" you want, consider a Walt Disney Travel Company package.

The Walt Disney Travel Company offers packages that include a stay at a Disney hotel and a Park Hopper ticket. It's possible to add extras, such as a character breakfast in the park or a guided tour of Disneyland park, as well as admission to another Southern California attraction, such as Sea World or Legoland. Purchase extras separately.

Besides booking guests into an official Disneyland Resort hotel, the Walt Disney Travel Company also works closely with dozens of Good Neighbor hotels and motels (see pages 45–50 for details), and they are included in its packages as well. To book a vacation package at the Disneyland Resort, contact a travel agent, or call the Walt Disney Travel Company at 714-520-5060.

The Disneyland Resort is also featured in a wide variety of non-Disney-run package tours, including those sponsored by individual hotels and airlines (United Vacations, Alaska Airlines Vacations, Southwest Vacations, and jetBlue Vacations offer packages, for instance). AAA Vacations (888-780-5185) offers packages to the traveling public, too.

This book's selective guide to Anaheim-area hotels and motels can help you decide initially which property best suits your party's travel style, needs, and budget (refer to the *Accommodations* chapter for guidance). Pick one, then contact a travel agent or the desired hotel directly to make a reservation or book a Disneyland Resort package. Be sure to inquire about deposit requirements, cancellation policies, and trip insurance (we highly recommend opting for trip insurance). Happy hunting!

What to Pack

Southern California isn't so laid-back that you only need to pack shorts, T-shirts, and sneakers. Nor is it a place that demands formal attire. Casual wear will suffice in all but the fanciest restaurants, and, even there, men can usually wear sports jackets without ties. Bathing suits are an obvious must if you plan to take advantage of your hotel's swimming pool or go for a walk on a long, surf-pounded Pacific beach. It's also a good idea to bring along a bathing suit cover-up and sunglasses (and don't forget the sunscreen). Tennis togs or golf gear may be necessary if you plan to hit the courts or the course. The weather in summer can be quite warm, but because Southern California air-conditioning is extremely efficient, you should take a lightweight sweater or jacket to wear indoors.

In winter, warm clothing is a must for evening; during nighttime visits to the parks, a heavy jacket may be a godsend. Whatever the time of year you visit, come prepared for the unexpected: Pack a light shirt and a warm jacket—just in case.

MAKING A BUDGET

Vacation expenses tend to fall into five major categories: (1) transportation (which may include costs for airfare, airport transfers, train tickets, car rental, gas, parking, and taxi service); (2) lodging; (3) theme park tickets; (4) meals; and (5) miscellaneous (recreational activities, souvenirs, toiletries, forgotten items, and expenses such as pet boarding, etc.).

When budgeting, first consider what level of service suits your needs. Some prefer to spend fewer days at the Disneyland Resort, but stay at a deluxe hotel like the Grand Californian or dine at pricier restaurants. Others want a longer vacation with a value-priced Good Neighbor hotel and less expensive meals. The choice is up to you. (Having said that, we do feel that a great deal of the Disney experience comes from staying on-property and recommend at least making room in your budget for accommodations at the somewhat more moderately priced Disneyland Hotel or Paradise Pier Hotel.)

Once you've established your spending priorities, it's time to determine your price limit. Then make sure you don't exceed it when approximating your expenses—without a ballpark figure to work around, it's easy to get carried away.

SAMPLE BUDGET

LODGING:

Disneyland Hotel: $460 per night (x 4 nights)

Lodging total = $1,840

THEME PARK TICKETS:

Adult 4-day Park Hopper ticket: $380 (x 2 people)

Child 4-day Park Hopper ticket: $360 (x 2 people)

Tickets total = $1,480

MEALS:

(two inexpensive and one moderate meal per day, plus one snack)

Average adult: $90 (x 5 days) (x 2 people)

Average child: $55 (x 5 days) (x 2 people)

Meals total = $1,450

MISCELLANEOUS:

Average adult: $65 (x 5 days) (x 2 people)

Average child: $45 (x 5 days) (x 2 people)

Miscellaneous total = $1,100

DISNEYLAND RESORT VACATION TOTAL* = $5,870

If you would like a lower hotel rate, consider a stay at one of Disney's Good Neighbor hotel partners. Room rates may start as low as $109.

Don't forget: Staying at a Disney hotel gives you priority admission to the theme parks (with a ticket).

Even if you stick to fast food, expect to spend at least $50 (adult) and $30 (child) per day.

Careful packing should cut down on miscellaneous expenses, which include forgotten toiletries such as toothpaste and the all-important sunscreen.

This is an example of a moderately priced budget for a family of four (two adults and two kids staying at the Disneyland Resort for four nights and five days during "off-peak" times), excluding transportation costs. Theme park admission prices are likely to increase in 2020.

* Includes round-trip transfers via Disneyland Resort Express bus. See page 23 for details. Be sure to include transportation costs (which vary widely) in your travel budget.

Money-Saving Strategies

COST-CUTTING TIPS

LODGING: The most important rule is not to pay for more than you need. Budget chains don't offer many frills, but they are usually clean and provide the essentials; many even have a swimming pool, albeit a small one. (Bigger isn't always better!)

You can also save by checking the cutoff age at which kids can no longer share their parents' room for free. Many hotels and motels allow children under age 18 to stay free. A few places have a cutoff age of 15 or 17, so it's best to find out before making a reservation. And ask about special rates or discounts, especially if you are a California resident, Disney Vacation Club or AARP member, or are in the military.

Hostels and RV parks also offer lower-priced lodging alternatives. Contact the Anaheim/Orange County Visitor & Convention Bureau at 855-405-5020 for a listing of those areas closest to the Disneyland Resort.

FOOD: The budget-minded (and who isn't?) should plan to have meals in coffee shops or fast-food restaurants, or save your splurges for the buffets to get your fill and your money's worth. If you want to try an upscale place, go for lunch; the entrées are often the same as those at dinner time, but may cost less.

Pack a picnic and enjoy meals outside. There's a small picnic area just to the left of Disneyland Park's entrance. (It's surrounded by trees—so it's easy to miss.) Snacks may be brought into the parks, but not glass bottles, knives, or beverages containing alcohol. Refillable plastic or metal cups and bottles are permitted. Coolers are allowed, but must be no larger than 24 inches long, 15 inches wide, and 18 inches high. Loose and dry ice are not permitted. Reusable ice packs are recommended. You can also save on meals by choosing lodging with kitchen facilities and opting to eat in some of the time. The savings on food may more than cover the additional cost of accommodations. Don't forget to pack snack items, too—especially when traveling with kids.

In the Anaheim area, a number of places offer refrigerators or kitchen facilities (look for suite hotels); some provide breakfast.

TRANSPORTATION: When calculating the cost of driving from your home to the Disneyland Resort, consider your car's gas mileage, the price of gasoline, and the expense of the accommodations and food

en route. If you are planning to fly, don't forget about the cost of getting from home to the airport and later to the hotel. Also factor in the cost of renting a car at your destination, if that's part of your plan. Remember to ask if your hotel charges for parking (rates tend to vary) or shuttle transportation to the Disneyland Resort—these daily charges can tack quite a bit onto a family's total vacation cost.

DISNEY DISCOUNTS

ANNUAL PASSPORT: Annual Pass–bearers may net savings on Disneyland Resort hotel rooms, restaurants, select merchandise throughout the parks and Downtown Disney, and select guided tours. Deluxe, Signature, Signature Plus, and Premier Annual Passholders may enjoy up to 20 percent discounts on merchandise at many Disneyland resort retail locations, and 10 to 15 percent on unlimited free PhotoPass downloads (refer to page 85). The Premier, Signature, and Signature Plus Annual Passes include parking. The Signature Plus Annual Pass includes the MaxPass benefit (refer to page 13). Current Annual Passholders may receive a savings when they renew their passes, too.

DISNEY VISA® CARDS: Cardmembers who pay with their Disney Visa Card may enjoy savings on merchandise, dining, and guided tours. Specifics are subject to change. Visit *DisneyRewards.com* or *DisneyDebit.com* for additional information.

AUTOMOBILE ASSOCIATION OF AMERICA (AAA): You don't have to be a member of the Auto Club to order a vacation package through AAA. Contact your regional AAA office for additional information.

BIRNBAUM COUPONS: The coupons at the back of this book will net you savings at several Downtown Disney spots. You're welcome!

Theme-Park Tickets

TICKET OPTIONS

One- through Five-Day Tickets allow admission to one Disneyland Resort theme park per day, while One- to Five-Day Park Hopper tickets allow admission to both parks and allow you to "hop" between parks. Theme park tickets generally expire 13 days after first use. Some tickets are subject to price changes during certain times of year.

The main types of annual passports are Deluxe, Signature, and Signature Plus versions. All afford the bearer shopping and dining discounts, as well as park-hopping (visiting both theme parks in one day). The big difference between annual pass types are blockout dates (select dates when the passholder may not enter the Disney parks).

The Signature Plus Annual Passport is valid for one year and has no blockout dates. The Signature Annual Passport is valid 350 days of the year with two blocked-out weeks surrounding the Christmas holiday. The Deluxe Annual Passport is valid about 320 days of the year, with blockout periods such as December holidays, Saturdays from March through August, and other peak times of year. Annual Passport blockout dates are park specific, with Disneyland Park blocked out more often than Disney California Adventure. For blockout date specifics and calendars, visit *disneyland.com* or use the Disneyland Resort mobile app or website. Premier passes allow entry to all Disney theme parks in the United States and come with the benefits of a Signature Plus pass. With the exception of the Deluxe pass, annual passports include theme park parking.

Annual passes may be purchased and renewed at all Disneyland Resort ticket windows and by visiting *www.disneyland.com* or the Disneyland mobile app. There are special passes for Southern California residents. Offers vary, so inquire in advance: call 714-781-4565 or visit *www.disneyland.com*.

PURCHASING TICKETS

Where to Buy Tickets: All tickets may be purchased at Disneyland Resort ticket booths. Long lines may be avoided by purchasing via the Disneyland app or *disneyland.com*. (You can print them, have them mailed, or pick them up at Will Call. The latter two options come with a fee.) Multi-day tickets may be sold at some Disney Stores, too. Advance-purchase tickets of 3 days or more include one "Magic Morning," allowing access to Disneyland Park one hour before posted opening time on a Tuesday, Thursday, or Saturday.

Tickets by Mail: Send check or money order and ticket request (plus a $10 fee for orders over $200) to Disneyland Ticket Mail Order Services, Box 61061, Anaheim, CA 92803. It's also possible to order by calling Ticketing & Reservations at 714-781-4400 (up to 30 days ahead). Allow 10 business days for processing.

Tickets by Phone: Call 714-781-4565 and have a major credit card handy. Allow at least 7 business days for delivery, and up to 10 during busy times of year.

Note that the Disneyland Resort ticket structure and pricing are likely to change in 2020. For updates, visit *www.disneyland.com*.

Ticket Prices

Although prices[†] will likely increase, the following should give you an idea of what you will pay for tickets in 2020. Note that 1-Day tickets purchased in 2020 must be used by 12/31/20. The first day of use of multi-day tickets must be on or before 12/31/20. Multi-day tickets must be used within 13 days of first use or by January 13, 2021, whichever occurs first. For updates, call 714-781-4565, or visit *www.disneyland.com*. All details are subject to change in 2020.

	ADULTS	CHILDREN*
1-Day Ticket (1 park)	$104/129/149	$98/122/141
1-Day Ticket (hopper)	$154/179/199	$148/172/191
2-Day Ticket	$225	$210
2-Day Ticket (hopper)	$280	$265
3-Day Ticket	$300	$280
3-Day Ticket (hopper)**	$355	$335
4-Day Ticket**	$325	$305
4-Day Ticket (hopper)**	$380	$360
5-Day Ticket**	$340	$320
5-Day Ticket (hopper)**	$395	$375
Deluxe Annual Passport		$799
Signature Annual Passport		$1,149
Signature Plus Annual Passport		$1,399
Premier Annual Passport		$1,949

† One-day prices are quoted in Value/Regular/Peak order. For dates, visit *www.disneyland.com*. Prices vary by date.
* 3 through 9 years of age; children under 3 free
** Includes one "Magic Morning" early Disneyland Park admission with select attractions on Tuesday, Thursday, or Saturday with advance purchase.
There is a single price (for adults and children) for annual passports.

Customized Travel Tips

TRAVELING WITH CHILDREN

When you tell your kids that a Disney vacation is in the works, the challenge is keeping them relatively calm until you actually arrive at the Disneyland Resort.

PLANNING: Get youngsters involved in plotting a Disneyland trip from the outset, putting each child in charge of a small part of the vacation preparation—such as visiting *www.disneyland.com*, choosing which attractions to see and in what order to see them, and investigating which other activities to include in your Southern California visit.

EN ROUTE: Certain resources can stave off the "Are we there yet?" chorus, such as travel games, books and magazines, and snacks to quiet rumbling stomachs. If you drive, take plenty of breaks along the way. If you fly, try to time your departure and return flights for off-peak hours and during the off-season, when chances are better that an empty seat or two will be available. During takeoffs and landings, encourage toddlers to suck on bottles or pacifiers to keep ears clear, and supply older kids with chewing gum, a lollipop, or water. And don't forget activities to keep them occupied.

IN THE HOTELS: Several Anaheim-area hotels offer special kids' programs. Some offer babysitting services or babysitting referrals year-round (fees apply).

IN THE THEME PARKS: The smiles that light up your kids' faces as they enter a Disney theme park should repay you a thousandfold for any fuss en route. No place in the world is more aware of the needs of little ones—or their parents—than this one.

Favorite Attractions: Fantasyland and Mickey's Toontown in Disneyland Park are great places to start with small kids, who delight in the bright colors and familiar characters. In Disney California Adventure, Cars Land, Disney Junior Dance Party!, and Monsters, Inc.—Mike and Sulley to the Rescue! have big kid

appeal. If you have children of different ages in your party, you may have to do some juggling or split the group up for a few hours so that older kids won't have to spend their whole vacation waiting in line for Dumbo. Some rides, like Snow White's Scary Adventures, may be too intense for some youngsters. (If they're afraid of the witch, skip the attraction.)

Strollers: They can be rented for $15 ($25 for two) at the Stroller Shop, located to the right of the entrance to Disneyland Park. This is the only place to rent a stroller for either park. If you leave the parks but plan to return later that day, keep the receipt and get another stroller at no additional charge.

Baby Care: Baby Care Centers feature toddler-size flush toilets that are quite cute—and completely functional. In addition, there are changing tables, a limited selection of formulas, baby foods, and diapers for sale, plus facilities for warming baby bottles (you can wash out your bottles here, too). A special room with comfortable chairs is available for nursing mothers.

The decor is soothing, and a stop here for a diaper change or feeding is a tranquil break for parent and child alike. The Baby Care Centers are located in Central Plaza, at the Castle end of Main Street in Disneyland, and near Ghirardelli Soda Fountain & Chocolate Shop in Disney California Adventure.

Changing tables and diaper vending machines are also available in many restrooms.

Note: Parents of toddlers should pack a supply of swim diapers. They are required for children who want to spend time frolicking in hotel pools.

Where to Buy Baby Care Items: Disposable diapers, baby bottles, formula, etc., are sold at Baby Care Centers in the parks. Pack as much of your own as possible—prices can be steep and the selection is small.

Lost Children: Youngsters should carry the mobile phone number for the parent or guardian who accompanies them to the parks. But even without it, when a child gets separated from his or her family or fails to

---

HOT TIP!

Pack kid-friendly snacks, such as fruit, cereal, breakfast bars, crackers, and water. Snack stands are plentiful at Disneyland Resort, but not always handy or cost-efficient.

show up on time, trained Cast Members and Disneyland Resort's security force follow specific procedures when they encounter a lost child. Please report lost children to a Cast Member (park worker), and Disneyland Resort security personnel will assist you.

Kids age 13 and younger will be escorted (by a Disney Cast Member) to the park's Baby Care Center, while a parent is contacted via mobile phone or otherwise directed to the Baby Care location. Kids older than 13 will be taken to City Hall in Disneyland Park or Chamber of Commerce just inside the entrance area of Disney California Adventure. Lost children found in the Downtown Disney District are taken to either the Disneyland Hotel or the Baby Care Center and Lost Children location inside Disneyland Park (near Plaza Inn).

TRAVELING WITHOUT CHILDREN

Disneyland Resort is as enjoyable for solo travelers and couples as it is for families for several reasons: Its ambience encourages interaction, and the attractions are naturally shared events.

PLANNING: Read Disneyland Resort literature carefully before you arrive to familiarize yourself with the area's layout and activities. Also, search for information about other places in Southern California that you intend to visit.

Food for Thought: Sightseeing takes lots of energy, and only healthy meals can provide it at a consistent level. Don't attempt to save money by skipping meals. Prices at the parks and nearby "off-property" eateries are relatively reasonable, and there are some healthy options, even in the fast-food restaurants. And don't forget to stay hydrated—running around theme parks all day is a lot of work.

Health Matters: If you visit in summer, avoid getting overheated. Protect yourself from the sun with a hat and plenty of sunscreen, rest in the shade often, and beat the midafternoon heat with a cold drink or a snack in an air-conditioned spot.

If you are injured or feel ill, speak to a Disney Cast Member or go to First Aid to see the nurse. *In case of emergency, call 911.* Above all, heed attraction warnings. If you have a back problem, heart condition, or other physical ailment, suffer from motion sickness, or are pregnant, skip rough rides. Restrictions are noted at attraction entrances, as well as on park guidemaps.

Lost Companions: Traveling companions can get separated. If someone in your party wanders off or fails to show up at an appointed meeting spot and cell phone communication is thwarted, head for City Hall in Disneyland park or Chamber of Commerce in Disney California Adventure park. Guests can leave and receive messages for one another during the day.

MEETING OTHER ADULTS: Downtown Disney, with its mix of restaurants and lounges, is a nice spot to mingle. While each of Disney's hotels has lounges worth visiting, Trader Sam's Enchanted Tiki Bar at the Disneyland Hotel is exceptionally engaging.

TRAVELERS WITH DISABILITIES

The Disneyland Resort is quite accessible to guests with disabilities, and, as a result, it makes a good choice as a vacation destination. But planning is still essential.

GETTING TO ANAHEIM

Probably the most effective means of ensuring a smooth trip is to make as many advance contacts as possible for every phase of your journey. It's important to make phone calls regarding transportation well before your departure date to arrange for any special facilities or services you may need en route.

The Society for Accessible Travel & Hospitality (SATH, 2175 Hudson St., Fort Lee, NJ 07024; *www.sath.org*) has member travel agents who book trips for travelers with disabilities, keeping special needs in mind. Membership costs about $49, or $29 for students and seniors (age 63 and older).

The following agencies specialize in booking trips for travelers with physical disabilities: Accessible Journeys (35 W. Sellers Ave., Ridley Park, PA 19078; *www.accessiblejourneys.com*; 610-521-0339 or 800-846-4537) and Ventures Travel (3600 Holly Lane N. #95, Plymouth, MN 55447; 952-852-0107 or 866-692-7400; *www.venturestravel.org/custom-trips*).

Hertz (800-654-3131), Alamo (800-651-1223), and National (888-273-5262) rent hand-controlled cars at Southern California airports. Order your car at least 72 hours in advance and confirm before arrival.

Though less direct, it is also possible to access the area by public transportation. All Anaheim Resort Transportation (aka ART, the official Disneyland Resort Shuttle Bus) routes provide access to the Disneyland Resort through the Main Transportation Center (visit *www.rideart.org* or call 888-364-2787). The same is true

Height Ho!

At attractions with age and/or height restrictions, a parent who waits with a child too young or too small to ride while the other parent goes on the attraction will have expedited boarding as soon as the first parent comes off. This is called the "rider switch" policy, and if lines are long, it can save a lot of time. Be sure to ask the attendant, and he or she will explain what to do.

for many of the routes covered by the Orange County Transportation Authority, the public bus company that serves Orange County (*www.octa.net*, or 714-560-6282). All ART and OCTA buses have lifts for travelers using wheelchairs.

Scootaround rents standard and electric wheelchairs, as well as motorized scooters. Pickup and delivery is available for all hotels in the Disneyland Resort area. Visit *www.scootaround.com*, or call 888-441-7575. A company called Wheelchair Getaways of California rents wheelchair-accessible vans and has pick-up and delivery options for most area hotels. Call 800-638-1912, or visit *www.wheelchairgetaways.com*.

LODGING

Most hotels and motels in Orange County have rooms equipped for guests with disabilities, with extra-wide doorways, grab bars in the bathroom for shower or bath and toilet, and sinks at wheelchair height, along with ramps at curbs and steps to allow wheelchair access. Unless otherwise indicated, all the lodging described in the *Accommodations* chapter (page 39) provide guestrooms for travelers with disabilities.

INSIDE THE DISNEYLAND RESORT

Cars displaying a "disability" placard will be directed to a section of each Disney parking lot, next to the tram pick-up and drop-off area.

Wheelchairs and Electric Conveyance Vehicles (ECVs) can be rented at the Stroller Shop outside the entrance to Disneyland Park. This is the only rental location for both theme parks. The price is $12 per day for wheelchairs, and $50 for ECVs, plus tax and a refundable $20 deposit. A few wheelchairs may be available to borrow from Disney's three hotels; inquire at the front desk. Quantities are limited. We recommend using your own wheelchair whenever possible.

Most waiting areas are accessible, but some attractions offer auxiliary entrances for guests who use wheelchairs or other mobility devices; guests may be accompanied by up to five party members using the special entry point. The Main Street train station is not wheelchair accessible. However, guests using wheelchairs may access the train in New Orleans Square, Mickey's Toontown, or Tomorrowland.

Accessibility information is provided in special brochures (see Park Resources, below). In all cases, guests with mobility disabilities should be escorted by someone in their party who can assist as needed.

In some theme park attractions, guests may remain in their wheelchair or Electric Conveyance Vehicle; in others, they must be able to transfer in and out of their wheelchair or ECV. In a few attractions, guests must leave their wheelchair or ECV and remain ambulatory during the majority of the attraction experience.

For Guests with Visual Disabilities: An audio tour and the *Braille Guidebook* are available upon request at City Hall in Disneyland Park and at Chamber of Commerce in Disney California Adventure. Both are free to use but require a $25 refundable deposit. A portable handheld device containing several services, including audio description, is available from Guest Relations at each theme park (a refundable deposit is required).

Trained service animals are permitted in most locations. Animals may not be permitted to ride some attractions. They may wait with a non-riding member of their party or in a portable kennel. For details, visit *disneyland.disney.go.com/guest-services/service-animals/*.

For Guests with Hearing Disabilities: Reflective captioning is available in the pre-show areas of select attractions—ask about it at the attraction entrance or visit *https://disneyland.disney.go.com/guest-services/hearing-disabilities/*.

Dozens of attractions provide hand-held captioning service. The system uses a wireless handheld receiver to display text in locations where fixed captioning systems are impractical, such as moving attractions. Receivers are available through Guest Relations and require a $25

Park Resources

Contact Guest Relations at 714-781-7290 for details on *Services for Guests with Visual Disabilities and Hearing Disabilities; Services for Guests with Service Animals;* and *Attraction Access for Guests Using Wheelchairs and Electric Conveyance Vehicles (ECVs)*, or use the Disneyland Resort mobile app or visit *www.disneyland.com*. Information is also available at City Hall in Disneyland and at Chamber of Commerce in Disney California Adventure park.

refundable deposit. For details, visit the website referenced in the previous paragraph or check at City Hall in Disneyland Park or Chamber of Commerce inside Disney's California Adventure.

Text typewriters (TTYs) are available to borrow from the three Disneyland Resort hotels. Inquire about them when you check in.

Sign Language interpretation is available by request for select special events with at least 14 days advance notice. Call 714-781-4636 (select option 1, and then option 0). Guests under age 18 must have parent or guardian permission to call.

A portable handheld device containing several services, including handheld captioning, may be borrowed at City Hall in Disneyland Park or Chamber of Commerce in Disney California Adventure park (a $25 refundable deposit is required).

DISNEYLAND RESORT TOURS

The following guided tours provide guests with a chance to explore Disneyland Park and Disney California Adventure in entertaining and informative ways. Annual Passholders and Disney Visa® Cardmembers receive a discount on select guided tours. Tours may be booked up to 30 days in advance. Availability is limited. For details or to book a tour, call 714-781-8687 or visit *www.disneyland.com*, or stop by City Hall (on Main Street in Disneyland Park) or Chamber of Commerce at Disney California Adventure. Theme park admission is required (but not included) for all guided tours:

• ***Walk in Walt's Disneyland Footsteps*** (9:30 A.M. daily): Led by a knowledgeable guide, the tour covers Walt's original theme park. In addition to your theme park ticket, expect to pay an extra $109 (per person, all ages) for the 3.5-hour tour. Guests travel through Walt's original Magic Kingdom, while hearing stories of the challenges, inspiration, and fun associated with all of his creations. The tour includes a meal on Main Street, a collectible button and pin, and a visit to the Disneyland Dream Suite in New Orleans Square. Details are subject to change. For updates, visit *www.disneyland.com*.

• ***Disney's Happiest Haunts Tour*** (Seasonal): Journey though both parks at dusk and prepare for a night of chilling tales and eerie sights on this 3-hour walking tour. Cost is about $85 per person and includes a souvenir keepsake and a Halloween treat. Guests should be at least 40 inches tall. The tour is not recommended for guests using wheelchairs or strollers. Participating guests ride Haunted Mansion and Big Thunder Mountain. Details are subject to change.

• ***Grand Circle Tour*** (Seasonal): All aboard! Get a behind-the-scenes view into Walt Disney's lifelong appreciation of trains and how they inspired some of his creations. One highlight of the 2-hour tour: a ride in a special parlor car on the *Lilly Belle* steam train. There is a guided walking tour and a sweet treat, too. Cost is about $85. To participate, guests must be at least 18 years old with government-issued photo ID.

• ***Holiday Time at the Disneyland Resort*** (Seasonal): This tour shares the history of Disneyland's holiday traditions and enchanting tales of holidays from around the world, includes visits to attractions that have had holiday makeovers, and offers special seating for the holiday parade, A Christmas Fantasy. Cost is about $85 per person and includes a pin, a warm beverage, and a gingerbread cookie.

• ***VIP Tour Services:*** A dedicated team is available to customize and guide your Disneyland Resort vacation: 714-300-7710.

How to Get There

Most visitors to Disneyland Resort arrive by car. Many who live nearby own an Annual Pass and often drive there to spend a day or weekend at the resort. But for those traveling any significant distance, it tends to cost less to fly than to drive, and can save time. During your days at Disneyland Resort, you won't need a vehicle. Rent a car for the days you plan to venture off Disney property, or rely on local tours to see the area sights. If you prefer to leave the driving to someone else, traveling to Disneyland by bus or train are alternatives.

BY CAR

SOUTHERN CALIFORNIA FREEWAYS: Driving just about anywhere in Orange County, or farther afield, requires negotiating a number of freeways and surface streets. But once you familiarize yourself with a few names and numbers, navigating through California becomes much more manageable.

The freeways are well marked and relatively fast, barring (common) traffic snags. That said, they can be rather frenetic. Major thoroughfares may merge with little or no notice. Monstrous traffic jams are common during morning and evening rush hours. And proper names of most roads change, depending on where you are. I-5, for instance, is called the Santa Ana Freeway in Orange County; in the Los Angeles area, it becomes the Golden State Freeway; to the south, it's the San Diego Freeway. It's a good idea to learn both the name and the route number of any freeway on which you plan to travel. Exit signs list a route number and either a direction or city name (but not always both).

HOT TIP!
Driving to Disneyland and looking for an address for the GPS? Look no further: 1313 S. Harbor Blvd., Anaheim, CA 92802.

It's also good to have an idea of the layout of the freeways. Several run parallel to the Pacific coast and are intersected by others running east and west. While this scheme is fairly straightforward, it is complicated by a couple of freeways that squiggle across the map.

CALIFORNIA DRIVING LAWS: Under state law, seat belts are required for all passengers; right turns at red lights are legal unless otherwise posted, as are U-turns at intersections; and pedestrians have the right-of-way at all crosswalks. By law, kids must be in car or booster seats until they reach the age of 8 or a height of 4 feet, 9 inches. And keep that phone in your pocket—it is illegal to use it while driving in California.

AUTOMOBILE CLUBS: Any one of the nation's leading automobile clubs will come to your aid in the event of a breakdown en route (be sure to bring your membership card with you), as well as provide insurance covering accidents, arrest, bail bond, lawyers' fees for defense of contested traffic cases, and personal injury. They also offer trip-planning services—not merely advice, but also free maps and route-mapping assistance.

MAPS/GPS: If you don't have a GPS app on your smartphone, know that some car rental agencies provide GPS systems and maps. Of course, it's still wise to familiarize yourself with the route beforehand. Routes can be plotted via *http://maps.yahoo.com*; *www.mapquest.com*; or *http://maps.google.com*.

BY AIR

Anaheim lies about 45 to 120 minutes southeast of Los Angeles by car. Most Disneyland Resort guests who arrive by plane disembark at Los Angeles International Airport (LAX), one of the world's busiest. It handles approximately 1,500 departures and arrivals daily of more than 59 commercial airlines. Major carriers serving Los Angeles include jetBlue, American, Delta, and United airlines.

Much closer to Anaheim, Orange County's John Wayne Airport is about a half-hour drive from Disney and is served by 7 commercial airlines and more than 200 flights a day. It is sometimes possible to find the same fare to John Wayne/Orange County Airport (SNA) as to LAX, and if it's a nonstop flight, so much the better. There aren't as many direct flights available, but given the proximity to the Disneyland Resort, it's worth considering. Another airport vying for attention is the

HOT TIP!

Freeway traffic updates can help you avoid a jam. Tune to 1070 AM (in Anaheim and Los Angeles).

Long Beach Airport (LGB). It is also relatively close to Anaheim, but few airlines serve it on a nonstop basis.

HOW TO GET THE BEST AIRFARE: Airfares seem to be forever in flux, changing often. That makes it important to shop around—or have your travel agent do so. It pays to keep these suggestions in mind:

• Check into all airlines serving your destination. See if you can get a lower fare by slightly altering the dates of your trip, the hour of departure, or the duration of your stay—or, if you live halfway between two airports, by leaving from one rather than the other or by flying into a different area airport.

• Weekend flights tend to bring higher prices. Fly midweek whenever possible. (Tuesdays and Wednesdays are usually best.)

• Purchase your tickets online. Airlines often offer lower fares or waive transaction fees when customers use their websites.

• Keep an eye on airline websites, social media sites, and newspapers for ads announcing special fares.

AIRPORT TRANSPORTATION: Friendly, reasonably priced, scheduled bus service is offered by Disneyland Resort Express (visit *https://dre.coachusa.com*, or call 714-978-8855 or 800-828-6699). It not only goes to the Disneyland Resort hotels and the properties in Anaheim, but also several hotels in Buena Park (7 miles away). Prepaid round-trip service is offered at a small discount. The standard-size bus stops are at each LAX airline terminal, outside baggage claim; look for the green bus stop signs on the center island and for DISNEYLAND RESORT EXPRESS above the windshield (the Disney theming makes the buses easy to spot). Note that this bus stops making airport pickups at about 6 P.M. (possibly earlier).

Those who fly into John Wayne Airport (named after one of Orange County's most famous residents), 16 miles from Disneyland, have an easier time of it. The ride into town takes half the time than from LAX. From baggage claim, head to the Ground Transportation Center. The coaches pick up from the ticket booth located to the left. Look for the full-size motor coach that has DISNEYLAND RESORT EXPRESS clearly displayed above the windshield.

SuperShuttle (visit *www.supershuttle.com*, or call 800-258-3826) also serves area airports. At Los Angeles International Airport, claim your luggage, then head to the SHARED RIDE VAN sign on the outer island and contact a blue-uniformed guest service rep for details. A van should arrive within 15 to 30 minutes.

At John Wayne Airport, proceed to the transportation center across the street and look for the island marked VAN SHUTTLE SERVICE. A van should arrive within 15 to 30 minutes. Advance reservations are required for pick-up at Long Beach. Here, vans collect passengers across from the main terminal in the car rental return lot. To return to any airport without an existing reservation, check with your hotel front desk the day before the departure for bus schedules and reservation information.

To the Disneyland Resort from the Airports

	Disneyland Resort Express Bus	SuperShuttle
Los Angeles International Airport (LAX)	$30 ($48 round-trip) per adult; $9 ($14 round-trip) per child ages 3–11.* It runs until about 6 p.m.	$17 per person (one way)
John Wayne Airport (SNA)	$20 ($35 round-trip) per adult; $7 ($11 round-trip) per child ages 3–11.*	$12 per person (one way)
Long Beach Airport (LGB)	Resort Express service is not available, but it's possible to take a Yellow Cab for about $52–$60 each way.	$33 for the first guest in the party, about $9 for each additional guest.

* For each paying adult, one child may ride for free. Children under 3 ride free. Prices are subject to change.

CAR RENTALS: Several major car rental agencies have locations at LAX, John Wayne, and Long Beach airports; in Union Station; at many hotels; and elsewhere in Anaheim. Expect to pay between $252 and $310 a week for an intermediate car (plus tax and insurance fees), and $50 to $102 for a 3-day weekend, with unlimited mileage. Some rental companies to choose from are Avis (800-331-1212), Budget (800-527-0700), Dollar (800-800-4000), Hertz (800-654-3131), Alamo (800-327-9633), and National (800-227-7368).

It pays to call agencies and check websites to get the best available deals. Be sure to ask about any special promotions or discounts. Loss Damage Waiver (LDW) coverage is essential for your protection in case of an accident, but it can add a lot to your bill (usually at least $9 a day). Most packages that include a rental car do not include LDW. If you have your own car insurance, check with your carrier to see what is covered.

An increasing number of major credit card companies offer free collision damage coverage for charging the rental to their card, and some may provide primary coverage. That means your credit card company may deal with the rental company directly in the event of an accident, rather than compensate you after your insurance has kicked in. It's worth a call to find out.

If you're renting a car at Los Angeles International Airport (LAX), the drive to the Disneyland Resort is only 31 miles, but it will take at least 45 minutes with light traffic, or up to two hours if the roads are congested. From John Wayne Airport (SNA), the drive takes about 25 minutes (without traffic). Expect a drive of about a half hour from Long Beach Airport (LGB)—again, that estimate does not factor in that tricky wild card known as Southern California traffic.

> ## HOT TIP!
> If you take a taxi, note whether or not the trip is metered or if there is a flat fee to your destination—and make sure you are charged accordingly.

BY TRAIN

It's possible to get to Anaheim by rail from L.A.'s Union Station using Amtrak's Pacific Surfliner train (*www.amtrak.com*; 800-872-7245) or L.A.'s Metrolink Orange County light-rail (*www.metrolinktrains.com*; 800-371-5465). Union Station is in downtown L.A. and is served by trains from all over the country.

You can get to Union Station from Los Angeles International Airport (LAX) by cab, by bus (LAX FlyAway Bus; *www.lawa.org/flyaway*; 866-435-9529), or by L.A.'s Metro subway (323-466-3876; *www.metro.net*; the system also serves Long Beach Airport). Hertz and Budget rental agencies have counters at Union Station; call companies directly for rates and hours.

The Anaheim train station is adjacent to Angel Stadium in Anaheim, which is about two miles from the Disneyland Resort. Yellow Cabs can be called from the station (714-999-9999). In addition, Hertz and Budget car rental agencies will pick up customers from the Anaheim train station; contact the companies directly for rates and operating hours.

BY BUS

Buses make sense if you're traveling a short distance, if you have plenty of time to spend in transit, if there are only two or three people in your party, and/or if cost-control is key.

Buses make the trip from Los Angeles and San Diego, though they usually make a few stops along the way. Travel from most other destinations usually requires a change of vehicle in L.A. Transfers are usually made at 1716 E. 7th St. at Alameda in downtown L.A.

The Anaheim Greyhound bus terminal is at 2626 E. Katella Ave.; *www.greyhound.com*; 800-231-2222. Yellow Cabs can get you to Disneyland from the bus terminal for about $12; 714-999-9999.

Southern California

0 5 10 15 20
Miles

To Palm Springs

San Bernardino

Riverside

San Bernardino Fwy.

Riverside Fwy.

San Juan Capistrano

To San Diego

San Diego Fwy.

San Clemente

Dana Point

Disneyland

Orange

Santa Ana

Irvine

Fullerton

Anaheim

Garden Grove

John Wayne
(Orange County)
Airport

Laguna Beach

Buena
Park

Garden Grove Fwy.

Costa
Mesa

Newport Beach

Balboa Peninsula

Fountain
Valley

Huntington Beach

PACIFIC OCEAN

Pasadena

Los Angeles

Long Beach
Airport

Long Beach

Santa Ana Fwy.

Burbank

Hollywood

Avalon

Beverly
Hills

Santa Monica Fwy.

Palos Verdes
Peninsula

Los Angeles
International Airport

Manhattan Beach

Redondo Beach

Santa Monica

Venice Beach

To Santa Barbara

CATALINA
ISLAND

Getting Oriented

Southern California's patchwork of small communities has undeniably blurred borders. The Disneyland Resort is in Anaheim, but you might not know if you were in that city or one of its immediate neighbors except for the signs. Buena Park lies to the northwest, Garden Grove to the south, Santa Ana to the southeast, and Orange to the east.

Farther south—in Huntington Beach, Newport Beach, Laguna Beach, and San Juan Capistrano—there's a bit more breathing room between communities. Heading northwest from Anaheim, you'll come to Los Angeles International Airport.

Continuing northwest into L.A., you'll find Santa Monica to the west, and, to the east, Beverly Hills, West Hollywood, and Hollywood. On the beach farther north and west is Malibu, and inland to the east are Burbank (home of the Walt Disney Studios) and Glendale. The San Fernando Valley lies farther north and a bit inland from Los Angeles proper, while Santa Barbara, Southern California's northern boundary, is on the coast, about two hours to the north.

North–South Freeways: There are two north-south thoroughfares: I-5 (the Santa Ana Freeway in the Anaheim area) runs from Vancouver, Canada, to San Diego, and is the main inland route in Southern California, linking Los Angeles and San Diego; I-405 (the San Diego Freeway) sprouts from I-5 north of Hollywood, veers south toward the coast, then rejoins I-5 at Irvine, a bit south of Anaheim.

East–West Freeways: Of the roads that intersect the two principal north-south arteries, one of the closest to the Disneyland Resort is Route 22, also known as the Garden Grove Freeway; it begins near the ocean in Long Beach and runs beyond the southern border of Anaheim. Route 91, called the Artesia Freeway on the west side of I-5 and the Riverside Freeway on the east, lies about eight miles north of Route 22.

Farther north you will reach I-10, called the Santa Monica Freeway from its beginning point near the Pacific shore in Santa Monica to just east of downtown Los Angeles. At this juncture, it jogs north and then turns east again, becoming the San Bernardino Freeway. The I-10 thoroughfare is located approximately 12 miles north of Route 91.

North of I-10 (anywhere from two to eight miles, depending on your location) is U.S. 101, which heads south from Ventura and then due east, crossing I-405. It is known as the Ventura Freeway until a few miles east of I-405, at which point the road angles south and becomes the Hollywood Freeway, and eventually merges into I-5.

HOW TO GET THERE: Disneyland Resort is on Harbor Boulevard between Katella Avenue, Disneyland Drive, and Ball Road, 31 miles south of downtown Los Angeles and 87 miles north of San Diego. Many visitors drive to Disneyland from elsewhere in Southern California, while those who come from farther away fly into one of the area airports, rent a car, and drive from there. Once at their hotel, guests may prefer to use the hotel's shuttle

Travel Times

To/From the Resort	Approx. Distance	Drive Time
Balboa	30 miles	40 min.
Buena Park	7 miles	12 min.
Carlsbad	50 miles	60 min.
Costa Mesa	20 miles	30 min.
Dana Point	30 miles	40 min.
Garden Grove	5 miles	10 min.
Huntington Beach	15 miles	25 min.
John Wayne Airport	16 miles	25 min.
Laguna Beach	30 miles	45 min.
Las Vegas	280 miles	5–6 hrs.
Long Beach	20 miles	30 min.
Los Angeles (downtown and airport)	31 miles	45–90 min.
Newport Beach	20 miles	30 min.
Palm Springs	180 miles	3–4 hrs.
San Diego	87 miles	90 min.
San Juan Capistrano	32 miles	45 min.
San Simeon	270 miles	5–6 hrs.
Santa Ana	5 miles	10 min.
Santa Barbara	110 miles	2–3 hrs.

Drive times are under optimal conditions; rain or rush-hour traffic will increase or even double the time.

or Anaheim Resort Transportation (ART) to and from the Disneyland Resort.

Southbound I-5 Exit: To get to Disneyland, southbound I-5 (the Santa Ana Freeway) travelers should exit at Disneyland Drive, turn left, cross Ball Road, and follow signs to the most convenient parking area.

Northbound I-5 Exit: Northbound travelers should exit I-5 at Katella Avenue, proceed straight to Disney Way, and then follow signs to the most convenient parking area.

From John Wayne/Orange County Airport: Take I-405 north to CA-55 north to I-5 north. Watch carefully for highway signs once out of the airport. Exit at Katella Avenue, head straight to Disney Way, then follow signs to the most convenient parking area.

From Los Angeles International Airport: Take I-105 east to I-605 north to I-5 south. Take Disneyland Drive exit toward Ball Road. Merge onto Disneyland Drive, and proceed to the most convenient parking zone (the Mickey & Friends parking structure or the Toy Story parking area).

Exit off Orange Freeway: Travelers on the 57 freeway should exit on Katella Avenue and proceed west. Turn right on Harbor Boulevard, and follow signs to the parking area.

ANAHEIM SURFACE STREETS: Disneyland is in the center of the Anaheim Resort, a 1,100-acre district. Disneyland is bounded by Harbor Boulevard on the east, Disneyland Drive (a segment of West Street) on the west, Ball Road on the north, and Katella Avenue on the south.

Harbor Boulevard, near Ball Road, is the most convenient place to pick up I-5 (Santa Ana Freeway) going north to Los Angeles. Katella Avenue, past Anaheim Boulevard, is the most convenient entrance to southbound I-5 going to Newport Beach and points south.

Note: Parking rules are strictly enforced in Anaheim. Be sure to park in a designated lot, feed the parking meter often, and heed all signs.

LOCAL TRANSPORTATION: The Orange County Transportation Authority (OCTA; 714-560-6282; *www.octa.net*) provides daily bus service throughout the area, with limited weekend service. Several different lines stop at the Disneyland Resort, but note that public transportation, while cost-efficient, may involve considerable waiting and transferring. At press time, the fare was $5 for a one-day unlimited pass. Seniors (age 65 and older) and people with disabilities pay $1.50 for a one-day pass. Exact change is required; pennies are not accepted.

Anaheim Resort Transportation, aka ART (visit *www.rideart.org*, or call 888-364-2787), is a multi-route guest transit system serving the Anaheim Resort area.

ART Passes may be purchased online and from many area hotels, public sales outlets, and various kiosk locations. Drivers do not sell passes. Adult fares are $5.50 for a one-day pass, $14 for three days, and $23 for a five-day pass. Kids ages 3 to 9 pay $2 for one day, $3 for three days, and $5 for five-day passes. There is no charge for baby passengers.

The Metro serves L.A. County and the major attractions of Orange County (323-466-3876; *www.metro.net*). Cost is about $1.75 each way (75 cents for seniors). A refillable TAP (Transit Access Pass) card, exact change, or a token is required. Tokens may be bought in bags of ten ($17.50) at locations throughout the L.A. area.

TAXIS: The only licensed taxi company that's officially authorized to serve Disneyland Resort is the Anaheim Yellow Cab Company (*www.yellowcab.com*; 714-999-9999). The fare to John Wayne Airport from Disneyland Hotel generally runs about $44, plus tip; if you're going to LAX, figure at least $99 (or more, depending on the traffic). The fare to and from Long Beach Airport runs approximately $68, plus gratuity. Prices for town cars are usually slightly higher. Taxis can be called to pick you up at train and bus stations. Lyft and Uber car-sharing services are also authorized to pick up and drop off guests—see the Hot Tip below for details.

HOT TIP!

Guests getting picked up or dropped off by car (including car-sharing services) should go to the drop-off/loading zone in the Downtown Disney parking area. Parking is free for the first 3 hours when you make a minimum $20 purchase and receive validation at any Downtown Disney location. Downtown Disney table-service eateries will validate up to 2 additional hours. After that, it costs about $14 per hour (charged in 30-minute increments). The maximum daily parking and lost ticket charge is about $56.

Planning Your Itinerary

For those lucky enough to live in the Los Angeles/Orange County area, the Disneyland Resort offers the opportunity to return frequently. Seasoned visitors and first-timers alike will do well to plan each step of their visit far in advance—make the travel arrangements as soon as vacation dates are set (refer to the Trip Planning Timeline below to make sure you don't miss any crucial steps), and then study the following chapters of this book to decide how you'd like to spend each day of the trip.

How many days should you spend with the Mouse and his pals? Well, that's up to you, but to experience the Disneyland Resort at its best, we recommend a stay of at least four full days—you will have enough time to see quite a few theme park attractions, parades, and shows (plus revisit all of your favorites), lounge beside your hotel's pool, enjoy a meal (possibly with Disney characters present), shop for souvenirs, and enjoy a rejuvenating spa treatment. If you'd like to visit other area attractions, add on one day for each excursion. But don't try to cram too much into one visit; this is your vacation, after all.

Once you've decided how many days you're going to dedicate to Disney, it's time to decide how you'll split up your time on-property. We suggest that you begin with a day at Disneyland Park (for the original and quintessential Disney experience), followed by a visit to Disney California Adventure. On the third day, return to Disneyland and hit the park's highlights, plus any attractions you missed, and save time for souvenir shopping. Day four should be dedicated to your preferred park and some downtime by the pool or in Downtown Disney. Evenings can be spent in a park, if it's open late, or in Downtown Disney's restaurants, lounges, and play zones. The options are plentiful.

On the following pages, we've provided full-day schedules to guide you through four days in the parks (with tips for families with young children and priorities for days when the lines are at their longest). The schedules are meant to be flexible and fun (not Disney boot camp), so take them at your own pace and plan breaks to relax: Have a Mickey Mouse ice cream bar, browse through the shops, smell the flowers, or just pick a bench and watch the crowds rush by.

Trip Planning Timeline

First Things First

◇ Make hotel and transportation reservations as far ahead as possible. Call 714-520-5050 to buy theme park tickets and to book Disney hotel accommodations (see pages 14 and 40 for details); remember that a deposit must be paid within 21 days of the reservation. Log all confirmation numbers in a notebook, and call to confirm before you leave home.

◇ Decide where you will be on each day of your vacation, and create a simple schedule.

6 Months

◇ Unless you opted for a vacation package that includes theme park admission, it's time to purchase your Disney park tickets (see page 17 for ticket options and ordering methods).

Up to 2 Months

◇ Find out theme park hours, the attraction refurbishment schedule, and details on any special events by visiting www.disneyland.com, using the (free) Disneyland Resort mobile app, or calling 714-781-4565.

◇ Make dining reservations (they're necessary at most table-service restaurants at the Disneyland Resort; call 714-781-3463), and add the information to your day-by-day schedule. Refer to the *Good Meals, Great Times* chapter for details on Disneyland Resort eateries.

2 Weeks

◇ Airline confirmation and travel vouchers should have arrived by now. Contact your travel agent or travel company if they haven't shown up yet.

1 Week

◇ Reconfirm all reservations and finalize your day-by-day vacation schedule.

◇ Add all your important telephone numbers (doctor, family members, house sitter) to your trip planning notebook, and be sure to bring it and your day-by-day schedule with you.

1 Day

◇ Place any tickets you may have purchased (and a valid, government-issued photo ID) in a carry-on bag.

DISNEYLAND PARK
ONE-DAY SCHEDULE

- Disneyland's breakfast options have expanded of late. If you don't nosh at the hotel, consider having a bite at Red Rose Taverne, Plaza Inn, or Carnation Cafe.

- Take in the sights as you walk down Main Street, but don't stop to shop now (you'll have time for that later). Instead, head straight to Adventureland's Jungle Cruise and Indiana Jones Adventure* before making your way to Splash Mountain* and The Many Adventures of Winnie the Pooh in Critter Country. (If you plan to dine at the Blue Bayou, be sure to make a reservation in advance by calling 714-781-3463.)

- Be sure to experience the park's newest land, Star Wars: Galaxy's Edge. Highlights include *Millennium Falcon:* Smugglers Run and Star Wars: Rise of the Resistance.

- Backtrack to New Orleans Square, and visit the Haunted Mansion* and Pirates of the Caribbean before breaking for lunch.

- Next, see the show at the Golden Horseshoe Saloon, then tackle Big Thunder Mountain Railroad* in Frontierland. (Don't ride Big Thunder on a full stomach.)

- Explore Fantasy Faire. Then walk through the Castle into Fantasyland and visit Snow White, Pinocchio, Peter Pan, and Mr. Toad. Be sure to see Alice, the Mad Tea Party, the Matterhorn,* and It's a Small World, too.

- Keep an eye on the time and try to fit the afternoon show or parade into your schedule.

- Visit Mickey's Toontown, making Roger Rabbit's Car Toon Spin* a top priority.

(Continued on page 30)

* Fastpass is available for this ride. Retrieve your time-saving Fastpass before visiting the land's remaining attractions. To learn how the system works, see page 58.

DISNEYLAND DELIGHTS

These attractions combine to form the quintessential Disneyland park experience:

Indiana Jones Adventure
Pirates of the Caribbean
Haunted Mansion
Big Thunder Mountain Railroad
Splash Mountain
Peter Pan's Flight
Matterhorn Bobsleds
It's a Small World
Star Tours—The Adventures Continue
Jungle Cruise
The Many Adventures of Winnie the Pooh
Buzz Lightyear Astro Blasters
Space Mountain
Fantasmic! (nighttime spectacular)
Mr. Toad's Wild Ride
Millennium Falcon: Smugglers Run

LINE BUSTERS

When the park is packed, the following attractions may have shorter waits: The Disneyland Railroad, Enchanted Tiki Room, Tarzan's Treehouse, The Many Adventures of Winnie the Pooh, *Mark Twain* riverboat, and The Disneyland Story—Presenting Great Moments with Mr. Lincoln.

IF YOU HAVE YOUNG CHILDREN

- First, head to Fantasyland and visit each area attraction (note that some are scary for small children) before heading to Mickey's Toontown. Then visit Critter Country to enjoy The Many Adventures of Winnie the Pooh.

- Take tykes to It's a Small World and King Arthur Carrousel. If you need cooling off, backtrack to Toontown and splash around at Donald's Boat.

- Ride the Jungle Cruise, then sing with the Tiki Birds in Adventureland and climb through Tarzan's Treehouse before returning to your favorite rides.

- Scope out a spot on a Main Street curb up to an hour before the parade. For smaller crowds, watch the parade from the viewing area near It's a Small World.

(Continued from page 29)

➭ Hop on the Disneyland Railroad and disembark in Tomorrowland. Hit the Finding Nemo Submarine Voyage, Buzz Lightyear Astro Blasters, and Space Mountain* before heading to dinner.

Note: If the park is open late, you can board the monorail in Tomorrowland and dine in Downtown Disney before returning to the park.

➭ After dinner, take the wheel of a hot rod at Autopia, then take flight at Star Tours—The Adventures Continue* and/or Astro Orbitor.

➭ Take little ones back to Mickey's Toontown before it closes for the day—it closes earlier than the rest of the park when there is a fireworks presentation (generally one hour before the show starts).

➭ On nights when Fantasmic! is presented, make a point of getting to New Orleans Square and the Rivers of America in plenty of time to see it—or, better yet, get a Fastpass assignment early in the day. (Check a park Entertainment Times Guide for the schedule.)

➭ Stroll back to Main Street. Shop, stop for dessert, see the Disneyland Story, and watch the fireworks light the sky over Sleeping Beauty Castle.

➭ If there's time, take a second spin on your favorite attractions.

MEET THE CHARACTERS

There are lots of places to mix and mingle with Disney characters in this park. Some of the better spots include Toontown (Mickey, Minnie, Donald, Goofy, and more), Critter Country (Pooh and pals), Fantasyland's Fantasy Faire (princesses), and around Town Square on Main Street, U.S.A. Check a park Times Guide for the schedule. And don't forget your camera!

TOP SHOPS

Whether you're browsing or buying, Disneyland is a shopper's paradise. Here are a few of the spots where wallets get a workout:

Candy Palace
Disneyana
Emporium
Main Street Magic Shop
Pieces of Eight
Pioneer Mercantile
Port Royal Curios & Curiosities
The Star Trader

HOT TIP!

If you'd like to meet Mickey Mouse, make a beeline for his Toontown house—the Big Cheese greets guests in the movie barn out back. For the shortest wait, get there soon after Toontown opens for the day.

* Fastpass is available for this ride. Retrieve your time-saving Fastpass before visiting the land's remaining attractions. See page 58 for details.

➰ Begin your California adventure by snagging a Fastpass for Guardians of the Galaxy—Mission: BREAKOUT!* or Radiator Springs Racers* (they tend to run out of Fastpass assignments early, as do Soarin' Around the World* and Toy Story Midway Mania!*). If you'd like to view an evening performance of World of Color, now's the time to pick up a show ticket. (You can do so at a machine near the Grizzly River Run attraction entrance.)

➰ Depart from Paradise Gardens Park and head to Cars Land. Do not miss Radiator Springs Racers*! If possible, visit Mater's Junkyard Jamboree before moving on to Hollywood Land. Enjoy a thrilling adventure at Guardians of the Galaxy—Mission: BREAKOUT! (in Hollywood Land).

➰ Refer to a Times Guide for the next performance of Frozen—Live at the Hyperion, and plan to arrive at the theater at least 20 minutes before the show. In the meantime, enjoy Monsters, Inc.—Mike & Sulley to the Rescue!, Mickey's PhilharMagic, and visit Disney Animation (be sure to meet Anna and Elsa and see a show called Turtle Talk with Crush). Take tots to the interactive Disney Junior Dance Party!

(Continued on page 32)

* Fastpass is available for this ride. Retrieve your time-saving Fastpass before visiting the area's remaining attractions. To learn how the system works, see page 58.

ADVENTURE ACES

If you're short on time, be sure to catch as many of the following four-star attractions at Disney California Adventure as possible:

Toy Story Midway Mania!
Radiator Springs Racers
Frozen—Live at the Hyperion
Soarin' Around the World
World of Color
Turtle Talk with Crush
Incredicoaster
Mater's Junkyard Jamboree
Guardians of the Galaxy—Mission: BREAKOUT!
Monsters, Inc.—Mike & Sulley to the Rescue!
The Little Mermaid—Ariel's Undersea Adventure
Mickey's PhilharMagic

IF YOU HAVE YOUNG CHILDREN

➰ Head straight to the Hollywood Land section of the park. Stop in to visit with Anna and Elsa before experiencing Monsters, Inc.—Mike & Sulley to the Rescue!, and Mickey's PhilharMagic. Head over to Disney Animation for Turtle Talk and Sorcerer's Workshop. Next, pay a visit to Disney Junior Dance Party! Check a park entertainment schedule and take in a performance of Frozen—Live at the Hyperion.

➰ Try the kid-friendly obstacle course on the Redwood Creek Challenge Trail.

➰ Mosey on over to Pixar Pier. Take a spin on the Jessie's Critter Carousel and go to Toy Story Midway Mania! before moving to the Paradise Gardens Park side of the lagoon. Be sure to hit these kid-pleasers: The Little Mermaid—Ariel's Undersea Adventure and Jumpin' Jellyfish.

➰ Finally, treat night owls to the World of Color water show. (The noisy water jets might spook some.) Warn kids that they may get a teeny bit wet.

DISNEY CALIFORNIA ADVENTURE
ONE-DAY SCHEDULE

(Continued from page 31)

LINE BUSTERS

When lines abound at Disney California Adventure, we suggest heading to the following attractions: Frozen— Live at the Hyperion, Redwood Creek Challenge Trail, Disney Animation, and Monsters, Inc.—Mike & Sulley to the Rescue! The line for The Little Mermaid—Ariel's Undersea Adventure often thins later in the day.

TOP SHOPS

Shopping at this park can be an adventure in and of itself. These are some of the spots that have earned their place in the spotlight:

Big Top Toys
Elias & Co.
Off the Page
Oswald's
Rushin' River Outfitters
Sarge's Surplus Hut
Trolley Treats

MEET THE CHARACTERS

Guests have many opportunities to catch up with favorite characters at Disney California Adventure. Among the best spots are Buena Vista Street (Mickey, Goofy, and Donald Duck), Hollywood Land (Anna, Elsa, Olaf, Captain America, and Spider-Man), Redwood Creek Challenge Trail (Chip and Dale), Cars Land (Mater, McQueen, and Red the Fire Engine), and Pixar Pier (Woody, Buzz, and Jessie). Check a park Times Guide for the day's schedule. Details are subject to change.

⇨ Make your way over to Grizzly Peak and experience Soarin' Around the World. Then get set to get wet on the drenching Grizzly River Run* white-water raft ride. If you're up for it (and wearing proper footwear), then tackle the Redwood Creek Challenge Trail.

⇨ Pick up some wine-pairing tips or sample California's finest at the Golden Vine Winery.

⇨ Explore the Pacific Wharf area before proceeding on to Pixar Pier's daredevil rides (don't ride on a full stomach!).

⇨ Work your way around Paradise Bay, making sure to take in The Little Mermaid—Ariel's Undersea Adventure.

⇨ Be sure to catch the delightful nighttime extravaganza World of Color.* Line up for a waterside viewing spot at least 45 minutes before showtime—and know that you might get a little wet if you are up close.

* Fastpass is available for this ride. Retrieve your time-saving Fastpass before visiting the area's remaining attractions. See page 58 for details.

A SECOND DAY IN DISNEYLAND PARK

Returning for a second or third day in each of the theme parks means more time to savor the atmosphere, try attractions you missed the first day, and revisit all the old and new favorites. Knowing that there will be a second day to play also makes for a less harried pace on day one.

➡ Start the morning with a character breakfast at the Plaza Inn (you can also share a morning meal with the characters outside the park at Goofy's Kitchen in the Disneyland Hotel, the Grand Californian's Storytellers Cafe, or PCH Grill in Disney's Paradise Pier Hotel).

➡ If you missed or would like to revisit Star Wars: Galaxy's Edge, get there early! It is a wildly popular realm.

➡ Head to Tomorrowland and experience Space Mountain,* Star Tours—The Adventures Continue,* Buzz Lightyear Astro Blasters, and visit other favorites.

➡ Navigate over to Mickey's Toontown. See the sights and spend some time mingling with resident Disney characters.

➡ Visit It's a Small World, enjoy the fanfare at the nearby show, Mickey and the Magical Map, and then tour Fantasyland.

➡ Stroll, shop, and take a lunch break on (or on your way to) Main Street, U.S.A.

➡ Ride a Main Street Vehicle up to Town Square and continue on foot toward Adventureland.

➡ Stop at the Enchanted Tiki Room and Tarzan's Treehouse before heading to New Orleans Square. There, the priorities are the Haunted Mansion* and Pirates of the Caribbean. Visit them and navigate over to Critter Country for Splash Mountain* and The Many Adventures of Winnie the Pooh.

➡ Meander through the shops of New Orleans Square, and then stop for a leisurely dinner at a nearby eatery. River Belle Terrace, the French Market, and the full-service Blue Bayou and Cafe Orleans are all solid options.

➡ Select a viewing spot about 45 minutes ahead for the evening's performance of Fantasmic! (if it is scheduled).

➡ Wait for the crowds to disperse at show's end and make your way to Big Thunder Mountain Railroad* for one last go 'round before the park closes for the night.

* Fastpass is available for this ride. To learn how the system works, see page 58.

A SECOND DAY IN DISNEY CALIFORNIA ADVENTURE

⇨ If you don't have an advance reservation for a table-service meal, stop for a hearty quick-service breakfast at Flo's V8 Cafe.

⇨ Cut through Hollywood Land and get a Fast-pass for Guardians of the Galaxy—Mission: BREAKOUT! Head to the wildly popular Cars Land, followed by Pixar Pier.

⇨ Thrill-seekers flip for the topsy-turvy Incredi-coaster,* and gamers of all ages will swoon over Toy Story Midway Mania!*

⇨ Take a lunch break at Lamplight Lounge, Flo's V8 Cafe, Award Wieners, Cocina Cucamonga, or Pacific Wharf Cafe; or, if the park is open late, head back to your hotel to relax or splash in the pool (be sure to retain your park ticket so that you can return later in the day). Another option is to spend the afternoon in Downtown Disney—most of its restaurants and shops open by noon (or earlier).

⇨ Your California Adventure picks up again with Soarin' Around the World* (located in Grizzly Peak Airfield), followed by a visit to The Little Mermaid—Ariel's Undersea Adventure, then on to Grizzly River Run* (if you don't mind the likelihood of getting more than a tad soggy).

⇨ Stop for the parade if one is offered today, then make your way over to Hollywood Land. En route, try to catch a performance by The Red Car Trolley News Boys (featuring a very special guest: Mickey Mouse).

⇨ Wander through the backlot, enjoying the impromptu entertainment, take in Turtle Talk with Crush, and meet Anna and Elsa inside Disney Animation. Olaf, Spider-Man, and Captain America may greet guests in Hollywood Land, too. Take a tour of Monstropolis at Monsters, Inc.—Mike and Sulley to the Rescue! and visit Mickey's PhilharMagic.

⇨ Plan to line up at least 20 minutes early for the musical stage show known as Frozen—Live at the Hyperion.

⇨ If time permits after the show, revisit some of your favorite attractions or search for last-minute souvenirs at the shops on Buena Vista Street.

⇨ Don't miss World of Color*—it's an extremely popular show. (Guests up front may get a little wet.) If possible, snag a show ticket for World of Color—and know that it will not interrupt any Fastpass assignments during your visit to the park. (Show tickets are dispensed from a Fastpass-like machine situated near The Little Mermaid— Ariel's Undersea Adventure.)

* Fastpass is available for this ride. To learn how the system works, see page 58.

Fingertip Reference Guide

BARBERS AND SALONS

One nearby spot at which hair may be cut or coiffed is Pure Escape Beauty Bar at the Hilton Anaheim Hotel (777 Convention Way; 714-740-4628).

CAR CARE

The Anaheim office of the Automobile Club of Southern California is located at 420 N. Euclid Street; *www.calif.aaa.com*; 714-774-2392. For emergency roadside service, call 800-400-4222.

DRINKING POLICIES

While Disneyland Park has lifted its long-standing no-alcohol policy (currently offering spirited beverages at Oga's Cantina), imbibing is an option at many spots at Disney California Adventure and at many venues within the Downtown Disney District. Alcohol may also be purchased in the lounges and restaurants of the three Disney hotels. The legal drinking age in the state of California is 21. (Legal proof of age is required.)

LOCKERS

Lockers of various sizes are available just outside the main entrance of the parks (our preferred location),

---

inside Disneyland on Main Street (behind the Market House), and inside Disney California Adventure (DCA) across from Guest Relations. Prices are $7, $10, $12, or $15 per day, depending on the locker's size. These storage facilities make it convenient to intersperse frolicking on the attractions with shopping; just make your purchases and stash them in a locker. Availability is limited, and during busy periods all the space can be taken well before noon. Disney California Adventure guests may stash items in lockers for free while they ride Grizzly River Run. The lockers are off to the side of the attraction's entrance.

LOST AND FOUND

Lost and Found is located to the left of the entrance to Disneyland Park. At any given time, a survey of the shelves might turn up mobile phones, cameras, umbrellas, strollers, handbags, sunglasses, baby shoes, jewelry, and even a few crutches, false teeth, and hubcaps. (Once, a wallet containing $1,700 in cash was turned in.) The Disneyland Resort will return lost items to guests who fill out a report. If you lose something at a hotel, contact the front desk.

MAIL

Postcards are sold in gift shops throughout Anaheim, in many shops and souvenir stands on Disneyland Resort property, and at the three Disneyland Resort hotels. Stamps are sold at all Disney hotels, too.

Cards that are deposited in the mailboxes in the Disney theme parks are picked up and delivered to the U.S. Post Office once a day, early in the morning. All items are postmarked Anaheim, not Disneyland. (By the way, don't forget to arrange for your own mail to be held by the post office or picked up by a neighbor while you're on vacation.) Due to the heavy volume, expect delivery to take much longer than usual—don't mail your rent from here.

Post Office: The U.S. Post Office that's closest to the Disneyland Resort is Holiday Station, a half-mile away (1180 W. Ball Rd., Anaheim; 714-533-8182). It's open from 9 A.M. to 5 P.M. weekdays only.

MEDICAL MATTERS

Blisters are the most common complaint received by Disney's First Aid departments, located at the north end of Main Street, U.S.A., next to Lost Children in Disneyland, and at the Chamber of Commerce near the entrance of Disney California Adventure. So be

---

HOT TIP!

To avoid the sometimes maddening congestion at the Main Street locker location, consider stowing your stuff at the lockers near the picnic area, just outside Disneyland Park's turnstiles. (They are on the left side of the entrance as you face the park.)

forewarned, and wear comfortable, broken-in shoes (bring a backup pair, too)—and pack extra Band-Aids, just in case.

If you have a serious medical problem while on Disney property, call 911 and contact any Disney Cast Member (aka employee). He or she will get in touch with First Aid to make further arrangements. First Aid, staffed with registered nurses, will supply breathing machines and crutches for guests. It will not dispense medication to anyone under 18 without the consent of a parent or chaperone.

It's always a good idea to carry an insurance card and any other pertinent medical information. Those with chronic health problems should carry copies of all their prescriptions, along with their doctor's telephone number.

Prescriptions: The pharmacy at CVS, about a mile from Disneyland Resort, is open 24/7 (480 South Main St.; 714-938-1200). The drive-thru pharmacy at Walgreens, about three miles from the Disneyland Resort, also operates 24 hours a day, seven days a week (12001 Euclid St., Garden Grove; 714-530-1071). At the intersection of Katella Ave. and Harbor Blvd., there is another 24/7 CVS with a pharmacy that's open Monday through Friday from 9 A.M. to 9 P.M., Saturdays and Sundays from 10 A.M. until 6 P.M. (1803 S. Harbor Blvd., Anaheim; 714-817-9116).

Refrigerator Facilities: In the Disney parks, insulin and antibiotics that must be refrigerated can be stored for the day at First Aid. (It does not store breast milk for nursing mothers.) Outside the theme parks, there are refrigerators in many of the area's hotels and motels. If your room doesn't have one, a fridge can usually be supplied for a nominal charge, or the hotel or motel may be able to store insulin in its own refrigerator. Inquire before you make the reservation.

MONEY

Cash, traveler's checks, Visa, American Express, Master-Card, JCB, Discover Card, Diner's Club, Disney gift cards, and Disney Dollars are all accepted as payment for admission to the theme parks, for merchandise purchased in shops, and for meals (except at select souvenir and food carts, where it's strictly cash). Personal checks may be used to pay for park admission. Checks must be imprinted with the guest's name and address, drawn on a U.S. bank, and accompanied by proper ID—that is, a valid driver's license or passport. Department store charge cards are not acceptable identification for check-writing purposes. Disney hotel guests who have left a credit card number at check-in can charge most expenses in the parks to their hotel bill.

Disney Dollars: First introduced by The Walt Disney Company in 1987, Disney Dollars were discontinued in 2016. However, those already in circulation are still accepted as cash at most Disneyland Resort, Walt Disney World, and Disney Store locations. So if you have Disney Dollars burning a hole in your pocket, rest assured you can still use that colorful cash. Note that change will be provided in U.S. currency, not Mickey money.

Disney Gift Cards: Available for purchase at many merchandise locations, these may be redeemed throughout the Disneyland Resort (though there are some exceptions at Downtown Disney, where select vendors are not equipped to accept cards).

Financial Services: Automated Teller Machines (ATMs) are located at each park's main entrance; in Disneyland at The Disney Gallery on Main Street, by the Fantasyland Theatre, by the Frontierland Stockade, and in Tomorrowland; in California Adventure at the Entry Plaza, in the Pacific Wharf region, at the restrooms near Goofy's Sky School, and in the Pixar Pier area of the park; in Downtown Disney by the LEGO store and Wetzel's Pretzels; and in all Disneyland Resort hotels. For details, inquire at a Guest Relations location.

Personal checks are not accepted in the parks. ATMs at the park entrances accept credit cards for cash advances. Note that the presence of a bank on Main Street is a tad deceiving: The bank offers no financial services.

American Express Cardmember Services: Cardholders can purchase American Express Travelers Cheques, American Express Gift Cheques, and American Express gift cards, and exchange foreign currency (for a fee) at the Altour/American Express Travel Representative Office: 240 Newport Centre Dr., Suite 116, Newport Beach, CA; 714-541-3318. This office is open Monday through Friday from 9 A.M. to 5:30 P.M. and on Saturday from 9 A.M. to 4 P.M.

Many Anaheim banks sell American Express traveler's checks, usually for a one percent fee.

Foreign Currency Exchange: Foreign currency may be exchanged (at the day's current exchange rate) at City Hall in Disneyland, Chamber of Commerce at Disney California Adventure, and at the front desk at each of the three Disneyland Resort hotels. Paper currency only.

PETS

Except for certified service animals, pets are not allowed in Disneyland or Disney California Adventure. However, non-poisonous creatures may be boarded in the Disneyland Pet Care Kennel, which is located by the entrance to Disneyland Park. Reservations are not necessary (the kennel rarely reaches capacity). Pets may be boarded for the day (no overnight stays). In addition to proof of rabies and distemper vaccinations, guests have to show proof of hepatitis and leptospirosis vaccinations for dogs over four months of age. Without proof of all four vaccinations, the dog will not be permitted entrance to the kennel. At press time, it cost about $20 per day, per pet. Cash only. To ask about the kennel rates during your visit, call 714-781-7662.

Disney personnel do not handle the animals, so the pet owners themselves must put their animals into the cages and take them out again. Guests are encouraged to visit and walk their pets several times a day. Kennel attendants are not responsible for walking any of the animals in their care.

Note: During busy seasons, there may be a morning rush, starting about 30 minutes before the theme parks open, so you may encounter some delay in arranging your pet's stay. Plan accordingly.

Outside the Disneyland Resort: If you would like to board a pet in the vicinity of the Disneyland Resort, please contact the Animal Inns of America, 10852 Garden Grove Blvd., Garden Grove, CA 92843; *www.animalinns.com*; 714-636-4455.

Some hotels and motels in the Disneyland Resort area accept well-behaved (preferably small) pets, but most do not allow guests to leave their animals in a room unattended.

To learn about other possibilities for pets, contact the Anaheim/Orange County Visitor & Convention Bureau; search "pets" at *www.visitanaheim.org*, or call 714-765-2800.

PHOTOGRAPHIC NEEDS

The Main Street Photo Supply Co. inside Disneyland can answer questions and charge most batteries (or you can bring your own charger and plug it in there). Disney California Adventure offers similar services. For anything more serious, rent a camera and have a factory-authorized shop do the work on your camera when you return home. If you've lost your lens cover, it's worth checking at Lost and Found (see page 35); they may not have your cap, but they often have extras.

Try not to take your camera on wet, rough, or bumpy rides. Stash it in a locker or with a non-riding member of your party. Note that selfie sticks are not permitted in Disney theme parks.

RELIGIOUS SERVICES

Catholic: St. Justin Martyr; 2050 W. Ball Rd., Anaheim, about two miles from Disneyland; *www.saintjustin.org*; 714-774-2595. Masses are presented in English and Spanish; call or check the website for times.

Episcopal: St. Michael's Episcopal Church; 311 W. South St., Anaheim; *http://stmichaels.ladiocese.org*; 714-535-4654; about seven blocks from Disneyland. Sunday services are at 8 A.M. and 11:30 A.M. (English). Call for mass times offered in Spanish.

Jewish: Temple Beth Emet; 1770 W. Cerritos Ave., Anaheim; 714-772-4720; *www.tbe-oc.org*; a few blocks from Disneyland. Services are held on Fridays at 6 P.M. and 9 A.M. on Saturdays.

HOT TIP!

Disneyland Resort offers a new package called MaxPass, which includes mobile booking and redemption of Fastpass assignments in Disneyland and Disney California Adventure—plus unlimited downloads of PhotoPass images. For details, visit *www.disneyland.com*. All details are subject to change in 2020.

Lutheran: Prince of Peace Lutheran Church; 1421 W. Ball Rd., Anaheim; *www.princeofpeaceanaheim.com*; 714-774-0993, about one mile from the Disneyland Resort. Sunday services are at 8 A.M. (traditional) and 10:30 A.M. (praise).

Non-denominational: The Kindred Community Church; 8712 E. Santa Ana Canyon Rd., Anaheim; 714-282-9941. Services are held on Sundays at 8:30 A.M. and 10:30 A.M.. The church is about 11 miles from Disneyland; *www.kindredchurch.org*.

United Methodist: Anaheim United Methodist Church; 1000 South State College Blvd., Anaheim; 714-776-5710; *www.anaheimumc.org*; Sunday morning services are held at 10 A.M. (traditional); approximately 3.3 miles from the Disneyland Resort.

SHOPPING FOR NECESSITIES

It's a rare vacationer who doesn't leave some essential at home or run out of it mid-trip. Gift shops in almost all the hotels stock items no traveler should be without, but they usually cost more than in conventional retail shops. One good source is CVS Pharmacy at 480 South Main St.; 714-938-1200.

Inside the theme parks, aspirin, bandages, suntan lotions, and other sundries are sold; just ask a Cast Member to direct you to the closest shop. Some items are also available at each park's First Aid location and Baby Care Center.

SMOKING POLICY

Disneyland Resort is a smoke-free zone. Smoking (of any kind) is not permitted anywhere within the boundaries of the Disneyland Resort. This includes Disneyland and Disney California Adventure theme parks, Downtown Disney District, and all three Disneyland Resort hotels (including guestrooms and balconies). A $250–$500 cleaning fee will be charged for smoking in hotel rooms, on balconies, or on patios. The smoking ban includes tobacco, e-cigarettes, and any products creating a vapor or smoke. Smoking of marijuana is prohibited. No exceptions. For more details, visit *disneyland.com*.

TELEPHONES

If you don't have a wireless phone handy (or charged), know that local calls from most pay phones in Southern California cost 50 cents. Most hotels in the area charge an average of a dollar or more for local, toll-free, and credit-card calls made from your room.

For long-distance calls, policies vary from hotel to hotel, but charges are always higher than they would be for direct-dial calls made from a pay phone. It makes the most sense to use a calling card when dialing long-distance from a room phone.

Phone Cards: Disney offers AT&T prepaid phone cards in values of $10 and $20. They can be purchased at select locations at the Disneyland resort hotels.

Wireless Phones: To ensure a dose of uninterrupted magic for you and those around you, stick to texting while visiting the parks and silence your ringer. You'll be glad you did.

TIPPING

The standard gratuities around Anaheim are about the same as in any other city of its size. Expect to tip bellhops about $1 to $2 per bag. Tip cabdrivers 15 percent; outstanding shuttle or tour bus drivers, $1 to $2. Valets usually get $1 to $3 when you pick up the car. In table-service restaurants, a 15 to 20 percent gratuity is generally the norm. If you are pleased with the condition of your room, it is customary to leave a gratuity of $2 to $5 per day for the housekeeper (leave a note with the tip to avoid confusion). Note that room service bills often include a gratuity.

WEATHER

Weather Information: For current weather forecasts, pay a visit to *www.weather.gov*, *www.weather.com*, or *www.wunderground.com*.

DID YOU KNOW?

The land on which Disneyland Resort stands was once occupied by groves of orange and walnut trees. Some of the original trees' descendants still call Disneyland home.

ACCOMMODATIONS

"Why do we have to grow up?" —Walt Disney

The welcome sign is always out at the Disneyland Resort hotels, where themed meals, amenities, and decor are definitely in character and add to the fun of a Disneyland vacation. And the resort's Disneyland Hotel and Grand Californian Hotel & Spa take staying at Disneyland to a lovely level of luxury.

In addition to the three hotels within the Disneyland Resort, there are dozens of properties in Orange County, known as Disneyland Good Neighbor hotels, that the Walt Disney Travel Company has handpicked to round out the Disneyland area lodging options. We have selected a bunch of these recommended hotels, based on services and proximity to the Disneyland Resort, to highlight in this chapter.

If the sole purpose of your trip is to visit Disney, plan to stay in Anaheim, either on Disneyland property or at one of the surrounding hotels. Once you arrive and check in, you won't need your car again until you leave. Complimentary transportation to and from the parks is provided by monorails and trams serving the Disneyland Resort, and by buses serving neighboring hotels, motels, and inns. If struck with a bit of wanderlust, know that Anaheim is within range of a host of Southern California destinations, including movie studios, museums, beaches, and more. Whatever your vacation goals, we've provided a variety of options in Anaheim, from old-fashioned to contemporary, simple to sublime.

Disneyland Resort Hotels

Fans of the Disneyland Resort are faced with a difficult decision. It isn't whether or not to stay on Disneyland Resort property (that's recommended if it's within the budget), but which of the three hotels to choose. Some factors to consider:

The whimsical pool area and character meals make the classic Disneyland Hotel appeal to the kids in the family (and the kid in us all).

Meanwhile, Disney's Paradise Pier Hotel sports a sunny facade to complement Disney California Adventure. Inside, Disney's influence is subtle, but it is possible to dine with characters.

The design team has really outdone itself with the Grand Californian Hotel & Spa. Located adjacent to Disney California Adventure theme park, the hotel's theming and style touch every detail, right down to the floorboards.

Whichever resort hotel you choose, one thing is certain—a stay on-property is sure to complete the overall Disney experience. From a resort information TV channel to wake-up calls from Mickey Mouse (or one of his pals), every detail reminds you that you're in Disney's land.

Exclusive Benefits: Some perks are reserved for guests staying at a Disneyland Resort Hotel. Perhaps the most significant of these is "Extra Magic Hour," which allows early entry into one of the parks (at no extra cost) on each morning of their stay (with a ticket). There's also preferred admission (with ticket) to a park if it reaches capacity. There's even an exclusive entrance to Disney California Adventure park, available only to guests staying at Disney's Grand Californian Hotel (a valid resort key card is required to use this park special entrance).

One of the most convenient perks is the ability to charge most expenses incurred at a Disney park back to the hotel room, if a credit card was provided at check-in. Purchases can be charged to the room from the time of check-in until 11 A.M. on the day of departure.

Shoppers may also enjoy having purchases delivered to their hotel's Bell Services Desk, where they can pick up their packages the next day—rather than having to tote them around the parks all day.

HOT TIP!

Rooms equipped for guests with disabilities are available at the three Disneyland Resort hotels, all of which are completely non-smoking. No exceptions.

Other on-property perks include continuous, in-lobby screenings of Disney's animated features (at all Disneyland Resort hotels), light-up "fireworks" on the headboards (at the Disneyland Hotel), and preferred access to a limited number of reservations for eateries and other guest experiences.

Check-in and Checkout: Check-in begins at 3 P.M. (4 P.M. for the Villas at Disney's Grand Californian), but guests who arrive early can check in, store their luggage at the Bell Desk, and go have fun. A photo ID is required at check-in. Checkout is at 11 A.M., and, again, bags can be stored until guests are ready to depart. Express check-out is available by leaving a credit card number at check-in.

Prices: Rates for standard guest rooms range from about $295 to $932. Concierge-level rooms start at about $438. Suites start from about $763 to $1,216. They fluctuate based on hotel, view, season, day of the week, etc. Self-parking costs $25 per day for registered guests at a Disneyland Resort hotel; valet parking costs $35 per day. Local calls, fitness center access, and unlimited Wi-Fi are available to all hotel guests.

Deposit Requirements: A deposit equal to one night's lodging (plus tax) is required at time of booking when making a "room only" reservation. Packages require a $200 deposit, due within 38 days of booking. Final payment is due 45 days prior to arrival. Packages booked within 30 days prior to final payment due date (45 days before arrival) don't require a deposit. If you prefer not to use a credit card to pay the deposit, call 714-520-5050 for details.

Cancellation Policy: For a room-only booking, the deposit will be refunded if the reservation is canceled at least 5 days before the scheduled arrival. If you need to cancel a package, expect to be charged a $200 cancellation fee, plus insurance cost (where applicable), if the package is canceled 29 days or less prior to your scheduled arrival.

Additional Costs: Portable playpen-like cribs are available upon request (no charge). Self-parking costs $25 per day, while valet parking is available for $35 per day. Note that there is no longer an additional fee for extra guests (up to room capacity).

Discounts: Annual Passholders may get special discounts throughout the Disneyland Resort. There may be discounts available to California residents, members of the military, and teachers, too—ask when you make your reservation. Disney Visa® Cardmembers can reap savings on merchandise, guided tours, and dining at the Disneyland Resort. For more information, visit *DisneyRewards.com.*

Packages: The Walt Disney Travel Company offers packages that feature a stay at one of the Disneyland hotels. Call 714-520-5050.

DISNEYLAND HOTEL: This fanciful resort adjacent to the Downtown Disney District was the first hotel erected at Disneyland Resort—way back in 1955. It has had many looks over the years, and the current one proves the old adage: Everything old is new again! While the motif is a tribute to yesteryear and highlights the original mid-20th-century style of the hotel, there are some decidedly 21st-century touches, such as colorful fiber-optic "fireworks" on many of the guest-room headboards.

The pool area is popular with guests of all ages. With a nod to iconic park signage, "Disneyland" is spelled out in familiar blocks atop a platform supporting two twisting water slides. Reminiscent of the original monorail station at the Disneyland Hotel, a replica monorail train sits at each pool slide's entrance. The larger of the big slides sits 26 feet high and stretches 187 feet. The area also has a two-lane, mini slide for younger guests, as well as bubble jets in which to play. There are two hot tub spas and six poolside cabanas, too (there's a fee for cabana use).

The hotel has nearly 1,000 rooms, including 60 or so suites, located in three towers. Most tower rooms have two queen beds, and many rooms can sleep up to five people (one of them on a daybed). The 11-story Adventure Tower looks toward Downtown Disney and

PHOTO BY JILL SAFRO

Disney California Adventure on one side and the main pool on the other. The 11-story Fantasy Tower offers rooms with pool views, but only on one side; guests on the other side look out over city rooftops, with Disneyland to the right, and the best view of the fireworks. The 14-story Frontier Tower's rooms provide city and courtyard views.

A monorail stop is a short walk away in neighboring Downtown Disney, which allows for extremely easy access to Disneyland (it drops guests off in Tomorrowland)—a nice convenience for guests who relish a break in their park-going with a trip to one of the hotel pools, or the Fitness Center. The workout room may be used by all registered resort guests (age 14 and above; guests under age 18 must be accompanied by an adult) and is accessed with a room key.

In the lobby of the Fantasy Tower, a large shop called Fantasia sells Disney souvenirs. Goofy's Kitchen, hosted by Chef Goofy and his pals, is an extremely popular buffet open for brunch and dinner; Steakhouse 55 offers breakfast, dinner, and afternoon tea in an elegant setting; The Coffee House provides beverages, snacks, and quick meals for guests on the go. Room service is available; and Tangaroa Terrace Tropical Bar & Grill, a tiki-inspired casual dining spot, serves three meals a day with a South Seas flair, as well as grab-and-go items. The adjoining bar, Trader Sam's, is a nice spot for drinks and appetizers. (For more about dining, see *Good Meals, Great Times*, beginning on page 109.)

The convention and meetings area, adjacent to Goofy's Kitchen and linked to the lobby via a photo-lined passageway, deserves a look for its Disney-related artwork, including a floor-to-ceiling collage of Disney collectibles and milestones. Created entirely from old toys, souvenirs, name tags, and other assorted memorabilia, it commemorates the colorful and unique history of Disneyland.

The hotel can provide safe-deposit boxes, currency exchange, and child-care referrals. An ATM is on the premises. Airport buses bound for Orange County and Los Angeles airports stop at the nearby Disneyland Resort transportation area on Harbor Boulevard (aka West Shuttle Area), as do tour buses, city, and county buses.

Guest rooms have 2 queen beds or one king bed, a flat-screen TV, small safe, coffeemaker, 24-hour room service, desk with a telephone, free Wi-Fi, hair dryer, iron with board, small (unstocked) refrigerator, and complimentary weekday newspaper.

Standard room rates start at about $393 to $600, depending on view and season; no charge for roll-aways. Concierge-level rooms start at about $670. Suites range from about $799 to $5,100 and up. (Higher rates are for specialty suites such as the Pirates of the Caribbean Suite and the Mickey Mouse Penthouse Suite.)

Self-parking costs $25 per day; valet $35 a day. Non-registered guests who dine at Story Tellers cafe receive 3 hours free parking with validation, while Napa Rose and Mandara Spa patronage includes 5 hours free parking with validation. Non-resort guests just visiting the hotel pay about $20 for the first hour and $10 for each extra hour to self-park (with a $60 maximum for 24 hours); $30 for the first hour and $10 for each additional hour of valet parking, with a $100 maximum. Note that all prices were correct at press time but are likely to change in 2020.

Disneyland Hotel, 1150 Magic Way, Anaheim, CA 92802; 714-956-6425 (to make reservations) or 714-778-6600 (front desk); *www.disneyland.com*.

DISNEY'S GRAND CALIFORNIAN HOTEL & SPA:
This hotel is in a prime location—right in the middle of the Disneyland Resort. It includes 948 recently renovated studio rooms, 44 suites, 50 Disney Vacation Club villas, and 3 swimming pools. The resort has its own special entrance to Disney California Adventure park and easy access to the Downtown Disney District.

A border of trees surrounds the six-story hotel, built as a tribute to the American Craftsman tradition of the early 1900s. Cedar and redwood paneling decorates the cavernous lobby, where display cabinets filled with original art and reproductions introduce guests to that rich period of art. The lobby's great hearth has a perennially lit fire. Furnishings throughout the hotel have warm colors and intricate textures.

Each deluxe guestroom and suite features a 55-inch TV, small safe, 24-hour room service, desk with a phone, Wi-Fi Internet access (no charge), USB chargers, coffeemaker (with coffee and non-dairy creamer), iron with board, and small (unstocked) refrigerator. The bathroom is equipped with a makeup mirror and hair dryer.

Most of the guestrooms in the hotel feature two queen beds with a sleeper chair or daybed, or a king bed with

a sleeper chair. The carved wooden headboards are made of quarter-sawn oak, a hallmark of Craftsman design. They feature a blossoming orange tree mural, complete with two familiar chipmunks frolicking in its branches. California-inspired artwork dots the room walls, including original designs of orange crate labels—paying homage to Disneyland Resort's history.

The Disney Vacation Club (DVC) villas reflect the same design as the hotel and are available to all guests when not occupied by DVC members. Each studio has a queen-size bed and queen-size sleeper sofa, plus a kitchenette with microwave, coffeemaker, and mini fridge. Larger (one-, two-, and three-bedroom) villas sleep 5 to 12 and offer dining areas, kitchens, laundry facilities, master baths with hot tub spas, and DVD players. They include a king-size bed in the master bedroom, a living room with queen-size sleeper sofa (and a sleeper chair in the one- and two-bedroom villas), and either two queen-size beds or a queen bed and a double sleeper sofa in extra bedrooms.

Guest services include 24-hour room service, laundry and dry cleaning (including same-day service), a fitness center, and a business center. The concierge level offers upgraded amenities and services. Guests can relax at the Fountain Pool and Redwood Pool (the two are adjacent) and make a splash at the Mariposa Pool, which includes a companion hot tub and 4 private cabanas that are available to rent throughout the day. The luxurious Mandara Spa features treatment rooms and a couples suite accented with Balinese-inspired art and textiles. The spa includes steam rooms and a nail salon. Acorn's Gifts & Goods, which sells apparel,

special-edition pins, toys, collectibles, and snacks, is located in the main lobby.

Among the dining options are the award-winning Napa Rose, which features California cuisine and wines, and Storytellers Cafe, open for three meals in an Old California setting and the backdrop for a character-hosted breakfast. A newly (and nicely!) refurbished quick-service eatery, White Water Snacks, supplies coffee drinks, made-to-order, and grab-and-go selections; a new poolside bar is a good choice for a light meal or snack. The Hearthstone Lounge doubles as a breakfast spot, serving coffee and pastries to guests heading into the park.

The hotel can provide safe-deposit boxes and currency exchange. An ATM is on the premises. Airport buses bound for Orange County and Los Angeles airports stop at the hotel's main entrance, as do tour buses, and city and county buses. Buses also stop at the nearby Disneyland Resort transportation center (aka East Shuttle Area).

Rates for standard guestrooms start at about $485, depending on the view, date, season, etc. Concierge rooms start at about $932; suites start at about $1,216. There are no rollaway beds, but portable playpen-like cribs may be requested (no charge). Self-parking costs $25 a day; valet parking is $35. Non-resort guests pay $20 for the first hour of self-parking and $10 for each additional hour (with a $60 maximum); $30 for the first hour of valet parking, and $10 for each additional hour (with a $100 max).

Disney's Grand Californian Hotel & Spa, 1600 S. Disneyland Drive, Anaheim, CA 92803; 714-956-6425 (for reservations) or 714-635-2300 (front desk); or visit *www.disneyland.com.*

PHOTO BY KEITH GROSHANS

DISNEY'S PARADISE PIER HOTEL: This property's facade reflects the cheery ambience and carefree style of California beachfront boardwalks. The smallest of the Disneyland Resort hotels, Paradise Pier is popular with businesspeople and families alike.

The hotel's two high-rise towers—one 15 stories, the other 14 stories—are juxtaposed to create a central atrium, which cradles the lobby and a larger-than-life

character sculpture. Mickey's familiar silhouette shows up in subtle ways in the hotel's beachy decor. Each of the 481 guestrooms, including 20 suites, features Disney touches, one king-size bed or two queen beds, plus a twin daybed in the sitting area (a particular convenience for families). The rooms on the cabana level open onto a large recreation area that includes a sundeck, swimming pool, slide, hot tub spa, children's play area, and snack bar. If you plan to spend a lot of time in or beside the pool, consider a concierge-level room on the second floor for direct access.

The Mickey in Paradise shop, a lounge, and a restaurant are on the ground level of the hotel. Disney's PCH Grill offers dinner and a morning meal dubbed Donald Duck's Seaside Breakfast. The Surfside Lounge serves breakfast, lunch, and dinner selections, along with a full-service bar and a variety of coffee drinks. Room service is offered, too. The hotel also has an exercise room, guest laundry service, a concierge lounge, and an ATM (fees may apply). A glass-enclosed elevator provides a bird's-eye view of the lobby and Disney California Adventure park.

The hotel is connected to the Disneyland Resort and Downtown Disney by a landscaped walkway. Guests (with valid admission tickets) can access the Disneyland theme park by taking the monorail from the Downtown Disney station. (The monorail transports guests in the park's Tomorrowland station.) Both Disneyland and Disney California Adventure theme parks are within a 10- to 15-minute walk.

Standard rooms accommodate up to five guests. Rates start at about $295 and vary depending on the view, date, season, etc. There is no charge for kids under 18 sharing their parents' room; no charge for rollaways or cribs. Concierge rooms start at about $433. Suites begin at about $763. Self-parking costs $25 per day; valet parking is $35.

Disney's Paradise Pier Hotel, 1717 South Disneyland Drive, Anaheim, CA 92802; 714-956-6425 (reservations) or 714-999-0990 (front desk); *www.disneyland.com.*

Disneyland Good Neighbor Hotels

With fewer than 2,500 hotel rooms available at the Disneyland Resort and tens of thousands of guests pouring through the parks each day, it's no wonder that a majority of visitors stay off Disney property. To make it easier for guests to narrow down their off-property choices, the folks at Disney have selected local hotels and motels that meet their standards and anointed them Disneyland Good Neighbor Hotels. Before receiving the Disney seal of approval, hotels are reportedly graded on amenities, services, decor, guest satisfaction, price, and location. All Good Neighbor hotels sell tickets to Disneyland Resort theme parks.

Ranging from small operations to big chains, Good Neighbor hotels proliferate along Harbor Boulevard, which flanks Disneyland resort on the east. From Harbor, it's a relatively manageable to walk to the Disneyland Resort. (If you're planning to walk to and from Disney's theme parks, be sure to inquire about the distance before you book your hotel.) A few hotels are on Ball Road, the Resort's northern boundary. Below Katella Avenue, which borders the resort to the south, side streets lead to the Anaheim Convention Center and major convention hotels. Divided into Superior, Deluxe, Moderate, and Suite categories, there are more than 40 Good Neighbor hotels in all. In the following pages, we describe some of our favorites. For the properties not detailed here, see page 50.

Prices: Expect to pay approximately $109 to $425 (plus tax), or more, per night for a hotel room for two adults and two kids (children usually stay in their parents' room for free), $79 to $270 for a motel room, and $50 to $85 for tent or RV camping. Prices drop a bit in winter; they are highest in the summer and over holidays. The hotel room tax in Anaheim, California, is 15 percent.

Additional Costs: When comparing accommodation costs, consider hidden zingers, like parking. Hotels usually charge for it ($14 to $24 a day; more for valet service). Many also charge a fee when more than four people occupy a room. Ask about telephone rates when you check in—hotel surcharges are notoriously huge. Many hotels offer free Wi-Fi. Be sure to ask.

Savings: You may be able to save money by staying in a hotel that offers complimentary breakfast and shuttle service to Disneyland. Discounts are sometimes

HOT TIP!

For updates and additional information about the Disneyland Resort's Good Neighbor hotels, visit *https://disneyland.disney.go.com/hotels/good-neighbor/*. To learn about vacation packages that may be offered during your planned visit, go to *https://disneyland.disney.go.com/vacation-packages/good-neighbor-hotel-package/*.

offered to those who belong to an automobile or retirement association.

Individual Needs: What is absolutely essential for one vacationer—and worth the extra cost—might seem completely frivolous to another guest: room service, on-site restaurants, live music, a suite, a kitchen, concierge service and amenities, large swimming pool, exercise room, or a place that accepts pets.

Packages: The Walt Disney Travel Company offers packages in conjunction with each of the (Disney vetted) Good Neighbor hotels—representing potentially big savings for travelers. For details or to book a Good Neighbor package, contact the Walt Disney Travel Company directly at 714-520-5060, or visit *https://disneyland.disney.go.com/vacation-packages/good-neighbor-hotel-package/*.

Note: The following establishments accept major credit cards and offer rooms for travelers with disabilities, unless otherwise indicated. Call directly to inquire about deposit requirements and cancellation policies. Rates given were correct at press time, but are subject to change and should always be confirmed by phone.

SUITE HOTELS

HYATT HOUSE AT ANAHEIM RESORT: This all-suite hotel around the corner from the convention center prides itself on its larger rooms, ranging from 355 to 795 square feet, which strongly appeal to families and those who will be staying more than a few nights. The 264 suites are decorated in neutral hues and earth tones, and range from standard to studio suites, one-bedroom or family suites. Breakfast is included, as are Wi-Fi service and a 24-hour workout room.

Suites offer either one king or two queen beds, bunk beds, sofa beds, 42-inch flat-screen TVs, and views of the nightly Disney fireworks. Spacious studio and one-bedroom Kitchen Suites have a fully equipped kitchen with a refrigerator, microwave, dishwasher, stove, small appliances, and utensils.

The hotel is home to H Bar, Starbucks, and Blaze Pizza. There is an outdoor pool, barbecue pit, and patio. Kid-friendly movies are shown at the pool deck. Rates range from approximately $149 to $425 per night. Parking costs $20 a day.

Hyatt House at Anaheim Resort, 1800 South Harbor Boulevard, Anaheim, CA 92802; 714-971-1800; *www.anaheimresort.house.hyatt.com*.

CLEMENTINE HOTEL & SUITES ANAHEIM: Nestled in a garden-like setting, this residential-style hotel, formerly the Residence Inn by Marriott, is about a half-mile from Disneyland Resort. The 200 spacious suites, set inside sunny orange and yellow buildings, are offered in different room configurations, including a studio suite (one queen bed and a sofa bed, which sleeps four), a one-bedroom suite (two queen beds and sofa bed, which sleeps six), and a bi-level loft suite (two queen beds, sofa bed, and king bed, and two bathrooms, which sleeps eight). All rooms have a flat-screen TV, full kitchen with stove, microwave, dishwasher, a full-size refrigerator, and cooking utensils. Rates range from $149 to $450. Cribs and baby gates are available; rollaway beds are not.

Facilities include a fitness center with cardio equipment (water and towels are available), swimming pool, kiddie pool, whirlpool, and a single adaptive sport court that can be used for tennis, basketball, or volleyball (equipment may be borrowed). There is a guest laundry, mini market, firepit and barbecue area, and small playground.

Complimentary amenities include a daily hot breakfast buffet, business center with free Internet and printing services, Wi-Fi in all suites, and free parking—a huge perk in this neck of the woods. There is also a

helpful Disney planning and information desk. Pets accepted for a flat fee of $100 per stay. Anaheim Resort Transit provides bus transportation for a fee.

Clementine Hotel & Suites Anaheim, 1700 S. Clementine St., Anaheim, CA 92802; *www.clementinehotel.com* or 714-533-3555.

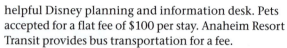

SUPERIOR HOTELS

ANAHEIM MARRIOTT: Conveniently located next door to the Anaheim Convention Center, the Marriott is a perennial favorite among conventioneers. The newly renovated guest rooms offer a residential feel and a SoCal vibe. Room amenities include a wall-mounted 55-inch flat-screen TV, sliding barn door entry to the bathroom, hardwood style floors, and a choice of one king-size or two double beds.

The main restaurant/lounge—nFuse—offers fresh California cuisine with a global twist, a full-service bar, and a pleasant area with sofas, a shuffleboard court, and a pool table. For a more casual bite, Slice Pizzeria offers custom-made pizza with house-made dough. The Market offers a wide variety of food and drink options, including Starbucks beverages, grab-and-go selections, juices, sodas, and more.

The Anaheim Marriott has its own dedicated Disney Planning Desk, a fitness center, outdoor pool, and whirlpool. The hotel is a couple of long blocks from the Disneyland Resort—for some, it is not within walking distance. Shuttle service to the Disney theme parks is provided by Anaheim Resort Transit for a fee; transportation to area airports may also be arranged.

Room rates for two start at $129 (there is no charge for children under age 18 sharing their parents' room); suites start at about $199; $20 per additional adult. Rollaway beds are $20 per stay, and cribs are free. Self-parking costs $25 per day; valet parking is $30 per day. The hotel is not pet-friendly.

> ## HOT TIP!
>
> If you stay in the 1300 to 1500 block of Harbor Boulevard, you can cross the street and walk to both theme parks. Of course, once you reach Disneyland Resort property, it's another 5- to 15-minute walk to get to Disney's theme park turnstiles.

Anaheim Marriott, 700 W. Convention Way, Anaheim, CA 92802; visit the hotel's website at *www.anaheimmarriott.com*, or call 714-750-8000 or 800-228-9290.

HILTON ANAHEIM: The 14-story glass exterior of this property reflects the Anaheim convention center, just steps away, while the enormous, welcoming lobby area invites the outdoors (and legions of conventioneers) inside. Hilton Anaheim, the largest hotel in the Anaheim resort area, boasts 1,572 rooms, including 93 luxurious suites, decorated in contrasting dark wood tones, with crisp white linens and warm wall coverings. Recent enhancements include a chic Lobby Lounge, fifth-floor Presidential Suite, a Chef's Table designed by architect John Gidding, a Disneyland Resort planning desk, and a Starbucks coffee shop.

The hotel's outdoor recreation area, located on the fifth floor, features a heated swimming pool, two whirlpools, and a kids' Splash Zone. Dining options include the MIX Restaurant & Lounge (with menus curated by award-winning Executive Chef Frederic Castan), and the Pool Grill & Bar for outdoor dining (the latter operates on a seasonal basis). There is also a modest food court that offers Baja Fresh, Sbarro, Just Grillin', and Submarina (sandwiches).

Add to that a business center, FedEx shop, and well-appointed boutiques (Travel Traders, Character Club, and Pure Escape Beauty Bar). The 25,000-square-foot Health Club & Spa at Hilton features state-of-the-art exercise equipment, daily fitness classes, an indoor saltwater pool, basketball court, whirlpool, steam room, sauna, and spa treatments (including massage).

Rates for a room with two queen beds range from $119 to $549 (there is no charge for kids under 18

when sharing their parents' room with existing bedding); suites run a bit higher. Ask about packages. There is no extra charge for cribs, but rollaway beds cost $35 per night. Self-parking costs $21 per day; valet parking, $26. Pets are not permitted.

Hilton Anaheim, 777 Convention Way, Anaheim, CA 92802; *www.hiltonanaheimhotel.com*; 714-750-4321 or 800-445- 8667.

HYATT REGENCY ORANGE COUNTY: The hotel, in Garden Grove, is one mile south of Disneyland Resort. Its dramatic, 17-story atrium encloses palm trees and greenery and houses the TusCA restaurant, Starbucks, a gift shop, Citrus Grove Deli, and OC Brewhouse. The hotel has 653 guestrooms (240 of which are suites). Rooms feature either a king-size bed or two queen beds, and modern design.

Amenities include coffeemaker, hair dryer, iron with board, plus free Wi-Fi. The one- and two-bedroom suites also have a living room, refrigerator, and microwave. Suites can accommodate up to 8 people.

Kids' Suites include a room for the little ones, complete with bunk beds and a TV. The parents' room has a king bed, TV, fridge, and microwave.

The hotel's impressive recreational facilities, located on the South Tower's third-story roof, include a heated swimming pool, a fitness center, basketball court, tennis court, and a firepit. Another outdoor pool and whirlpool are on the ground floor of the North Tower. This hotel offers a Disney planning and information desk. Transportation to and from the Disneyland Resort is provided for a fee.

Room rates start at about $137 (there is no additional charge for children under age 18 occupying their parents' room), plus $25 for each additional adult; $179 and higher for suites. There is no charge for cribs. Self-parking is $28 per day; valet parking is $36 per day.

Hyatt Regency Orange County, 11999 Harbor Blvd., Garden Grove, CA 92840; *www.orangecounty.regency .hyatt.com*; 714-750-1234.

ANAHEIM MAJESTIC GARDEN HOTEL: With its turrets and Tudor design, this 489-room hotel looks a bit like a castle, surrounded by grounds that incorporate three courtyards, a rose garden, and koi pond. The lobby has an exotic fish tank and free Internet service in a comfy, contemporary setting. There's a restaurant, cocktail lounge (with happy hour), and deli/gift shop.

The hotel, which recently underwent an $8 million renovation, has 463 rooms and 26 suites. The rooms—all large (490 square feet on average)—have two queen- or one king-size bed, cable TV, in-room movies, voice mail, iron, fridge, hair dryer, and coffeemaker (with coffee). Most of the guest rooms are designed to capture the hotel's castle theme with backdrops evoking an enchanted forest. Each suite has a sitting area with a sofa bed. Nearly all of the rooms can be connected to another to accommodate large parties.

The hotel has a full-service restaurant, arcade, outdoor heated pool and whirlpool, state-of-the-art fitness center, guest laundry, and conference rooms. It has a Disney planning and information desk, too. Airport transportation is available for a fee. Room rates start at $119 during off-season to $275 during peak season. Self-parking costs $18 per day. This property is pet-friendly. Check-out time is 11 A.M. The hotel offers free (and frequent) shuttle service to the Disneyland Resort (otherwise known as The Dream Machine).

Anaheim Majestic Garden Hotel, 900 S. Disneyland Dr., Anaheim, CA 92802; 714-778-1700; *www.sheraton.com/Anaheim* or *www.majesticgardenhotel.com*.

SHERATON PARK HOTEL AT THE ANAHEIM RESORT:

This 14-story tower is easy to spot, and the 490 rooms and six suites have balconies (some large, some small) that have a view of the pool or the Disneyland Resort (and its fireworks). Rooms offer either one king or two queen beds, refrigerator, iron, coffeemaker, and hair dryer.

The hotel has a lobby bar, Disney planning desk, Morton's The Steakhouse, Park 55 Cafe, and a snack bar. There's also a 24-hour fitness center, pool, whirlpool, and poolside bar.

Shuttle service to Disneyland is provided by Anaheim Resort Transportation (for a fee). Room rates run $149 to $234, depending on occupancy and season; suites start at $850. Rollaways cost about $15 extra; cribs are available free of charge. Self- and valet parking range from $21 to $26 daily.

Sheraton Park Hotel at the Anaheim Resort, 1855 S. Harbor Blvd., Anaheim, CA 92802; call 714-750-1811 or 866-837-4197; or visit *www.marriott.com/SNAPS*.

MODERATE HOTELS

ANAHEIM CAMELOT INN & SUITES: Directly across the street—and a relatively short walk away—from the Disneyland Resort, this hotel, with its shingled roof, clock tower, turrets, and window boxes, looks like something out of a Bavarian village. Each of the 121 rooms and suites has a 47-inch TV, microwave, mini fridge, coffeemaker, safe, free Wi-Fi, hair dryer, and an iron with board. It also has a gift shop, mobility scooter and stroller rental shop, and a guest laundry facility (fees apply). There is a pool (with a view of the Matterhorn Bobsleds attraction in Disneyland park), whirlpool, and terrace sundeck. Complimentary luggage storage is available in the lobby. While there's no on-site eatery, there are many family-friendly places to eat within walking distance.

Deluxe standard rooms, most with two queen-size beds, range from $159 to $299 year-round; family suites start at about $229 and accommodate up to six people, but they have only one bath. All rooms have a sleeper chair. Cribs are available for free. The front desk is staffed 24 hours a day. Adjoining rooms are usually available upon request. There is no shuttle service, but it is possible to walk to the Disneyland Resort entrance via Harbor Boulevard. Anaheim Resort Transit provides transportation to Disneyland Resort (for a fee). There is a daily fee for parking.

Anaheim Camelot Inn & Suites, 1520 S. Harbor Blvd., Anaheim, CA 92802; call 714-635-7275 or 800-828-4898, or visit *www.camelotinn-anaheim.com*.

FAIRFIELD BY MARRIOTT ANAHEIM RESORT: Fronted by palms and pines, this inviting 467-room hotel—fresh off a lobby renovation—is about a 7– to 10–minute walk to the Disneyland Resort theme park entrances. Its rooms, all accented with Disney artwork, are in two towers (one tower is nine stories high; the other, eight). Each room has a king-size bed or two queen beds, child-size sleeper sofa, smart TV, free high-speed Internet, an iron and board, a hair dryer, refrigerator, and coffeemaker (with coffee).

Other facilities include a fitness center, heated pool, whirlpool, gift shop, free Wi-Fi in the lobby and other public areas, arcade, Seattle's Best Coffee, and Pizza Hut Express. The rooms may be occupied by up to five people, and rates start at about $149; cribs are available.

Anaheim Fairfield Inn by Marriott, 1460 S. Harbor Blvd., Anaheim, CA 92802; call 714-772-6777 or 800-228-2800, or go to *www.fairfieldinnanaheimresort.com*.

COURTYARD MARRIOTT ANAHEIM THEME PARK ENTRANCE: Located across the street from Disneyland Resort is the first entirely "family-geared" Courtyard. All rooms sleep up to six and feature bunk beds, two separate showers in the bathroom, and a 47-inch TV with Netflix and Pandora radio. Guestrooms at this property start at a roomy 500 square feet. Suites are available, too. This is the only four-star hotel within true walking distance of the two Disneyland theme park entrances (about a 10-minute walk, give or take). Dining options include the Bistro Restaurant & Bar, Starbucks, and a lobby lounge. There is a modern fitness center, two laundromats, and a gift shop on the premises. Rates for a double room start at about $259.

The 20,000-square-foot Surfside Waterpark has four super slides and two tot-friendly twin slides; a 400-gallon "drench bucket" that spills water on folks below; a 42-foot lap pool; and a hot tub perched on a sundeck. The pool deck offers a good view of the Disneyland Resort fireworks.

Courtyard Marriott Anaheim Theme Park Entrance, 1420 S. Harbor Blvd., Anaheim, CA 92802; visit *www.anaheimcourtyard.com*, or call 714-254-1442.

BEST WESTERN PLUS STOVALL'S INN: This inn is known for its fanciful topiary garden. The property features 288 guestrooms, complimentary continental breakfast, fitness room, business center, and a pair of pools (one is heated), two whirlpools, a wading pool, and a gift shop. Room configurations include two queen, one king, or two double beds, and a bathroom with a separate sink and lots of counter space. Room service is available from 6 A.M. until 10 P.M. daily.

Accommodations come with a mini refrigerator, microwave, single-serving coffee/tea maker, hair dryer, iron (with board), and TV. Room rates for up to five guests run $79 to $149. Rollaways are $15; cribs are free. Parking costs $10 a night (one car per room).

Best Western Plus Stovall's Inn, 1110 W. Katella Ave., Anaheim, CA 92802. Visit *www.stovallsinn.com*, or call 714-778-1880 or 800-854-8177, ext. 3.

CANDY CANE INN: There's a lot to like about this sweet, two-story hotel—fountain out front, relaxed ambience, wrought-iron touches, and lots of flowers. Located down the street from Disneyland Resort's entrance (a manageable walk for adults and non-toddlers), the Candy Cane Inn is family run and well maintained.

Each of the 171 rooms, most of which face a courtyard, has a refrigerator, safe, free Wi-Fi, coffeemaker, iron, hair dryer, and two queen beds with custom bedding. Add to that a guest laundry (fees apply), pool, gazebo-covered whirlpool, and fitness center. Free continental buffet breakfast is served daily. Premium rooms also have robes, microwaves, in-room breakfast, turndown service, and 2 P.M. checkout. Sightseeing services are available, as is free shuttle service to and from the Disneyland Resort. Transportation to airports can be arranged. Parking is free.

Rates for a double room with two queen-size beds range from about $109 to $199, depending on the season. Rollaways, available in deluxe and premium rooms, are $20; cribs are free. The inn is located across the street from a shopping area with fast-food eateries.

Candy Cane Inn, 1747 S. Harbor Blvd., Anaheim, CA 92802. Visit *www.candycaneinn.net*, or call 714-774-5284 or 800-345-7057.

HOWARD JOHNSON ANAHEIM HOTEL AND WATER PLAYGROUND: This property's lush landscaping is a big reason to stay here. Flowers and trees proliferate; a central fountain anchors the four, two-story units. The hotel is close to Disneyland and local eateries. For a fee, Anaheim Resort Transit offers shuttle service to and from Disneyland. (At press time, the hotel was midway through an extensive room renovation.)

The 296 non-smoking rooms are divided among several buildings on 7 acres. Most have two queen beds, and all have a fridge, microwave, safe, and free Wi-Fi. The rooms are relatively spacious. Most rooms have a full balcony. Family suites are available.

There is a heated pool with a hot tub, plus Castaway Cove—a splashy pirate playground featuring slides, water cannons, toddler pool, and fountains. There are 2 guest laundries and a gift shop. Rates range from $149 to $229, depending on the season. Parking is free until 3 P.M. on day of checkout (one vehicle per room, no RVs). Rollaways cost $15 per day; cribs are free.

Howard Johnson Anaheim Hotel and Water Playground, 1380 S. Harbor Blvd., Anaheim, CA 92802; Visit *www.hojoanaheim.com*, or call 714-776-6120 or 800-422-4228.

TROPICANA INN & SUITES: This hotel is across from the pedestrian crosswalk to the Disneyland Resort (it's about a 10-minute walk). Each of its 197 rooms has a 43-inch flat-screen TV, coffeemaker (with coffee), fridge, small safe, microwave, hair dryer, iron, and free Wi-Fi. Standard rooms have two queens and a single sleeper chair. Guests may use a computer in the lobby free of charge. Some rooms have a view of Disney fireworks.

The inn has a cafe/shop combo known as The Cove on Harbor Market and Coffee House. It carries food, drinks, apparel, souvenirs, and sundries. There are many eateries in the area (some within walking distance). Anaheim Resort Tranportation provides shuttle service for a fee. There is a daily fee for self-parking.

The inn has a heated Junior Olympic pool, whirlpool spa, and a guest laundry (fees apply). Room rates are about $159 to $299. Suites sleep up to 8 guests and range from $229 to $399. Some suites have kitchens.

Tropicana Inn & Suites, 1540 S. Harbor Blvd., Anaheim, CA 92802; *www.tropicanainn-anaheim.com*; 714-635-4082 or 800-828-4898.

The Rest of the Best

Here's a roundup of the remaining Good Neighbor hotels. They have amenities and rates similar to those described in this chapter. However, some are a bit far from the Disneyland Resort.

Note: The various properties that boast Good Neighbor status are subject to change during the year; visit *www.disneyland.com* for updates.

SUPERIOR HOTELS

- Delta Hotels by Marriott Anaheim Garden Grove, 12021 Harbor Blvd., Garden Grove; 714-887-5555
- Sheraton Garden Grove Anaheim South Hotel, 12221 Harbor Blvd., Garden Grove; 714-703-8400

DELUXE HOTELS

- Country Inn & Suites by Radisson Anaheim, 1640 Clementine St., Anaheim; 714-598-0600
- Courtyard by Marriott Anaheim Resort, 2045 S. Harbor Blvd., Anaheim; 714-740-2645
- Desert Palms Hotel & Suites Anaheim Resort Convention Center, 631 West Katella Ave., Anaheim; 714-535-1133
- Hampton Inn & Suites Anaheim/Garden Grove, 11747 Harbor Blvd., Garden Grove; 714-703-8800
- Hilton Garden Inn Anaheim/Garden Grove, 11777 Harbor Blvd., Garden Grove; 714-703-9100
- Holiday Inn–Anaheim Resort, 1915 S. Manchester Ave., Anaheim; 714-748-7777
- Holiday Inn Hotel & Suites, 1240 S. Walnut St., Anaheim; 714-535-0300
- Hyatt Place at Anaheim Resort, 2035 S. Harbor Blvd., Anaheim; 714-750-4000
- Red Lion Hotel Anaheim, 1850 S. Harbor Blvd., Anaheim; 714-750-2801

MODERATE HOTELS

- The Anaheim Hotel, 1700 Harbor Blvd., Anaheim; 714-772-5900
- Anaheim Portofino Inn & Suites, 1831 S. Harbor Blvd., Anaheim; 714-782-7600
- Best Western Plus Anaheim Inn, 1630 S. Harbor Blvd., Anaheim; 714-774-1050
- Best Western Plus Park Place Inn & Mini Suites, 1544 S. Harbor Blvd., Anaheim; 714-776-4800
- Best Western Plus Pavilions, 1176 W. Katella Ave., Anaheim; 714-776-0140
- Best Western Plus Raffles Inn & Suites, 2040 S. Harbor Blvd., Anaheim; 714-750-6100

- Castle Inn & Suites, 1734 S. Harbor Blvd., Anaheim; 714-774-8111
- Clarion Hotel Anaheim Resort, 616 W. Convention Way, Anaheim; 714-750-3131
- Cortona Inn & Suites, 2029 S. Harbor Blvd., Anaheim; 800-416-6819
- Four Points by Sheraton Anaheim, 1221 S. Harbor Blvd., Anaheim; 714-758-0900
- Grand Legacy at the Park, 1650 S. Harbor Blvd., Anaheim; 714-772-0440
- Motel 6 Anaheim Maingate, 100 W. Disney Way, Anaheim; 714-520-9696

SUITE HOTELS

- Anaheim Marriott Suites, 12015 Harbor Blvd., Garden Grove; 714-750-1000
- Doubletree Suites by Hilton, 2085 S. Harbor Blvd., Anaheim; 714-750-3000
- Embassy Suites Anaheim-North, 3100 E. Frontera St., Anaheim; 714-632-1221
- Embassy Suites Anaheim-South, 11767 Harbor Blvd., Garden Grove; 714-539-3300
- Holiday Inn Express & Suites Anaheim Resort Area, 1411 S. Manchester Ave., Anaheim; 714-844-2801
- Homewood Suites by Hilton, 2010 S. Harbor Blvd., Anaheim; 714-750-2010
- Homewood Suites by Hilton Anaheim–Main Gate Area, 12005 Harbor Blvd., Garden Grove; 714-740-1800
- Hyatt House Anaheim Resort Convention Center, 1800 S. Harbor Blvd., Anaheim; 714-791-1800
- Residence Inn by Marriott Anaheim/Resort Area, 11931 Harbor Blvd., Garden Grove; 714-591-4000
- Residence Inn by Marriott Anaheim Resort/Convention Center, 640 W. Katella Ave., Anaheim; 714-782-7500
- SpringHill Suites Anaheim Maingate, 1160 W. Ball Road, Anaheim; 714-215-4000
- SpringHill Suites by Marriott Anaheim Resort Convention Center, 1801 S. Harbor Blvd., Anaheim; 714-533-2101
- Staybridge Suites, 1855 S. Manchester Ave., Anaheim; 714-748-7700

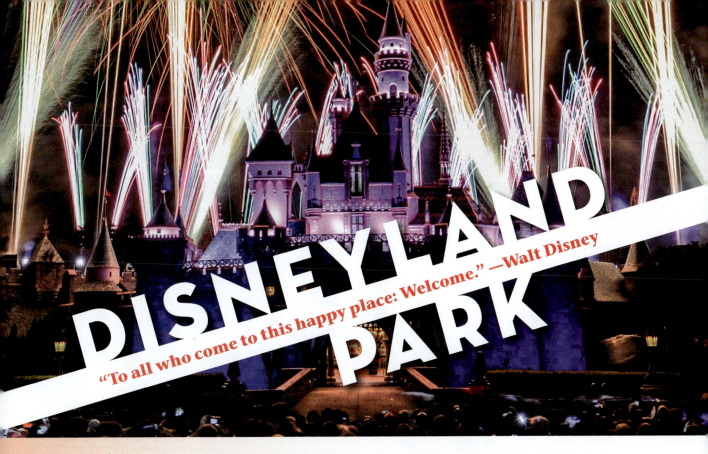

DISNEYLAND PARK

"To all who come to this happy place: Welcome." —Walt Disney

When you wish upon a star, your dreams come true. That's how the song goes, and it's always possible in Disneyland—Walt Disney's own dream come true. He envisioned "a place of warmth and nostalgia, of illusion and color and delight." The result: a place where imagination is given free reign, grins and giggles are encouraged, and everyone can see the world through a child's eyes.

The undisguised pleasure on the faces of park-goers reveals that they have fallen under the spell of a turreted pink castle; the oompah of a band marching down Main Street, U.S.A.; the clip-clop of a horse-drawn trolley; a close-up encounter with Mickey and Minnie; and a fireworks spectacle more fantastic than an elaborate, pyrotechnic dream.

Those who first entered Disneyland as wee ones now return with their own kids—and grandkids—to find the park of their memories unchanged in spirit and heart. Shows and attractions have come and gone since it opened in back in 1955 and whole new "lands" have been added, while many beloved classics endure. The newest neighborhood, Star Wars: Galaxy's Edge, promises high-flying intergalactic adventures for generations to come. Of course, the overall enchantment that guests experience when they walk through the portals of "the happiest place on earth" remains constant. That may well be Disneyland park's most enduring accomplishment. Enjoy!

DISNEYLAND PARK

Getting Oriented

Disneyland Park's layout—a basic hub-and-spokes configuration—is simple, but it was quite innovative when the park opened in 1955. The design makes getting around easy, though it's not altogether effort-less, since the numerous nooks, crannies, and alley-ways can be a bit confusing at first.

The hub of the theme park's wheel is Central Plaza, which fronts Sleeping Beauty Castle. From it extend five spokes leading to nine "lands": Main Street, U.S.A.; Adventureland; Frontierland; New Orleans Square; Critter Country; Fantasyland; Mickey's Toontown; Tomorrow-land; and Star Wars: Galaxy's Edge (a new land that opened in 2019). As you face Sleeping Beauty Castle, the first bridge to your left takes you to Adventureland; the next one, to Frontierland and New Orleans Square. To your right, the first walkway goes to Tomorrowland, and the next one—known as Matterhorn Way—leads to Fantasyland and on to Mickey's Toontown. If you cross the Castle's moat and walk through the archway, you'll reach Fantasyland. Critter Country occupies its own cul-de-sac, extending north from New Orleans Square. Star Wars: Galaxy's Edge is just beyond Critter Country (and may be accessed from there, as well as from Fantasyland and Frontierland).

Study the map at left to familiarize yourself with the layout of the park. When you arrive, ask for an Enter-tainment Times Guide, which includes details about the times and locations of the day's entertainment, as well as how to meet Disney characters. Entertainment info is available via the Disneyland Resort app, too.

PARKING

Guests are directed to park vehicles in the Mickey and Friends parking structure or the Toy Story lot on Harbor Boulevard. If one parking area is full, a Cast Member will direct you to one that isn't. Courtesy tram service transports guests from the parking deck only.

Parking areas open an hour before the park does—but getting a space can take a while if there are a lot of folks also hoping to get a head start on the day. Guests using wheelchairs will be directed to a special parking area and have access to ramps in the tram-loading area.

Parking Fees: Guests arriving in regular passenger vehicles pay about $25 to park for the day. (The fee for oversize vehicles is $30, and the cost for buses and trucks with extended trailers is $35.) Preferred parking starts at $40. You may leave the lot and return later the same day at no additional charge. (Hold on to your parking stub as proof of payment.) Prices are subject to change. Note that there is a courtesy shuttle to the parks from the Toy Story parking lot; the Mickey and Friends Parking Structure is within walking distance.

Lost Cars: Even if you take careful note of where you parked, you might have trouble remembering the exact spot when you return later. If this happens, contact a Cast Member and tell her or him approximately when you arrived for the day. With that information, park-ing lot personnel can usually help figure out the car's general location.

GETTING AROUND

The Disneyland Railroad's five narrow-gauge trains make a loop around the park, stopping at Main Street, U.S.A., New Orleans Square, and Tomor-rowland. It takes about 20 minutes to come full-circle on the train. Horse-drawn streetcars, horseless carriages, and a motorized fire engine make trips up and down Main Street, U.S.A.

To travel outside Disneyland Park, consider the sleek monorail, which glides between Tomorrowland and Downtown Disney. From Downtown Disney, you can walk to any of the three on-property hotels—the Disneyland Hotel, Disney's Paradise Pier Hotel, and Disney's Grand Californian Hotel & Spa.

The Grand Californian Resort & Spa is a short walk to the Disneyland entrance and has its own entrance to Disney California Adventure. (The gate is reserved exclusively for Grand Californian Hotel guests—you will have to flash a valid Grand Californian room key to use it.) Note that the theme parks require separate admission, unless you have a Park Hopper ticket; see page 55 for ticket pricing and structures.

Disneyland Park Primer

BABY FACILITIES

The Baby Care Center, on Main Street, U.S.A., by First Aid, provides changing tables, high chairs, toddlers' toilets, and a nursing area. Bottles can be warmed here, and baby powder, diapers, formula, and food are sold. There are no napping facilities or babysitting services.

FIRST AID

First Aid is at the north end of Main Street, next to the Baby Care Center. A nurse is on duty during park operating hours. In case of medical emergency, notify a Cast Member and call 911. The center can store medications that require refrigeration and provide special containers for the disposal of hypodermic needles.

GUIDED TOURS

Several tours originate from the Guided Tour Gardens, just left of City Hall. They include the ever-popular *Walk in Walt's Disneyland Footsteps* and the *Grand Circle Tour*, which focuses on Disney trains. There are also seasonal tours: *Disney's Happiest Haunts* for the Halloween season, and *Holiday Time at the Disneyland Resort*. Park admission is required for all tours. For more details, flip to page 21.

HOURS

Disneyland park is usually open daily, year round. Monday through Thursday hours are generally from about 10 A.M. to 8 P.M., Friday and Sunday from about 9 A.M. to 10 P.M., Saturday from 8 A.M. to 11 P.M., with extended hours during the summer months and holiday periods. For specific operating hours, visit *www.disneyland.com*, or call 714-781-4565.

During the busy spring break, summer, and Christmas holiday seasons, it's especially wise to arrive first thing in the morning so that you can visit the popular attractions before the lines get long. If you arrive at Disneyland too late, the parking structure and surrounding lots could be more crowded than usual; this is almost always the case in the summer months and during the last week of December.

INFORMATION

Cast Members at City Hall, Guest Relations kiosks (Fantasyland and New Orleans Square), and the Central Plaza Information Board can answer questions (or help plot your day so that you can make the most efficient use of your time and see what attractions truly interest you). Specifics on services and safety considerations have been compiled in Disneyland's guidemap; ask for it when you enter the park.

Information Board: A valuable planning resource, Central Plaza Information Board (aka the Tip Board) is located on Main Street, U.S.A. (near the Jolly Holiday Bakery Cafe). It lets you know how long the waits are for most park attractions, what (if anything) is not operating that day, and where and when park entertainment will take place. Cast Members can answer questions and provide information about eateries and hotels in the Disneyland Resort. They can help locate favorite Disney characters, too.

LOCKERS

Storage lockers are outside the main entrance (on the left) and on Center Street (about halfway up Main Street). Inside-the-park lockers cost about $7 or $10 per day, depending on size. Items may be stored during park hours only. You'll also find a kiosk from which to rent smartphone power packs. The cost is $30 per day and includes unlimited pack-swapping, plus power cords for iPhones and Android devices. The lockers outside the park cost $7, $10, $11, $12, and $15 per day.

LOST & FOUND

Disneyland Resort's Lost & Found department is located on the left side of the Disneyland park entrance. If you realize that you have lost something after you have departed the Disneyland Resort, call 714-817-2166 between 8 A.M. and 8 P.M.

PHOTO BY JILL SAFRO

MONEY MATTERS

Cash and traveler's checks are accepted at all food and shopping spots at Disneyland Resort. American Express, Visa, MasterCard, JCB Card, and Discover Card are accepted at shops and eateries (cash only at some vending carts).

Main Street's City Hall can assist with foreign currency exchange, as well as traveler's check cashing. Disneyland Resort hotel guests may charge almost any purchase made in the theme park back to their hotel bill if they gave a credit card number at check-in.

Disney gift cards are sold in many Disneyland park shops, Disney Stores, and from *disneygiftcard.com*. Cards are accepted at Disney hotels, Downtown Disney, Disney California Adventure, and at Disneyland (as are Disney Dollars). They are also valid at Walt Disney World in Florida and at U.S. Disney Store locations. Note that Disney Dollars are no longer sold.

There are four Automated Teller Machines (ATMs) within Disneyland. The first, encountered when entering the park, is near the Disneyana shop at the Bank of Main Street building. (Though one might expect the Bank to be, well, a bank, it is not. It's a shop.)

PACKAGE CHECK

There's no need to lug bags around. Guests of any Disneyland Resort hotel may have packages delivered to their hotel (no charge). Disneyland Park day guests may store bulky purchases at one of these locations, free of charge: The Stroller Shop, Pioneer Mercantile, Port Royal, and The Star Trader.

SAME-DAY RE-ENTRY

All Disneyland park guests have their picture taken upon initial entry to the park. (The photo is immediately linked to their ticket.) This makes for speedy and convenient re-entry, with the presentation of said park ticket. If you'd like to visit two parks on one day, you'll need to purchase the "hopper" option prior to entering the first park. (Disneyland and Disney California Adventure are within walking distance of each other, which allows for hassle-free hopping between the parks.) Note that hand stamps are no longer required for re-entry to either Disneyland Resort theme park.

SMOKING RULES

The Disneyland Resort is a smoke-free zone. Smoking (of any kind) is not permitted anywhere within Disneyland Resort boundaries—this includes all of Disneyland Park, Disney California Adventure, Downtown Disney, the Disneyland hotels, and the esplanade between the theme parks. The ban includes tobacco, e-cigarettes, and any products creating a vapor or smoke. Smoking of marijuana or other illegal substances is prohibited. No exceptions.

STROLLERS & WHEELCHAIRS

Strollers ($15) and wheelchairs ($12 with a $20 refundable deposit and a credit card) may be rented outside the entrance of Disneyland Park (on the right). Electric Conveyance Vehicles (ECVs) cost $50 for the day, with a $20 deposit and major credit card. Wheelchair and ECV supplies are limited. Misplaced strollers may be replaced at the park's entrance and at The Star Trader shop in Tomorrowland.

SECURITY CHECK

All guests are subject to a thorough security check before entering Disneyland Resort. All bags are searched and guests must pass through a metal detector. For more about Park Rules, visit *www.disneyland.com/parkrules*.

Expect car trunks to be searched when entering Disney parking facilities.

Guests checking into a Disneyland Resort hotel must present valid government-issued photo ID.

Ticket Prices

Although prices† will likely increase, the following should give you an idea of what you will pay for tickets in 2020. Note that 1-Day tickets purchased in 2020 must be used by 12/31/20. The first day of use of multi-day tickets must be on or before 12/31/20. Multi-day tickets must be used within 13 days of first use or by January 13, 2021, whichever occurs first. For updates, call 714-781-4565, or visit *www.disneyland.com*. All details are subject to change.

	ADULTS	CHILDREN*
1-Day Ticket (1 park)	$104/129/149	$98/122/141
1-Day Ticket (hopper)	$154/179/199	$148/172/191
2-Day Ticket	$225	$210
2-Day Ticket (hopper)	$280	$265
3-Day Ticket	$300	$280
3-Day Ticket (hopper)**	$355	$335
4-Day Ticket**	$325	$305
4-Day Ticket (hopper)**	$380	$360
5-Day Ticket**	$340	$320
5-Day Ticket (hopper)**	$395	$375
Deluxe Annual Passport		$799
Signature Annual Passport		$1,149
Signature Plus Annual Passport		$1,399
Premier Annual Passport		$1,949

† One-day prices are quoted in Value/Regular/Peak order. For dates, visit *www.disneyland.com*.
* 3 through 9 years of age; children under 3 free
** Includes one "Magic Morning" early Disneyland Park admission with select attractions on Tuesday, Thursday, or Saturday with advance purchase.
There is a single price (for adults and children) for annual passports.

Main Street, U.S.A.

This pretty thoroughfare represents Main Street America in the early 1900s, complete with the gentle clip-clop of horses' hooves on pavement, melodic ringing of streetcar bells, and strains of nostalgic tunes such as "Bicycle Built for Two" and "Coney Island Baby."

The sounds of brass bands, a barbershop quartet, and ragtime piano fill the street. An old-fashioned steam train huffs into a handsome brick depot. Rows of picturesque buildings line the street. Authentic gaslights, which once lit up Baltimore and St. Louis, flicker at sundown in ornate lampposts lining the walkways, and the storefronts—painted in a palette of pastels—could not be more inviting. Walt Disney was a master of detail: throughout Main Street, even the doorknobs are historically correct.

To make the buildings appear taller, a set designer's technique called forced perspective was employed. The first floor is seven-eighths scale (this allows guests to enter comfortably); the second story is five-eighths scale; and the third, only half size. The dimensions of the whole are small enough for the place to seem intimate and comforting, yet the proportions appear correct. (Forced perspective was also used to make the Matterhorn and Sleeping Beauty Castle seem taller than they are.)

The following attractions are listed in the order in which you'll encounter them while walking from the entrance up Main Street, toward Sleeping Beauty Castle.

CITY HALL: Before strolling up Main Street, U.S.A., stop briefly at the Information Center at City Hall, on the west side of Town Square, to find entertainment schedules, make dining reservations, or get advice to help you plan your Disneyland day. City Hall is also an excellent meeting place if members of your party separate and plan to regroup later in the day.

FIRE DEPARTMENT: Next door to City Hall, this was Walt Disney's home away from home during the construction of Disneyland. His private apartment, on the top floor, looks just the same as when Walt called it home. It's decorated with antiques and items he and his wife Lillian picked up during their travels around the world. A light flickers in the window in Walt's

memory. The apartment is not open to the public, but guests are welcome to visit the firehouse. Kids love—and are welcome—to climb on the fire wagon parked inside the firehouse. It's a realistic copy of a truck from the early 1900s and provides a great photo opportunity.

DISNEYANA: This treasure chest of a shop has wares representing creative efforts from throughout the Walt Disney Company, often including never-before-seen art, displayed in an ever-changing exhibit area. Disney artists and Imagineers make appearances here. And the park bench from which Walt dreamed up Disneyland is on display! It used to be near the Griffith Park merry-go-round in Los Angeles.

DISNEYLAND RAILROAD: Walt Disney loved trains so much he actually built a one-eighth-scale model of one, the Carolwood Pacific, in the backyard of his home. So it was only natural that his first theme park include a railroad—five narrow-gauge steam trains have circled Disneyland Park since it opened in 1955. Two of the locomotives were built at the Walt Disney Studios, while three had other lives before finding a home at Disneyland.

Guests who ride the train between Tomorrowland and Main Street, U.S.A., are in for a few surprises. In

1958 Walt Disney added a diorama of the Grand Canyon, depicted from its south rim on a seamless, handwoven canvas that is 306 feet long and 34 feet high, and is covered with 300 gallons of paint. The accompanying music is the "On the Trail" section of American composer Ferde Grofé's *Grand Canyon Suite*.

The Disneyland Railroad experience was recently enhanced a bit. It now travels across an elevated trestle, affording panoramic views of five new waterfalls gracing the Rivers of America. Disneyland veterans may also spot some old Frontierland friends along the way.

THE DISNEYLAND STORY, PRESENTING GREAT MOMENTS WITH MR. LINCOLN: The Disneyland Opera House makes the perfect backdrop for a tribute to the "happiest place on earth," and the man who created it, one Walter Elias Disney. A unique collection of art, models, and mementos—as well as a film—marks more than 60 years of Disneyland magic. After taking a walk down Disney memory lane, guests may pay a visit to the 16th president of the United States. Yes, Abraham Lincoln is here (in realistic, Audio-Animatronics form). After a brief presentation about the Civil War, "Mr. Lincoln" stands up and delivers a stirring discourse about liberty, the American spirit, and the challenges facing the nation. It's exceptionally au courant for an 18th-century allocution.

MAIN STREET VEHICLES: Main Street's motorized fire wagon, horseless carriages, and horse-drawn streetcars lend the thoroughfare a real touch of nostalgia, while at the same time giving guests a lift from one end of the street to the other. The fire truck is modeled after those that might have been discovered on an American Main Street in the early 1900s, except that it has seats where the hose was meant to be carried.

The horse-drawn streetcars, inspired by those in 19th-century photographs, carry up to 30 passengers each. Most of the horses that pull the cars are Belgians

Save Time in Line!

For those of us who'd prefer not to waste precious time standing in line for theme park shows and attractions, Disneyland's Fastpass is nothing short of a miracle. The system lets guests forgo the task of waiting in a long line for many theme park shows and attractions at the Disneyland Resort.

How? There are two ways to book Fastpass. The first—and free—method is to visit a Fastpass booth (located near the entrance of participating attractions) and slip a valid park ticket into the Fastpass machine.

In return, guests get a slip of paper with a time printed on it (in addition to the safe return of their park ticket). That time—for example, 4:05 P.M. to 5:05 P.M.—represents the "window" in which guests are invited to return to the attraction and practically walk right on—without standing in a long line! Latecomers will not be accommodated.

Once you use your Fastpass to enter an attraction (or the time on it has passed), you can get a new Fastpass time for another attraction. It's also possible to get a Fastpass for a second attraction two hours after the first one is issued.

For example, if one Fastpass was issued at 2 P.M., you can get a Fastpass for another attraction or show at 4 P.M. Sound confusing? It won't be once you've tried it.

Disney's Fastpass service, as described above, is free to everyone bearing a valid theme park ticket. It should be available during peak times of the day, and all peak seasons. We've placed a Fastpass symbol (**FP**) beside the listings for all of the attractions that were participating at press time. Note that the addition of MaxPass (see below and page 13) means that traditional Fastpass assignments are more popular than ever—get to those in-park kiosks as soon as possible.

The second way to reserve Fastpass assignments—a service known as MaxPass—costs about $15 per person, per day, and is done via mobile device with the Disneyland app. MaxPass includes unlimited downloads of the day's PhotoPass images (turn to page 85 of this book).

Traditional, free-of-charge Fastpass is expected to be offered throughout 2020. We recommend using it whenever possible. For more information, call 714-781-4565 or visit *www.disneyland.com*. All details are subject to change in 2020.

(characterized by white manes and tails and lightly feathered legs) and Percheron draft horses.

MAIN STREET CINEMA: This small, standing-room-only movie theater features classic, early Mickey Mouse cartoons. The six animated shorts, which play continuously throughout the day, were originally aired before feature films. There are no seats in the theatre, but it is still a pleasant spot to soak up some Disney nostalgia.

PENNY ARCADE: This place is more of a candy shop than an arcade, but the air of nostalgia remains. Those who have frequented it in the past will be happy to find Esmeralda front and center, ready as always to tell your fortune. The arcade still has Mutascopes, machines that feature hand-cranked moving pictures and require a penny to operate.

Save some change for the arcade's penny presses. You insert a penny (plus a few other coins to pay for the service), and the penny will be flattened and imprinted with the image of Sleeping Beauty Castle or the face of one of the Disney characters.

CENTRAL PLAZA: Main Street, U.S.A., ends at Central Plaza, the hub of the park, and four of the park's lands are directly accessible from here. At its center stands the Walt and Mickey Partners statue. It's one of the park's most popular picture spots.

One of Disneyland's Information Centers is located here, near the entrance to Adventureland. Besides the information desk, there is a handy Information Board, (aka Tip Board) updated frequently, that posts wait times for many attractions, which attractions offer Fastpass, what (if anything) is not operating that day, and where and when park entertainment will take place. They offer park Times Guides, too.

PHOTO BY JILL SAFRO

Adventureland

For someone who grew up in Marceline, Missouri, around the turn of the 20th century, as Walt Disney did, the far-flung regions of the world must have seemed most exotic and exciting. So it's not surprising that when he was planning his new park, he designated one area, called Adventureland, to represent all the (then) remote and mysterious corners of the world.

The original South Seas–island ambience all but disappeared with the opening of the Indiana Jones Adventure in 1995, and Adventureland became a 1930s jungle outpost. Today, the entrance to the Jungle Cruise is a walk-through headquarters, with old photographs and radios playing big band music interrupted by news flashes about Professor Jones's latest exploits and discoveries. Shops here sell wares that are meant to appeal to modern-day adventurers.

WALT DISNEY'S ENCHANTED TIKI ROOM: Introduced in 1963, this was the first of the park's Audio-Animatronics attractions and the precursor of more elaborate variations, such as "Great Moments with Mr. Lincoln" and the above-mentioned Dr. Jones. Housed in a vaguely Polynesian complex situated at the entrance to Adventureland, the 15-minute show has been given a spiffy face-lift.

The stars are four feathered emcees (José, Michael, Pierre, and Fritz), backed up by a company of pastel-plumed parrots and an eclectic chorus of orchids, carved wooden tiki poles, tiki drummers, singing masks, bird-of-paradise flowers, macaws, Amazon parrots, toucans, fork-tailed birds, cockatoos, and several other species.

The 225 performers all sing and drum up a tropical storm with so much animation that it's hard to resist a smile. Their repertoire includes "In the Tiki, Tiki, Tiki Room," "Let's All Sing," and "Aloha to You."

JUNGLE CRUISE: The spiel delivered by the skipper on this seven-minute river adventure has its share of corny jokes, but your navigator may turn out to be a natural comic with a funny delivery. Just remember that the cornball humor is part of the fun.

As jungle cruises go, this one is as much like the real thing as Main Street, U.S.A., is like life in an actual small town—long on loveliness and short on the visual distractions and minor annoyances that constitute the bulk of human experience. There are no venomous vipers and no Montezuma's revenge. And the Bengal tiger and king cobras at the ancient Cambodian ruins, and the great apes, gorillas, crocodiles, alligators, elephants, hippos, and lions in the water and along the shores represent no threat to passersby—though according to maintenance crews, they are almost as much trouble as real ones.

Movie buffs should note that Bob Mattey, who helped develop these jungle creatures, also worked on the giant squid for the Disney film *20,000 Leagues Under the Sea*, the man-eating plants in many Tarzan movies, and the menacing mechanical shark in *Jaws*.

The large-leafed upright tree in the Cambodian ruins section of the attraction is a Sacred Fig (*Ficus religiosa*), the same species of tree under which Buddha received enlightenment in India many centuries ago.

TARZAN'S TREEHOUSE: The 80-foot-tall, 150-ton *Disneyodendron semperflorens grandis*, or "large, ever-blooming Disney tree," which cradled the Swiss Family Treehouse from 1962 to mid-1999, currently embraces another lofty dwelling: Tarzan's Treehouse, inspired by the book by Edgar Rice Burroughs and Disney's 1999 animated feature *Tarzan*. Overlooking the Jungle Cruise and the Temple of the Forbidden Eye (the setting for the Indiana Jones attraction), this moss-and-vine-covered "high-rise apartment" shelters Tarzan, his adoptive mom, Kala (the ape), and Jane.

An area at the base of the tree has been designed around the scientific equipment that Jane and her father brought to the jungle. Nearby, a makeshift wooden staircase crafted from shipwreck salvage and a weathered suspension bridge provide easy access to the treehouse itself.

Jane's drawings, displayed throughout the compound, reveal the story of Tarzan's survival and coming-of-age in the wild. (But could there be trouble in paradise? That lout of a leopard, Sabor, is lurking somewhere in the tree!) By the time guests plant their feet on terra firma once more, they will have hit new heights—not unlike a certain high-flying hero himself—and gotten acquainted with some of the characters (both human and animal) who have shared in some of Tarzan's notorious exploits.

Note: Tarzan's Treehouse requires guests to climb quite a few stairs. Just a heads-up.

BIRNBAUM'S ★BEST★ INDIANA JONES™ ADVENTURE: FP

Hidden deep within the dense jungles of India, the Temple of the Forbidden Eye was built long ago to honor the powerful deity Mara. According to legend, Mara could "look into your very soul" and grant the "pure of heart" one of three gifts: unlimited wealth, eternal youth, or future knowledge. But legend also issues a rather stern warning: "A terrible fate awaits those who gaze upon the eyes of Mara!" Dr. Jones would only comment, "Records indicate that many have come, but few have returned."

Now *you* can take an expedition through the ancient temple ruins in this attraction based on the George Lucas/Steven Spielberg films. The experience, including the pre-show and queue area, can take more than an hour (without a Fastpass), though the ride itself lasts about 3½ minutes. You follow the jungle path through Dr. Jones's cluttered encampment, then enter the temple via the path marked by his original team. In the queue area, a newsreel tells of Jones's latest expedition. What it does not reveal is that Indy has entered the temple and disappeared.

Following in his footsteps, you will see warning signs that indicate there still may be booby traps that have not yet been disarmed. (The fun is in ignoring the warnings and letting the spikes fall where they may.) Inside the temple, guests board 12-passenger vehicles reminiscent of 1930s troop transports. One person sits by the wheel and serves as the expedition driver, but not until all are securely fastened in their seats for the twists and turns ahead. Hold on to your hat!

The search for Indiana Jones is on, and an encounter with the fearsome Mara is unavoidable. The trip reveals a world of mummies, glowing fires, falling lava, worrisome snakes, and poisonous darts.

Surprises lurk around every bend, and escape is only temporary (just as in the movies), as you suffer an avalanche of creepy crawlies, traverse a quaking suspension bridge, and find yourself on a collision course with a giant rolling boulder that threatens to flatten everything in its path. At the end of the ride, Indy himself is waiting for you, with a flippant parting remark, such as "That wasn't so bad" or "Next time you're on your own" or "Tourists. Why'd it have to be tourists?"

Thanks to the creative wizardry of Disney Imagineers, no two rides are exactly the same, so each time you enter the Temple of the Forbidden Eye, the overall experience may be slightly different. Hang on!

Note: Pregnant women and guests who suffer from heart conditions, motion sickness, sore necks or backs, and have other physical concerns should avoid this wild and exceptionally bumpy attraction. Guests must be at least 46 inches tall to board; children under age 7 must be accompanied by a person who is at least 14 years old. Spooked by snakes? There are more than a few in here. They may not be real, but they're still rather creepy.

New Orleans Square

Though New Orleans Square did not figure in the Disneyland layout until 1966, it's certainly among the park's most evocative areas. This would be true even if it were home to just the superb Haunted Mansion and Pirates of the Caribbean. But there's also its picturesque site on the shores of the Rivers of America, and its architecture, a pastiche of wrought iron, pastel stucco, French doors, and beckoning verandas.

Not to be missed are the pleasant open-air dining spots; the charming Blue Bayou restaurant overlooking the moonlit lagoon inside Pirates of the Caribbean; the unique assortment of boutiques; and the music—lively jazz and Dixieland, performed in traditional New Orleans style.

As you relax on a warm evening, snacking on beignets and mint juleps, images of Disneyland-as-amusement-park may evaporate. Just as Main Street, U.S.A., makes the theme park a great place to shop, New Orleans Square makes it a fine spot to spend a few relaxing hours. Those perpetual click-click sounds emanating from the railroad station are the Morse code version of the actual dedication speech Walt Disney gave on the opening day of Disneyland back in 1955. It begins: "To all who come to this happy place; welcome."

The attractions that are described on the following pages are listed in the order in which you would encounter them while strolling from east to west in Disneyland's New Orleans Square.

BIRNBAUM'S ★BEST★ PIRATES OF THE CARIBBEAN: The most swashbuckly adventure you'll find at Disneyland, this 16-minute boat ride transports guests through a series of sets portraying a rowdy pirate raid on a Caribbean village. Bursting with cannon fire, stolen loot, a gluttonous feast, and a raucous band of unruly mercenaries, Pirates of the Caribbean has been a fan favorite for more than half of a century. It was the last attraction built under Walt Disney's direct creative supervision.

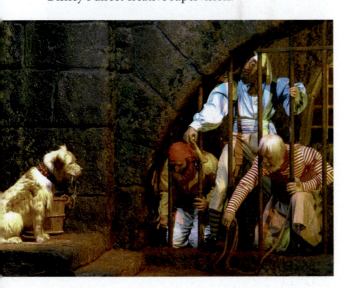

The experience begins with a voyage through a bayou, where will-o'-the-wisps glow just above the grasses. Fireflies twinkle nearby, while stars spangle the twilight-blue sky overhead. The attention to detail nearly boggles the mind. The Audio-Animatronics cast includes plastered pigs whose legs actually twitch in their soporific contentment, singing marauders, and wily wenches. The observant will note a couple of familiar rapscallion residents. Yep, that beloved scallywag Captain Jack Sparrow has dropped anchor here, as has his nefarious nemesis, Captain Barbossa. And there's a new pirate in town—the famous redhead resident of this attraction has teamed up with the local marauders! Redd hopes to help the townspeople "unload" their valuables at the Mercado Auction.

While it's by no means the most politically correct attraction, the theme song, "Yo-Ho, Yo-Ho (A Pirate's Life for Me)," manages to transform some blatant buccaneering into a rousing time for all. A must—again and again.

BIRNBAUM'S ★BEST★ HAUNTED MANSION: FP In a British radio interview, Walt Disney once explained how sorry he felt for those homeless ghosts whose hauntable mansions had fallen to the wrecker's ball. Feeling that these lost souls sorely needed a place of their own, he offered this Haunted Mansion, unquestionably one of Disneyland's top

HOT TIP!

Haunted Mansion Holiday kicks off in early September and runs through the New Year. It features Jack Skellington from *Tim Burton's The Nightmare Before Christmas*, as well as holiday decor galore. Silly, seasonal sight gags abound.

attractions. From its stately portico to the exit corridor, the special effects are piled on to create an eerie, but never terrifying, mood. Just frightfully amusing.

Judicious applications of paint and expert lighting effects heighten the shadows that play ghoulishly on the walls outside. The jumble of trunks, chairs, dress forms, and other assorted knickknacks in the attic are left appropriately dirty, and extra cobwebs, which come in convenient liquid form, are strung with abandon. The eerie music and the slightly spooky tones of the Ghost Host often set small children to whimpering, and soon their Mickey Mouse ears have been pulled tightly over their eyes. Still, the spirits that inhabit this house on the hill—999 in all—are a tame lot for the most part, though they are always looking for occupant number 1,000. Any volunteers?

What makes the seven-minute attraction so special is the attention to, and abundance of, details—so many that it's next to impossible to take them all in during the first, or even the second or third, time around. In the Portrait Chamber—a room full of fearsome-looking gargoyles that adjoins the chandeliered and lace-curtain-adorned foyer—it's fun to speculate on whether the ceiling moves up or the room moves down. (It's one way here and the opposite way at the Haunted Mansion's counterpart at Walt Disney World's Magic Kingdom park.)

Once in your Doom Buggy, look for the bats' eyes on the wallpaper, the tomb-sweet-tomb plaque, and the rattling suit of armor in the Corridor of Doors. Can you spot a Hidden Mickey in the haunted dining room? And keep your eyes peeled for the infamous "Hatbox Ghost" in the attic scene. Absent from the manse for decades, he's made a creepy comeback!

Then there are the dead plants and flowers and broken glass in the Conservatory, where a hand reaches out of a half-open casket; the terrified cemetery watchman and his mangy mutt in the Graveyard; the ghostly teapot that pours spectral tea; the ectoplasmic king and queen on the teeter-totter; the bicycle-riding spirits; the transparent musicians; and the headless knight and his supernatural Brunhilde. Nice stuff all.

The mansion was constructed in 1963, based on the historic Evergreen House in Baltimore, Maryland; the attraction opened in 1969. The signature song "Grim Grinning Ghosts" was composed especially for the Haunted Mansion attraction.

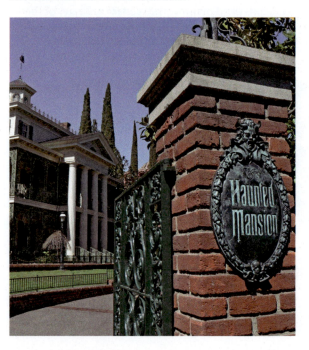

PHOTO BY JILL SAFRO

Frontierland

This is the America experienced by the pioneers as they pushed westward: rough wilderness outposts and dense forests, and rugged mountains delineating the skyline.

The sights in Frontierland are just about as pleasant as they come in Disneyland, and the atmosphere as relaxing.

FRONTIERLAND SHOOTIN' EXPOSITION: This shooting gallery, set in an 1850s town in the Southwest Territory, is completely electronic. Eighteen rifles are trained on Boothill, a mining town complete with a bank, jail, hotel, and stables. They fire invisible infrared beams that trigger silly results whenever they strike the red, reactive targets. The most challenging target is the moving shovel, which, when struck, causes a skeleton to pop out of a grave. There are nearly 100 targets on which to test your marksmanship.

Note: Park admission does not include use of the Frontierland Shootin' Exposition. Pay a buck for about 25 shots—then fire away (price subject to change).

BIRNBAUM'S ★BEST★ BIG THUNDER MOUNTAIN RAILROAD: FP Hold on to your hats and glasses, because this here's the wildest ride in the wilderness! Inspired by peaks in Utah's Bryce Canyon and Arizona's Sedona, Big Thunder Mountain is entirely a Disney creation. The name comes from an old Indian legend about a sacred mountain in Wyoming that thundered whenever anyone tried to excavate its gold. The attraction took five years of planning and two years of construction, and it cost about as much to build as the rest of the original Disneyland attractions put together.

As roller coasters go, this one is relatively tame. It's short on steep climbs and precipitous drops that put hearts in throats and make stomachs protest, but long on tight curves that provoke giggles of glee. Adding to the appeal of this thrill ride is the scenery that the runaway mine train passes along the way: a pitch-black bat cave, giant stalactites and stalagmites, a waterfall, a natural-arch bridge that affords fine views over the Big Thunder landscape, and mine walls ready to cave in.

The queue area sets the scene of the quaint mining town, with two hotels, a newspaper office, dance hall, saloon, and general store. If you listen closely, you may hear a local barmaid flirting with a miner to the tune of "Red River Valley" or "Listen to the Mockingbird."

As you approach the loading area, notice the brownish stone walls on each side of you. They were made from a hundred tons of real gold ore from the former mining town of Rosamond, California, which also yielded the 10-foot-tall stamp mill designated "Big Thunder Mine 1880."

Note: Pregnant women and guests who have heart conditions, weak backs, are prone to motion sickness, or other limitations should not ride. Guests must be at least 40 inches tall to experience Big Thunder Mountain Railroad. Kids under age 7 must be accompanied by a guest age 14 or older.

MARK TWAIN RIVERBOAT: One of the original Disneyland attractions, this five-eighths-scale vessel circumnavigates Tom Sawyer Island. Along the way, it passes the River Belle Terrace, the Royal Street Veranda, piney Critter Country, a waterfall, abandoned railroad tracks, and lovely dense woods filled with alders, cottonwoods, maples, and willows that might have been found along the Missouri frontier more than a century ago. Moose, elk, and (real) ducks complete the scene. The 14-minute ride offers a pleasant respite from the crowds. And if you manage to get one of the few chairs in the bow, the *Mark Twain* also provides a rare opportunity to rest your feet.

GOLDEN HORSESHOE SALOON: Tongue-in-cheek humor and Western flair are the key ingredients in the acts featured at this venue. The hall itself is resplendent with chandeliers, polished floors and banisters, and a long brass railing. Walt Disney kept a private box here, just to the left of the stage, on the upper level.

Performance times vary. Check a park Times Guide for the schedule or pay a visit to City Hall when you arrive at Disneyland park.

There is no assigned seating inside; all of the seats are good, though those up front or on the balcony are perhaps the best.

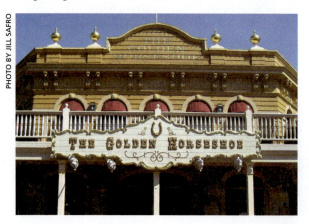

SAILING SHIP COLUMBIA: A full-scale replica of the 10-gun, 3-masted "Gem of the Ocean," the *Columbia* operates seasonally and on busy days at Disneyland. The original ship, built in Plymouth, Massachusetts, in 1787 and christened the *Columbia Rediviva* ("freedom reborn"), was the first American craft to circumnavigate the globe. (Back then, that took three years to do!)

Disney's *Columbia*, dedicated in 1958 and renovated in 1984, was the first ship of its kind to be built in more than a century. It circumnavigates the Rivers of America in 15 minutes. It has a steel hull and a deck planked with Douglas fir, and measures 110 feet from stem to stern, with an 84-foot mainmast. Usually moored at Fowler's Harbor, opposite the Haunted Mansion, the sailing ship towers majestically above the tree-tops of Frontierland.

Below Decks: The *Columbia*'s maritime museum, found below the main deck, celebrates the dedication and sacrifice of the brave explorers who filled in the final details of the world's map. It has historical displays and re-creates the living conditions of 18th-century sailors, based on reports in the ship's log and in letters between the captain and the owners.

PIRATE'S LAIR ON TOM SAWYER ISLAND: Yes, you read that right—there has been a pirate invasion in Frontierland. Tom Sawyer Island has been transformed into a pirate-y paradise, complete with hidden treasure, creepy caves, and shipwrecks.

The only way to reach the island is by pirate-piloted raft. Once there, guests have many areas to investigate. Among them is Smuggler's Cove, which incorporates the island's beloved bridges and invites guests to man the bilge pumps in an effort to raise sunken treasure. Then there's the Castle Rock lookout point, with its spyglasses and peepholes (perfect for spying on scally-wags or fellow park guests); Will Turner's Blacksmith Shop offers a glimpse at some of his works in progress; Dead Man's Grotto is a dark and labyrinthine set of caves sporting some spooky yet snazzy special effects. Purists are pleased by the preservation of Tom and Huck's Tree House. (Tom Sawyer Island is the only attraction designed by Walt Disney himself.)

Small signs point to places of interest on the island. Time spent here is worthwhile and could unexpectedly encompass some of your happiest moments in Disneyland.

Note: Tom Sawyer Island closes early to allow for Fantasmic! preparation. Check at the dock for excursion times, particularly the last raft departure of the day.

Critter Country

Lush, shady forests of pines, locusts, white birches, coastal redwoods, and evergreen elms surround Critter Country, one of the most pleasant corners of Disneyland. In 1972, this land debuted as Bear Country, the backwoods home of the since-departed Country Bear Playhouse. From 1956 through 1971, the area was called the Indian Village, complete with teepees and a dance circle, and was considered part of Frontierland.

PHOTO BY JILL SAFRO

In 1989, the zone welcomed foxes, frogs, geese, rabbits, crocodiles, and many of the other critters that make up the Audio-Animatronics cast of Splash Mountain. To make the furry residents feel at home, Disney Imagineers rechristened the area Critter Country. Observant guests will spot scaled-down houses, lairs, and nests tucked into hillsides and along the river.

BIRNBAUM'S
★BEST★

SPLASH MOUNTAIN: FP The fourth peak in Disneyland's mountain range of thrill rides—along with Big Thunder Mountain, the Matterhorn, and Space Mountain—Splash Mountain is unlike the other three attractions, where passengers ride roller-coaster-style cars down tubular steel tracks. In this 9-minute ride, they board hollowed-out logs and drift on a waterborne journey through backwoods swamps and bayous, down waterfalls, and finally (here's where the speed picks up) over the top of a super-steep spillway at the peak of the mountain into a briar-laced pond five stories below.

Splash Mountain is based on the animated sequences in Walt Disney's 1946 film *Song of the South*, and the principal characters from the movie—Brer Rabbit,

Brer Fox, and Brer Bear—appear in the attraction courtesy of Disney-created Audio-Animatronics technology. In fact, Splash Mountain's stars and supporting cast of 103 performers number almost as many as those in Pirates of the Caribbean attraction, which has 119 Audio-Animatronics characters.

Comparisons to Pirates of the Caribbean are particularly apt, as Splash Mountain was consciously designed to be a "How do we top this?" response to the popular, long-running pirate adventure. Splash Mountain broke new ground on several counts. Besides its impressive number of animated characters, it also boasts one of the world's tallest and sharpest flume drops (52½ feet at a 47-degree angle). That drop makes for one of the fastest rides ever operated at Disneyland Park.

PHOTO BY KEITH GROSHANS

▶

One other twist makes Splash Mountain unique in the annals of flumedom: After hurtling down Chickapin Hill, the seven-passenger log boats hit the pond below with a giant splash—and then promptly sink underwater (or appear to), with just a trace of bubbles left in their wake.

Splash Mountain's designers didn't only borrow the attraction's characters and color-saturated settings from *Song of the South*, they also included quite a bit of the film's Academy Award–winning music. In fact, the song in the attraction's finale, "Zip-a-Dee-Doo-Dah," has become something of a Disney anthem over the years. The voice of Brer Bear is performed by none other than Nick Stewart, the same actor who spoke the part in the film when it was released in 1946.

Keep in mind: The hotter the day, the longer the lines, so go early or late.

Note: Guests must be at least 40 inches tall to ride Splash Mountain. Kids under age 7 must be accompanied by a guest age 14 or older.

DAVY CROCKETT EXPLORER CANOES: Part attraction, part workout, the Davy Crockett Explorer Canoes requires teamwork and elbow grease to make the trip around the Rivers of America. The 25-foot-long canoes hold 20 passengers at a time and they are definitely not on a track. Modeled after the boats used by early Native Americans and European explorers, the canoes are powered entirely by handheld paddles. Though the helmsman and the sternman guide the rowing, guests' contributions are vital when it comes to completing the 2,400-foot voyage. Small children must wear (provided) life jackets.

Note: Davy Crockett Explorer Canoes operate on select days, and it closes at dusk. Check at the landing for excursion times.

THE MANY ADVENTURES OF WINNIE THE POOH: There's a cuddly critter in town, and he goes by the name of Winnie the Pooh. In this whimsical attraction, everyone's favorite honey-lovin' cub treats Disneyland park guests to a wild and whimsical 3½-minute tour of his home turf.

The attraction features a most unlikely form of transportation: beehives. They whisk (and bounce) guests through the Hundred Acre Wood, where the weather's most blustery. The wind is really ruffling the feathers of one of the locals. It seems Owl's treehouse has been shaken loose and just may topple to the ground—and onto the beehives below.

Similar sight gags abound, from a bubble-blowing Heffalump (hey, this is Disneyland) to a treacherous flood that threatens to sweep Tigger, Piglet, and the rest of the gang away. When the Pooh bear saves the day, it's time to celebrate—and everyone is invited to the party.

Note that, like many other Fantasyland attractions, this Critter Country ride has a few scenes that take place in near darkness. Some timid youngsters may find these moments a bit unsettling. (If your kids can handle the likes of Mr. Toad's Wild Ride and Pinocchio's Daring Journey, they should be within their comfort level while in the Hundred Acre Wood.)

Fantasyland

Walt Disney called Fantasyland a timeless land of enchantment. We couldn't agree more. The skyline, dominated by the peak of the Matterhorn, bristles with chimneys and weather vanes, turrets and towers. At the center of it all, as if deposited here by an itinerant carnival, is the regal King Arthur Carrousel.

Note: Parents of young children should be aware that many of Fantasyland's attractions—while tame—have moments that take place in the dark. (In fact, they are often referred to as "dark rides.") These include Peter Pan's Flight, Mr. Toad's Wild Ride, Alice in Wonderland, Snow White's Scary Adventures, Pinocchio's Daring Journey, and Storybook Land Canal Boats.

PHOTO BY JILL SAFRO

SLEEPING BEAUTY CASTLE: Rising above the treetops at the end of Main Street, U.S.A., it could be a figment of your imagination or a mirage created by Tinker Bell's pixie dust. Closer inspection proves this architectural confection is as real as the swans in the moat surrounding it. A composite of medieval European castles, primarily in the French and Bavarian styles, Sleeping Beauty Castle, the gateway to Fantasyland, is constructed of concrete, with towers that rise 77 feet above the moat. Trimmed in 22-karat gold leaf, it appears shiny even on gray days. The structure seems larger than it really is due to the use of forced perspective, down to the bricks.

From the Central Plaza, you're actually looking at what was originally intended to be the back of the castle; Walt Disney decided it was prettier that way and had the builders turn it around.

The drawbridge, lowered when the park first opened in 1955, is like a real one—though it has been raised (and lowered again) only once since that day. The historic event took place in 1983, at the re-dedication ceremony for Fantasyland.

Outside the castle, juniper is planted around the water's edge; it's one of the few green plants that the swans won't eat. One of the two graceful trees to the right of the drawbridge bears hundreds of tiny yellow flowers in spring, and the other is covered with lavender flowers for several weeks in early summer.

CASTLE WALK-THROUGH: This classic Disneyland experience features additional scenes and enhanced special effects. The show, which features a series of dioramas, tells the story of *Sleeping Beauty*—including the magic of fairies Flora, Fauna, and Merryweather and the sinister spells of the evil Maleficent.

Guests enter the walk-through from the right, on the Fantasyland side of the castle. Note that it is rather dark inside (which may spook tots) and there are some stairs to climb. Guests who are unable to do stairs or navigate the narrow passageways of the castle may experience the walk-through "virtually" in a special room on the ground floor.

FANTASY FAIRE: Once upon a time . . . in a storybook village nestled beside Sleeping Beauty Castle, folks of all ages were invited to mix and mingle with Disney characters and enjoy a live (and lively!) stage show. That time is now, and the guest list includes you. The Royal Hall and The Royal Theatre are the highlights of Fantasyland's newest neighborhood.

THE ROYAL HALL: Behind the richly detailed facade of this regal residence, you'll find a gorgeous gothic interior fit for a princess. A rotating group of royals is always on hand to greet guests. Expect favorites such as Belle, Cinderella, Snow White, and more.

THE ROYAL THEATRE: Bring your funny bone to this theatre—the antics on stage are meant to make you chuckle. The show features a madcap and original retelling of a classic and beloved Disney tale. The action recently regaled tales from *Beauty and the Beast* and *Tangled*. The theatrical yarns are presented by Mr. Smythe and Mr. Jones, Renaissance bards with vastly vaudevillian vigor, and a multitasking cast. It's fun for the whole family. Tales change periodically. Shows typically last about 22 minutes. The Royal Swing Big Band Ball takes place on select evenings. Check a park Times Guide for the performance schedule.

PIXIE HOLLOW: Where do Disney fairies live? In Pixie Hollow! Disneyland guests may enter the world of Tinker Bell and her friends. As guests walk along the garden path, they feel as though they are shrinking down to fairy size as the landscape gets larger and larger. Open daily, this miniature realm is extra sparkly on summer nights, when it glows with the "magic" of pixie dust. You'll find Pixie Hollow between the Castle and the entrance to Tomorrowland.

SNOW WHITE WISHING WELL & GROTTO: Tucked off Matterhorn Way, at the eastern end of the moat around Sleeping Beauty Castle, this is one of those quiet corners of the park easily overlooked by guests. (Though not everyone, as it is a popular spot to "pop the question.") If you stand by the wishing well, you might hear Adriana Caselotti, the original voice of Snow White, singing the lovely melody "I'm Wishing," written for Walt Disney's Oscar-winning 1937 film.

F.Y.I.: Any coins tossed into the well go to children's charities—so your wish will help fulfill other wishes.

PETER PAN'S FLIGHT: "Come on, everybody, here we go! Off to Never Land!" This attraction is one of the park's loveliest—and consistently one of the most popular. Based on the story by Sir James M. Barrie about a boy with an immunity to maturity and an affinity for flying—by way of Disney's 1953 animated feature—the ride's effects soar to celestial heights. Pirate ships embark from the Darling kids' nursery and carry travelers through the clouds and into a starry sky.

Water ripples and gleams softly in the moonlight; the lava on the sides of a volcano glows with almost the intensity of the real thing. After an ephemeral few minutes, the ships drift back into reality, an unloading area that is all the more jarring after the magic of the trip through Never Land.

Of the approximately 350 miles of fiber optics throughout Fantasyland, the majority is used in this ride. The twinkling London scene is an enlarged model of an authentic map of the city.

This attraction is atop the popularity list with guests of all ages and usually has a line consistent with its status. Head here first thing in the morning, or late in the day (after little ones have gone to bed).

MR. TOAD'S WILD RIDE: Based on the 1949 Disney film *The Adventures of Ichabod and Mr. Toad*—which was inspired by Kenneth Grahame's classic novel *The Wind in the Willows*—this simple, zany attraction is housed in an English manor bristling with ornate chimneys that really smoke. The wild, low-tech ride is experienced from the perspective of the eccentric but lovable Mr. Toad.

Of course, he is as inept a driver as you'd expect a toad to be. During the excursion, you crash through the fireplace in his library, burst through a wall full of windows, careen through the countryside, charge head-long into a warehouse full of TNT, lurch through the streets of London, then ram into a pub and veer out again. During the 2-minute journey, you'll also be berated by a judge in court, nearly collide head-on with a railroad train, and be banished to a fiery inferno. (Some effects may be too intense for tots.)

DID YOU KNOW?

There is a shadow of Sherlock Holmes (complete with pipe and cap) in the second-story window of the Constabulatory building inside the Mr. Toad's Wild Ride attraction (in Fantasyland).

ALICE IN WONDERLAND: This Fantasyland staple has been revamped and revitalized. It features a new Alice figure, animated flowers, and a rolling hedgehog. It is Alice in *Wonderland*, after all!

Traveling in oversize caterpillars, visitors fall down the rabbit hole and embark upon a bizarre adventure in that strange world known as Wonderland. They come face-to-face with Tweedledum and Tweedledee, a garden filled with singing roses, the Cheshire Cat, the Queen of Hearts and her playing-card soldiers, the White Rabbit, and other characters from Lewis Carroll's beloved story *Alice's Adventures in Wonderland*.

At the end of the nearly four-minute ride, a giant un-birthday cake explodes (thanks to a dynamite "candle"), providing a suitable finish to this sweet interlude. It's understandably popular with the under-age-7 demographic.

PHOTO BY MIKE CARROLL

MAD TEA PARTY: The sequence in Walt Disney's 1951 release *Alice in Wonderland* in which the Mad Hatter hosts a tea party for his "un-birthday" is the theme for this ride—a group of colorful oversize teacups whirling wildly on a spinning tea table. Festive Japanese lanterns hang overhead. One of the park's original attractions, this dizzying ride lasts only 1½ minutes—but it may feel a bit longer!

Note: The teacups may look mild, but it's a good idea to let a reasonable interval pass after eating before you take one for a spin.

BIRNBAUM'S ★BEST **MATTERHORN BOBSLEDS:** FP Though it's 100 times smaller than the actual peak, Disney's version of the Matterhorn is still a credible reproduction. The use of forced perspective makes the snowy summit look much loftier than the approximately 147 feet it does reach. Even the trees and shrubs help create the illusion. Those at the timberline are far smaller than the ones at the bottom.

The ride itself, like the Space Mountain and Big Thunder Mountain Railroad attractions, has to be counted among the most thrilling at Disneyland. At the time the Matterhorn Bobsleds were dedicated, in 1959, they were considered an engineering novelty because their dispatch system allowed more than one car to be in action at once. The ride was also the world's first tubular steel roller coaster. This classic is also considered Disney's first thrill ride. The old favorite has enhanced snow-caps, lighting, and visual effects.

The somewhat jolting adventure begins with a dramatic climb into the frosty innards of the mountain, then makes a speeding, twisting, turning descent through a cloud of fog and past giant icicles and ice crystals. The wind howls as you hurtle toward a brief encounter with the Abominable Snowman (take note of the effects!). The speed of the downhill flight away from the creature seems greater than it really is because much of the journey takes place inside tunnels. Splashdown is in an alpine lake.

A Magical Show

Mickey and the Magical Map is a live, musical spectacular presented in The Fantasyland Theatre. Each 22-minute performance features appearances by Disney pals such as Rapunzel, Mulan, Tiana, King Louie, and Sorcerer Mickey (of course!). The show is offered on select days. Check a Times Guide, *disneyland.com*, or the Disneyland Resort app for showtimes.

Note: Pregnant women and guests who suffer from weak backs (the seats are hard and the ride is bumpy), heart conditions, motion sickness, or other physical limitations should not take the ride. Guests must be at least 42 inches tall. Kids under age 7 must be accompanied by an adult.

PHOTO BY JILL SAFRO

STORYBOOK LAND CANAL BOATS: This 7-minute cruise through Monstro the Whale and past miniature scenes from Disney's animated films is not one of Disneyland's major attractions, yet few who take the trip would deny that the journey is one of the park's sweetest. No detail was spared, from the homes of the Three Little Pigs, to the Old English village of Alice in Wonderland (where the White Rabbit boasts his very own mailbox), to the London park that Peter Pan and Tinker Bell flew over with Wendy, John, and Michael Darling on their way to Never Land.

Other storybook locales include the marketplace where Aladdin met Princess Jasmine, the Seven Dwarfs' home and jewel mine, and Cinderella's castle. At the end of the cruise, the boat drifts past Geppetto's village, Prince Eric and Ariel's castle, King Triton's castle— and *Frozen*'s Kingdom of Arendelle.

BIRNBAUM'S ★BEST★ **IT'S A SMALL WORLD:** **FP** The background music for this attraction is cheerful and singsong, sometimes maddeningly so. It does grab your attention, starting with the cheery facade, embellished with stylized representations of the Eiffel Tower, the Leaning Tower of Pisa, Big Ben, the Taj Mahal, and other landmarks. The 30-foot-tall clock with the loud ticktock and the syncopated swing is frosting on the architectural cake. The whirring of gears that marks every quarter hour alone warrants a trip to the attraction's plaza.

Boats carry guests into a land filled with more than 300 Audio-Animatronics dolls representing children (and popular Disney characters) from 100 regions of the world. It's a pageant for the eyes, even if the ears grow weary. (If you find yourself humming "It's a Small World" for the next several hours, you can blame Richard M. and Robert B. Sherman, the Academy Award–winning composers of the music for *Mary Poppins*, among many other Disney scores.)

Topiary figures in the shapes of a giraffe, elephant, rhinoceros, lion, horse, and other friendly beasts bid guests farewell at ride's end.

PHOTO BY MIKE CARROLL

FP = Fastpass attraction (see page 58)

Note that It's a Small World is transformed inside and out between Thanksgiving and New Year's to become as close to a winter wonderland as you're likely to find in Southern California. The dolls even sing "Jingle Bells" along with "It's a Small World."

CASEY JR. CIRCUS TRAIN: One of the key sequences in the film *Dumbo*, in which an engine named Casey Jr. pulls a circus train up a steep hill, became the inspiration for this 3½-minute train ride that circles Storybook Land. The Storybook Land Canal Boats are better for viewing the landscaping and miniature details there, but it's worth a ride inside one of the wild-animal cage cars. Each train has two of them—plus a real caboose. Listen as the engine chugs, "I think I can" and then, "I thought I could" as it negotiates the hill.

PHOTO BY JILL SAFRO

DUMBO THE FLYING ELEPHANT: As beloved a symbol of Fantasyland as Sleeping Beauty Castle, this ride reminds all who see it of the baby elephant immortalized in Disney's 1941 feature film. In it, Dumbo discovers that his large ears actually enable him to fly.

A mechanical marvel, Dumbo the Flying Elephant is full of filigreed metalwork, with a system of cogs, gears, and pulleys. Brass pipes spew water from the base, and music is supplied by a vintage band organ housed in a small, ornate structure nearby. That figure atop the ride is Dumbo's trusty sidekick, Timothy Mouse.

SNOW WHITE'S SCARY ADVENTURES: Ornamental stone ravens perch on carved stone skulls atop a stone tower, and hearts pierced through with swords lie at the base of the twisted pillars that support this brooding building. The two-minute ride inside includes several fairly frightening scenes. In one, the Queen changes into a scary old hag before your eyes; in another, this wicked witch has the nerve to tempt you with a (likely) poisoned apple.

PHOTO BY KEITH GROSHANS

After passing a brief and happy scene in the Seven Dwarfs' cottage, ride vehicles travel through a creepy dungeon, visit a workshop where the Queen labors over her bubbling cauldron, and then venture into the Frightening Forest, where moss-draped trees point talon-like branches at passersby. The visit to the diamond mine, where the Seven Dwarfs work, is more beautiful than scary because of the sparkling gems glowing in the darkness.

It all ends in true storybook fashion: As the evil Queen attempts to roll a boulder down the side of a mountain to crush the dwarfs below, she gets struck by lightning (thanks to a convincing strobe effect) and tumbles over the edge of a cliff, leaving Snow White, her Prince, and their seven sidekicks to live happily ever after, as depicted in the mural near the exit. The music is taken from rare recordings used to create the film's original soundtrack.

Note: This attraction can be too intense for some children. Snow White's adventures really are scary!

PINOCCHIO'S DARING JOURNEY: Based on Disney's 1940 animated feature, this is a 3-minute morality play of sorts, with Jiminy Cricket serving as host and guide. Pinocchio, who is the creation of the toymaker Geppetto, pays a somewhat scary visit to Pleasure Island and discovers the right way to live.

As the ride vehicles move from the cheerful land of popcorn and Ferris wheels to the seamy world of Tobacco Road, Pleasure Island hues are replaced by drab shades of brown and gray. Here, little boys are turned into donkeys and sold to work in the salt mines.

Pinocchio escapes that fate, nearly becomes supper for Monstro the Whale, and winds up back home in the care of Geppetto—another happily-ever-after ending. The final scene, in which the Blue Fairy turns into a cloud of sparkles

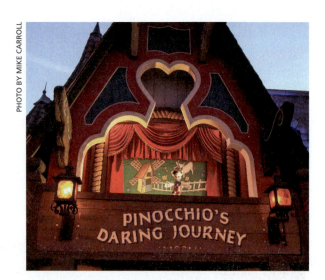

PINOCCHIO'S DARING JOURNEY

and then disappears, leaving a smattering of pixie dust on the floor, is partially accomplished via fiber optics.

Note: This attraction may be a bit frightening to some toddlers (not to mention those of us who may be spooked by the concept of turning into a donkey).

KING ARTHUR CARROUSEL: Guests come upon this graceful park landmark as they stroll toward the Sleeping Beauty Castle passageway into Fantasyland. One of the few attractions in the park that is an original rather than a Disney adaptation, the carrousel contains 68 horses—all movable, as Walt Disney wished. Carved in Germany over a century ago, no two horses are exactly alike, and they are as pampered as the live Belgian horses on Main Street, U.S.A. The ornamentation on them is gold, silver, and copper leaf. The nine hand-painted panels on top of the carrousel's main face tell the story of Princess Aurora, aka Sleeping Beauty.

Disneyland Park FastPass Attractions

Long lines got you down? Not to worry—some of the major Disneyland attractions offer Fastpass. (For an explanation of this time-saving, line-skipping system, turn to page 58.) We've listed some of those "E-ticket" crowd-pleasers below. (The attractions listed here may change and Fastpass may not be offered at all times during the year. All admission tickets must be activated at the park entrance before they can be used to obtain Fastpass assignments inside the theme park. Star Wars: Galaxy's Edge attractions did not offer Fastpass [or MaxPass] when they first opened, but that may change in 2020. Check *www.disneyland.com* for updates.)

ADVENTURELAND
Indiana Jones Adventure

CRITTER COUNTRY
Splash Mountain

FANTASYLAND
Matterhorn Bobsleds
It's a Small World

FRONTIERLAND
Big Thunder Mountain Railroad

MICKEY'S TOONTOWN
Roger Rabbit's Car Toon Spin

NEW ORLEANS SQUARE
Haunted Mansion

TOMORROWLAND
Space Mountain
Star Tours—The Adventures Continue
Buzz Lightyear Astro Blasters

Mickey's Toontown

Disneyland lore tells us that when Mickey Mouse burst onto the movie scene in 1928 in *Steamboat Willie*, the first synchronized-sound cartoon, his success was so great that his busy schedule demanded he practically live at the Walt Disney Studios. Thirty cartoons later, in the early 1930s, he was one tired mouse, so he moved into a quiet residence in a "toon only" community south of Hollywood. Over the years, many toon stars gravitated to Mickey's Toontown, as it quickly became known. Minnie Mouse, Pluto, Goofy, Roger Rabbit, Chip, Dale, and Gadget all live here, and Donald Duck docks his boat, the *Miss Daisy*, on Toon Lake.

One afternoon, while Mickey Mouse and his close friend Walt Disney were relaxing on Mickey's front porch, Walt revealed his idea for a theme park that would appeal to "youngsters of all ages." Mickey suggested that he build it next to the secret entrance to Toontown, and the rest is history. Disneyland opened to the public in 1955, but little did anyone realize while they were drifting through It's a Small World that they were right next door to Mickey's Toontown.

In 1990, Mickey and his friends decided to open up their neighborhood and their homes to non-toons, and, in preparation, all of Toontown received a new coat of ink and paint. The grand opening took place in January 1993.

Legend aside, the development of Mickey's Toontown was a real challenge: to create a three-dimensional cartoon environment without a single straight line. Yet, as topsy-turvy as it is, Mickey's Toontown is a complete community, with a downtown area, including a commercial center and an industrial zone, plus a suburban neighborhood. The best part is that everything is meant to be touched, pushed, and jumped on. Kids do just that, while adults relish the attention to detail and the assortment of gags. Much here is interactive, from the mouse-hole covers to the mailboxes.

This booming toontropolis is home to seven attractions, a duo of shops, and three fast-food eateries. The attractions are described in the neighborhood sections that follow; the shops, in the Shopping section later in this chapter; and the quick-service eateries, in the *Good Meals, Great Times* chapter of this book.

Guests enter this colorful land by walking under the Toontown train depot. The attractions are listed as they are encountered when strolling counterclockwise.

HOT TIP!

There are no full-service restaurants in Toontown, just a few fast-food places with window service, and limited outdoor seating. So don't plan on having an elaborate meal here.

DOWNTOWN TOONTOWN

In Toontown's "business" zone, an animated taxi teeters off the second-floor balcony of the Cab Co. A runaway safe has crashed into the sidewalk, and crates of rib-ticklers, ripsnorters, slapsticks, and wisecracks wait for passersby to lift the lids. At the Fireworks Factory, a plunger sets off quite a response when pressed; it's a good thing the Toontown Fire Department is located right next door.

Lift the receiver of the police telephone outside the Power House (home to all sorts of electrifying gizmos— open the door at your own risk), and you might hear a voice over the toon police car radio, announcing, "Someone put mail in the box, and the box does not like it. Please respond post haste." Or step on the mouse-hole cover near the post office, and you might hear, "How's the weather up there?" or "Is it time to come out now?"

You never know just what to expect once inside Toontown—but it's all bound to be goofy.

ROGER RABBIT'S CAR TOON SPIN: **FP** This chaotic, rollicking ride combines the technology of the Mad Tea Party teacups (cars here spin a full 360 degrees) and the tracks of Fantasyland attractions, such as Mr. Toad's Wild Ride. Benny the Cab and Roger Rabbit join the dizzying chase, which takes guests through the back alleys of the toon underworld made famous in the film *Who Framed Roger Rabbit*. The mission of each car is to save Jessica Rabbit from the evil weasels while avoiding the dreaded Dip.

If the spinning teacups over at Fantasyland's Mad Tea Party make your head spin (or worse), you should probably sit this one out.

ROGER'S FOUNTAIN: In this farcical fountain, a statue of Roger Rabbit is suspended in midair, afloat on a column of water erupting from a broken fire hydrant that he seems to have crashed into. (Roger's still holding the steering wheel from the cab he was driving.) Surrounding the hydrant, four floating taxicab tires serve as inner tubes for fish spouting arcs of water up into the air. The fountain is (appropriately) located near Roger Rabbit's Cartoon Spin.

POST OFFICE: Each kooky mailbox actually speaks in the voice of the character whose mail it receives— Mickey Mouse, Minnie Mouse, Roger Rabbit, Jessica Rabbit, Donald Duck, and Goofy. Together, they can create quite a cacophony.

Near the Post Office, a letter box pipes in with comments like, "Don't just stand there—mail something!"

TOON SQUARE

Located between the downtown area and the residential section of Toontown, this district is home to local businesses and institutions, including the Toontown Skool, the Department of Ink & Paint, and the 3rd Little Piggy Bank. Toontown's three eateries— Clarabelle's Frozen Yogurt, Pluto's Dog House, and Daisy's Diner—stand side by side on the square.

TOWN HALL: Toon residents emerge from this municipal building and proceed to the bandstand out front to greet guests, entertain with their antics, and provide more relaxing photo opportunities than are often available elsewhere in Disneyland.

When a character is about to arrive, the "Clockenspiel" above City Hall may spring to life: Mallets ring bells, toon hands pull whistles, and figures of Roger Rabbit and Mickey Mouse pop out of cannons, blowing horns that, in turn, produce bouquets of flowers.

GOOFY'S GAS: From the looks of it, any traveler would think twice about refueling at this station— or risk their vehicle getting goofed up. On the other hand, it does house Toontown's public restrooms and telephones, and that's an important location to know (though we don't recommend making any important business calls here).

The wacky water fountain beside the Goofy's Gas station dispenses refreshing H2O.

PHOTO BY JILL SAFRO

MICKEY'S NEIGHBORHOOD

The homes in this district sit at the base of the 40-foot-tall Toon Hills, which have their own version of the famous Hollywood sign. The attractions are described as a guest would pass them while walking counter-clockwise from Mickey's Fountain.

MICKEY'S FOUNTAIN: A statue of the world's most famous mouse stands at the center of a pool surrounded by toon-style musical instruments, creating a whimsical centerpiece for the Toontown residential area.

MINNIE'S HOUSE: It's hard to miss Minnie Mouse's House. This lavender-and-pink creation has a sweet-heart theme for the sweetheart inside. Here, guests can peek at Minnie's living room with its chintz sofa and sophisticated magazines (*Cosmousepolitan* and *Mademouselle*) on the coffee table.

There are messages from Goofy and Mickey on the answering machine in the hallway. Guests are invited to create new fashions for Minnie on the computer in her dressing room.

In Minnie's kitchen, a cake in the oven rises when a knob is turned, pots and pans clank out a melody when the stove is switched on, and the dishwasher churns when a button is pushed. The Cheesemore refrigerator is stocked with an assortment of dairy products, including Golly Cheeze Whiz, and the shopping list left on the outside of the fridge hints at this mouse's cheeses of choice. Be sure to check out the cookies on Minnie's kitchen table (and be prepared for a practical joke, courtesy of Ms. Mouse).

As you leave Minnie's House, you'll pass the wishing well in her yard. Don't think you're imagining things: It's been known to share a few parting thoughts.

MICKEY'S HOUSE: A short path leads from Minnie's backyard to the front door of Mickey's House. The welcoming yellow dwelling with a tile roof, huge green door, and green shutters is home to the toon who started it all. Not only is Mickey's face on the mailbox out front, but his welcome mat is in the instantly recognizable shape of three circles—his head and ears.

In the living room stands a player piano and a curio cabinet filled with all manner of memorabilia, including Mickey's baby shoes and a picture of him with his friend Walt Disney, as well as some of Pluto's treasures—a bone and a half-eaten shoe. In the laundry room, the washing machine chugs merrily away, and laundry supplies, such as Comics Cleanser and Mouse 'n' Glo, are at the ready.

PHOTO BY JILL SAFRO

From here, make your way through the greenhouse and into Mickey's backyard, where you'll see Pluto's doghouse and a garden with mysteriously disappearing carrots. If you want to meet the Mouse, be sure to visit the movie barn out back.

MICKEY'S MOVIE BARN: Ever industrious, Mickey has transformed the old barn in back of his cottage into a workplace, and guests are welcome to visit him here. The first stop is the Prop Department, where colorful costumes and props from some of his famous cartoons are stored.

In the Screening Room, a bumbling Goofy projects movie clips from a few "remakes" currently in progress, among them *Steamboat Willie* and *The Sorcerer's Apprentice*. Mickey is hard at work on a soundstage, but happy to take a break. Starstruck park guests enter in small groups for a photo and autograph session with Toontown's "famouse" resident.

Note: You can't get to Mickey's Movie Barn without going through his house. This attraction is a must for die-hard fans of the Mouse.

CHIP 'N' DALE TREEHOUSE: Just past Mickey's House stands the home of that jolly chipmunk duo, Chip and Dale. Styled to look like a redwood tree, this high-rise accommodates guests of all ages—but it's best enjoyed by small children. A spiral staircase leads to the lofty perch, whose windows provide a fine view of Mickey's Toontown.

GADGET'S GO COASTER: Gadget is the brilliant inventor from the TV cartoon *Chip 'n' Dale's Rescue Rangers*. So it's only fitting that some of her handiwork is within view of their treehouse. Gadget, the ultimate recycler, has created this coaster from an assortment of gizmos that once served other purposes. Gigantic toy blocks are now support beams for the tracks; hollowed-out acorns have become the cars of the train; and bridges have been created from giant combs, pencils, paper clips, and such. The thick steel tracks give the impression of a tame ride, but there are a few thrills, right up to the final turn into the station. This experience is exciting but rather brief (one minute), so if the line is long, save it for later.

Note: Guests must be at least 35 inches tall to ride Gadget's Go Coaster. Those under the age of 7 must be accompanied by a person age 14 or older. Pregnant

women should skip the trip. It may be a small coaster, but the 51-second ride is wilder than one might expect.

DONALD'S BOAT: Donald Duck's houseboat, named for his fair-feathered friend (Daisy), is docked in Toon Lake, adjacent to Gadget's Go Coaster. Parents can relax in a small, shaded seating area near a waterfall while their children explore the boat, which looks a whole lot like its owner.

See if you can recognize Donald's eyes in the large portholes of the pilothouse, his jaunty blue sailor's cap in the roof of the cabin, and his face in the shape of the hull. Would-be sailors can climb the small rope ladder or the spiral staircase up to the pilothouse to steer the wheel that turns the compass or to toot the boat's whistle.

GOOFY'S PLAYHOUSE: Located beside the *Miss Daisy*, this playground is just for kids. The garden outside Goofy's house boasts an odd assortment of delights: giant stalks bearing popcorn guarded by a Goofy-style scarecrow, spinning flowers, a leaky garden hose, and a patch with watermelons and pumpkins. Inside, young visitors can peek into Goofy's cupboards, climb on his furniture, and tickle the keys of the piano (doing so yields "goofy" sound effects rather than musical notes). Across the street is Goofy's Gas. It's not an actual filling station, but is a convenient place to take little ones for a pit stop—it's a restroom.

TOON PARK: This tiny soft-surface enclave next to Goofy's Playhouse supplies a safe play area for toddlers. Adjacent seating gives parents and other guests an inviting place to rest and enjoy the youngsters' antics. Stroller parking is nearby.

Tomorrowland

When Walt Disney was alive, the future seemed simple: We would all dress in Mylar and travel in flying saucers. The Tomorrowland he created in the '50s was set in the distant year of 1987, part Buck Rogers and part World's Fair. The current incarnation of Tomorrowland retains that spirit and is based on a classic vision of the future, one that looks at it from the perspective of the past. The result is an innocent and hopeful place—imagine, for instance, a planet that renews itself. Visit Tomorrowland today, and you enter a realm more in keeping with the rest of Disneyland than with the sterile, less positive future world often depicted in contemporary films.

Cross the bridge into this land and enter a visually engaging terrain, where the palette of colors is not otherworldly, but still forward-thinking. Futuristic boulders and dreamlike architecture coexist with apple, orange, lemon, and pomegranate trees that line pathways created from gray, mauve, and burgundy bricks. This landscape fires up the intellect as much as the imagination.

Galileo Galilei, Leonardo da Vinci, Jules Verne, H.G. Wells, and Walt Disney would have felt right at home here. Aldous Huxley probably wouldn't have.

Several of Tomorrowland's attractions are also located at Walt Disney World in Florida: Space Mountain, Star Tours—The Adventures Continue, Astro Orbitor, and Buzz Lightyear Astro Blasters (known in Walt Disney World as Buzz Lightyear's Space Ranger Spin). Other classic Tomorrowland attractions include Finding Nemo Submarine Voyage, the Disneyland Monorail, and Autopia.

A replica of the Moonliner, a Tomorrowland icon from 1955 to 1966, sits on the site of its predecessor. Monorail trains glide to and from the Downtown Disney district, while traditional Disneyland Railroad trains chug their way into the Tomorrowland station, a vibrant reminder that the past is indeed prologue (trains stop at Main Street and New Orleans Square, too).

The following attractions were operating at press time, but some may not be open in all of 2020. Check *www.disneyland.com* for Tomorrowland updates.

PHOTO BY JILL SAFRO

HOT TIP!

To maximize your scoring potential at the Buzz Lightyear attraction, aim for targets that are lit up, moving, or far away. They tend to yield the most points.

ASTRO ORBITOR: Towering high above the entrance to Tomorrowland, this big whirligig with spinning orbs and speeding starships is a fitting symbol for Tomorrowland. Astro Orbitor, modeled on a drawing made by Leonardo da Vinci almost five centuries ago, is the successor to Rocket Jets, which gave Disneyland guests a lift for 30 years. Each ride vehicle accommodates two passengers (or two adults and one small child), who can maneuver it up and down while spinning clockwise for 1½ minutes, reveling in sweeping views of Tomorrowland, (Main Street's) Central Plaza, the Matterhorn, and Sleeping Beauty Castle.

Note: The minimum age to ride Astro Orbitor is one year. Children under the age of 7 have to be in the company of an adult.

BIRNBAUM'S ★BEST★ **BUZZ LIGHTYEAR ASTRO BLASTERS:** 🅵🅿 The evil Emperor Zurg is up to no good—and it's up to that Space Ranger extraordinaire Buzz Lightyear and his Junior Space Rangers (that means you) to save the day.

So goes the story line of Tomorrowland's video game–inspired spin through the toy universe. The adventure is experienced from a toy's point of view. Guests begin their 4½-minute tour of duty as Space Rangers at Star Command Action Center. This is where Buzz gives his team a briefing on the mission that lies ahead. Then it's off to the Launch Bay to board the ride vehicles. The ships feature dual laser cannons, glowing lights, and a piloting joystick.

In addition to Buzz and the evil Emperor, you may recognize some other toy faces swirling about—the little green, multi-eyed alien toys, best known for their awe of "the claw." The Little Green Men have been enlisted to help in the fight against Zurg.

Once Junior Space Rangers blast off, they find themselves surrounded by Zurg's robots, who are mercilessly ripping batteries from toys. As Rangers fire at targets, beams of light fill the air. For every target hit, you will be rewarded with sight gags, sound effects, and points. The points, which are tallied automatically, are accumulated throughout the journey. Although the vehicles follow a rigid "flight" path (they're on a track), the joystick allows riders to maneuver the ships, arcing from side to side or spinning in circles while taking aim at their surroundings.

When the star cruiser arrives at Zurg's spaceship, it's showdown time. Will good prevail over evil? Or has time run out for the toy universe? And will you score enough points to be a Galactic Hero? (Most people improve their scores with a little practice.)

PHOTO BY JILL SAFRO

BIRNBAUM'S ★BEST★ **STAR TOURS—THE ADVENTURES CONTINUE:** 🅵🅿 Inspired by George Lucas's blockbuster series of Star Wars films, this is one of the most exciting attractions in Tomorrowland. It offers guests the opportunity to ride on droid-piloted StarSpeeders—the exact same type of flight simulator used by military and commercial airlines to train pilots—and explore the galaxy in a 3-D adventure. The action here takes place throughout the time period covered by the major Star Wars movies. The best part? There are dozens of different adventures to experience here—multiple visits will likely yield multiple surprises.

This is a rather turbulent trip—seat belts are definitely required. Passengers must be free of back problems, heart conditions, motion sickness, and other physical limitations to ride. Guests under 40 inches tall may not ride. Pregnant women must skip this one. If you have a young child, make sure he or she understands the significance of wearing 3-D glasses (and keeping them on) before you board the attraction—it's a concept lost on most tots.

STAR WARS LAUNCH BAY: Star Wars Launch Bay offers an immersive atmosphere in which to experience both the Light and Dark sides. Housed in the space formerly occupied by Innoventions, Launch Bay features props, videos, and movie memorabilia celebrating Star Wars and the recently reawakened Force. In addition to Light and Dark galleries, guests may meet characters such as everyone's favorite Wookiee, Chewbacca, plus Kylo Ren and that menacing Sith Lord, Darth Vader. Details are subject to change at any time in 2020.

BIRNBAUM'S ★BEST★ SPACE MOUNTAIN: **FP** When Space Mountain first opened in 1977, it quickly rocketed to the top of just about everyone's list of favorite attractions—where it remains to this day. While the classic facade and essence of the attraction remain intact, the experience is decidedly 21st century. Brave voyagers blast off from a realistic launch port. Once they've shot through a disorienting tunnel, riders will have a close encounter with a meteorite. After that, it's all about screeching through the darkness, past spinning stars and whirling galaxies. Add to that an edgy soundtrack (which is synchronized to each ride vehicle), and you've got one out-of-this-world attraction.

If your courage fails you, just ask an attendant to direct you to the nearest escape route (aka "the chicken exit"). Space Mountain is an extremely popular attraction—get a Fastpass if you can.

Note: Pregnant women and guests who have weak backs or necks, heart conditions, motion sickness, or any other physical limitations must sit this one out. Children under age 7 must be accompanied by an adult. Guests must be at least 40 inches tall to experience Space Mountain.

F.Y.I.: *Mercury 9* and *Gemini 5* astronaut Gordon Cooper worked with Disney Imagineers to create Space Mountain. He wanted to give guests a realistic feeling of actual space flight. Mission accomplished!

AUTOPIA: The only attraction left from the original Tomorrowland, Autopia was dubbed "The Freeway of the Future" back in 1955. Kids have always loved guiding the small sports cars around the twisting roadways (for them, a top speed of seven miles per hour is thrilling). The Tomorrowland and Fantasyland roadways now comprise a single attraction (yes, there were two Autopias; the one in Fantasyland opened in 1959 to accommodate spillover crowds). Guests travel in restyled race cars through 21st-century terrain, experiencing a series of happy roadside surprises along the way. Featuring a real working gas pedal and steering wheel, each car can seat 2 adults or 3 children and navigates curves and inclines just like the real thing. Don't let the lack of a brake pedal scare you—to slow down or stop, simply ease off the accelerator. This attraction is quite popular with those who've not yet reached Driver's Ed age.

Notes: Guests must be at least 54 inches tall to drive alone. Folks who are at least 32 inches tall are also invited to drive, as long as they are accompanied by someone who is at least 54 inches tall. Kids under age 7 must be accompanied by someone at least 14 years of age. Pregnant women; guests with heart, back, or neck problems; and those sensitive to motion should not ride. Intentionally bumping the vehicle in front of you is not permitted.

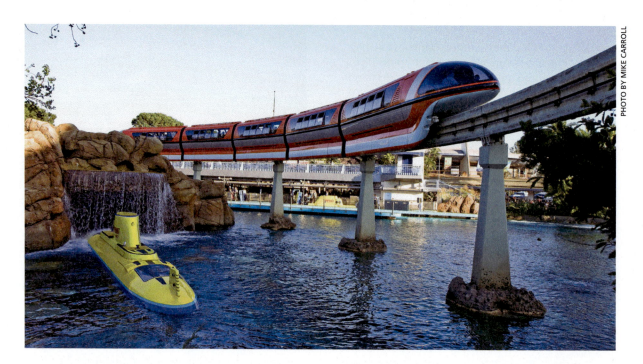

DISNEYLAND MONORAIL: Who doesn't love the monorail? The first daily operating monorail in the Western Hemisphere was a novelty when it was introduced at Disneyland in 1959. Today, it's still a thrill to watch them glide through the park. The sleek, Mark VII trains were designed to evoke images of their 1959 predecessors. Straddling a concrete beamway, the monorail has rubber tires—which enable it to glide quietly—as well as braking wheels atop the beam and guiding and stabilizing wheels on either side.

The 2½-mile-long "highway in the sky" is a distinctive and integral part of Tomorrowland. The electrically powered ride takes guests around the periphery of Tomorrowland, over to Downtown Disney and its diverting activities, and then back to Tomorrowland.

For a special experience, inform the Cast Member on the boarding ramp that you'd like to sit up front in the pilot's cabin. It can usually accommodate up to five passengers. If all the seats are taken, you can always wait for the next monorail and try your luck again.

By boarding the monorail in Tomorrowland, you are actually leaving Disneyland Park. If you get off at the Downtown Disney station, be sure to retain your valid park ticket. You will need to show it (and photo ID) to reboard the monorail or pass through Disneyland Park's turnstiles. Know that walking back to the park is an option—as Disneyland is about a 5-minute stroll from the Downtown Disney monorail station.

BIRNBAUM'S ★BEST★ FINDING NEMO SUBMARINE VOYAGE: Uh-oh. It seems that curious little clownfish has wandered off again. And this time he's done so in Tomorrowland's submarine lagoon. The good news is the subs that used to take guests to the North Pole now provide the perfect means for monitoring the fin-challenged fish and his high-spirited underwater hijinks.

The submarine adventure begins as a quiet expedition to observe an undersea volcano. But faster than you can say, "All drains lead to the ocean," our frisky friends from *Finding Nemo* start floating and fluttering in front of a personal porthole. The whole gang's here, including Nemo's overprotective dad, Marlin; the faithful-if-forgetful royal blue tang, Dory; that totally awesome turtle dude, Crush; and more. They're on a quest to catch up with their buddy Nemo, and you're invited along for the slightly frenetic, completely kinetic undersea search. Oh, and remember that volcano you were going to observe? It erupts.

Will you survive the sub-shaking volcanic quaking and find Nemo? Yep. They don't call this "the happiest place on earth" for nothing.

This whimsical experience is appropriate for guests of all heights and ages, provided that the guests are claustrophobia-free. Several moments may be too intense for some tots.

> ## HOT TIP!
>
> **A trip on the monorail yields panoramic views of the Disney California Adventure theme park and its neighbor, the Grand Californian resort. However, it does not stop at either place.**

Star Wars: Galaxy's Edge

There's a wondrous new adventure zone in the heart of Disneyland Park—Star Wars: Galaxy's Edge! The brand-new land is set on the planet Batuu, a remote outpost on the far reaches of the galaxy. As the story goes, Batuu was once a busy crossroads along the old sub-light-speed trade routes. Now, thanks to the rise of hyperspace travel, Batuu has pretty much fallen off the radar. It's far from deserted, however. In fact, the largest settlement on the planet, Black Spire Outpost, has become quite the haven for folks who prefer to fly under the radar: smugglers, rogue traders, and space-traveling adventurers. It's also an excellent destination for anyone trying to avoid the ruthless First Order. Each invites guests to live out their own Star Wars adventures.

The new land is accessed via pathways connected with Fantasyland, Critter Country, and Frontierland. For updates, use the Disneyland Resort mobile app, or visit *www.disneyland.com*. There are two bona fide E-Ticket attractions here—*Millennium Falcon: Smugglers Run* and Star Wars: Rise of the Resistance.

BIRNBAUM'S ★BEST★

MILLENNIUM FALCON: SMUGGLERS RUN: Are you eager to jump into hyperspace on the "fastest hunk of junk in the galaxy"? Here's your chance to take the controls of Han Solo's beloved bucket of bolts, the *Millennium Falcon!*

It seems Hondo (from the animated shows *Star Wars: The Clone Wars* and *Star Wars Rebels*) is running a "legitimate business" out of a spaceport and he needs extra flight crews to make some runs for him—provided they don't ask too many questions. That's where you come in.

Before entering the cockpit of the legendary starship, you and five fellow crew members are assigned a role. There are three roles (pilot, gunner, and engineer) and one goal: complete the mission without banging up the ship. At the end of the thrilling (and bumpy) flight, your crew will receive a point total—and a few choice words from Hondo.

Guests must be at least 38 inches tall to ride this attraction and should be free of motion sickness and any other health issues. Expectant mothers are advised to skip *Millennium Falcon:* Smugglers Run.

> ## HOT TIP!
> When Star Wars: Galaxy's Edge opened in May of 2019, Fastpass was not offered for either of its E-ticket attractions. However, Fastpass may be added at any time. Check *disneyland.com* for updates.

BIRNBAUM'S ★BEST★

STAR WARS: RISE OF THE RESISTANCE: What happens when Star Wars heroes and villains end up on the same planet? A *massive* battle breaks out!

In one of the most ambitious adventures ever produced by Disney Imagineering, this immersive attraction places you in the middle of an epic battle between the First Order and the Resistance—including a face-off with the infamous Kylo Ren.

The journey takes guests aboard a full-size transport shuttle and a Star Destroyer. It's a thrilling and harrowing adventure—and not for the faint of heart. To ride, guests should be free of health issues (including pregnancy and motion sickness), and at least 40 inches tall. For additional information, visit *disneyland.com*.

Shopping

Until you get to know Disneyland park, you might not expect that anyone would visit just to go shopping. But among Southern Californians, it's a definitely top draw for the Disney-themed merchandise and gift items. Mickey Mouse paraphernalia, such as key chains, mugs, T-shirts, hats, and other such souvenirs, is found here in abundance, of course, but there are some surprises, such as character-inspired costumes for kids, wireless phone accessories and items for the office, plus upscale items, such as art collectibles, jewelry, products for the home, and custom-made lightsabers.

MAIN STREET, U.S.A.

CANDY PALACE: An old-fashioned pageant in pink and white, this shop is alluring at any time of day, but never more than when the candy-makers are at work in the glass-walled kitchen confecting candy canes, chocolate-covered strawberries, caramel apples, toffee, fudge, and other temptations for anyone with a sweet tooth. The products made on the premises are available for purchase, along with a veritable bounty of chocolates, licorice, taffy, and other treats.

CHINA CLOSET: If you're in the market for kitchenware, mugs, figurines, picture frames, snow globes, or Christmas ornaments, this is the place to go.

CRYSTAL ARTS: Glasses and pitchers, frames, trays, and other mementos can be engraved (for free) and monogrammed while you wait, or you can get them unornamented. The shop also sells glass miniatures, bells, and paperweights. To save ten percent off your purchase, be sure to use the Arribas Brothers coupon at the back of this book.

DISNEYANA GIFTS: Serious collectors and the simply curious alike will discover rare and unusual Disney merchandise here, such as limited-edition art and hand-painted cels inspired by Disney animated classics. Popular pieces have included sculptures from the Walt Disney Classics Collection. This amusing shop is located in the Bank of Main Street building, next to the Main Street Opera House.

Note: Disney sketch artists often drop by the shop to sign reproduction artwork, sculptures, or recently published books.

DISNEY CLOTHIERS, LTD.: Disney character merchandise has always been popular, but if you want something a little more stylish, this is where to find it. The spot caters to fashion-conscious shoppers with a love for Disney-themed gear. Almost every item in the selection of men's, women's, and children's clothing and accessories sold here incorporates Mickey and Minnie in some way.

DISNEY SHOWCASE: Featuring the latest seasonal merchandise (Disney style), this shop also offers hats, shirts, home decor items, park logo merchandise, and assorted souvenirs. Personalization is offered (for a fee).

EMPORIUM: Much like an old-time variety store, this large and bustling shop offers an incredible assortment of wares, and it is home to Disneyland logo selections. Decorative figurines, mugs, home decor, clothing, plush toys, character hats, jewelry, and a variety of souvenirs make up the bulk of the stock.

PHOTO BY JILL SAFRO

NEW CENTURY JEWELRY: Among the delicate offerings here are 14-karat-gold charms of Tinker Bell, Donald Duck, and Minnie Mouse. The marcasite character jewelry is subtle and somewhat sophisticated.

NEWSSTAND: While no actual news is offered here (No news is good news, right?), this stand stocks a small selection of Disney-themed souvenir items.

PENNY ARCADE: Adjacent to the Gibson Girl Ice Cream Parlor is a virtual Coney Island of food and fun. Fresh-made treats fill ornate shelves, and scrumptious saltwater taffy is available in an array of flavors. To add to the classic carnival atmosphere, old-fashioned arcade games that still cost a penny to play and a Welte Orchestrion line the walls. And for a mere 25 cents, you can have beloved fortune-teller Esmeralda predict your future. Good stuff.

SILHOUETTE STUDIO: Working at the rate of about 60 seconds per portrait, Disneyland's silhouette artists truly are a wonder to behold. Individual and group portraits are available.

FORTUOSITY SHOP: Merchandise in all shapes and sizes, including trendy fashions and accessories like Mickey Mouse watches and character-laden novelty clocks, beckons from this unique emporium.

MAD HATTER: This hat shop stocks Mickey Mouse ear hats in black and various colors and designs. You can even get your name stitched on the back. They've got Goofy, Stitch, and princess hats, too.

MAIN STREET MAGIC SHOP: Small but well stocked with gags and tricks—and books about how to pull them off—this shop has the wherewithal to inspire budding illusionists. In the market for an invisible pooch? A magic wand? An ice cube with a bug in it? This place has it all.

MAIN STREET PHOTO SUPPLY CO.: Should a Disneyland PhotoPass photographer snap your mug, this is the place to preview, peruse, and print it. You can also find frames, and photo albums. Camera batteries may be charged here, too (for free).

MARKET HOUSE: This Disney version of an old-fashioned general store is actually a cleverly themed Starbucks coffee shop. Stop here for fresh-brewed coffee and specialty drinks, plus cookies, cake pops, sandwiches, salads, savory snacks, and much more.

20TH CENTURY MUSIC COMPANY: This little place carries a selection of collector pins and pin lanyards, plus books, classic Disney music, and DVDs.

NEW ORLEANS SQUARE

CRISTAL D'ORLEANS: Glasses and chandeliers, decanters, tiaras, glass slippers, pitchers, and paperweights are typical treasures here. All engraving (and some monogramming) is done free of charge. To save ten percent off your purchase, use the Arribas Brothers coupon at the back of this book.

Get Your Ears Done Here

Since Disneyland first opened in 1955, there has been no more coveted souvenir than a pair of Mickey Mouse ears personalized with the lucky owner's name—or that of a family member. And never have there been more styles to choose from. Most can be embroidered for a nominal fee at both locations of the Mad Hatter (in Fantasyland and on Main Street), the Gag Factory in Toontown, Tomorrowlanding in Tomorrowland, and other select locations. The shops will not embroider company names on hats.

LE BAT EN ROUGE: Looking to cross a few Disney-themed items off your shopping list? You've come to the right place. Some of the merchandise may have a New Orleans flair, too. Expect clothing, jewelry, and other accessories.

LA MASCARADE D'ORLEANS: A compact and brightly lit showcase for PANDORA products, this shop has a variety of its signature items: necklaces, rings, earrings, and charm bracelets—many with a Disney theme. In fact, some items are Disney Parks exclusives.

MLLE. ANTOINETTE'S PARFUMERIE: This fragrant boutique carries classic and chic fragrances for men and women. The parfumerie "blends the essence of French-style elegance with American-style spontaneity." It's in the heart of New Orleans Square.

PIECES OF EIGHT: Wares with a pirate theme are purveyed at this shop beside the Pirates of the Caribbean exit. There are items such as pirate rings, ships' lanterns, caps, plus fake knives and rubber skulls. You will also discover T-shirts, key chains, glasses, and other souvenir items imprinted with the Pirates of the Caribbean logo. In the market for a pirate sword? Look no further. And, for the right price, you may be able to fill a bag with colorful pirate booty. *Arrrrrrrrrrrr!*

PORT ROYAL CURIOS AND CURIOSITIES: Ready to give your treasured Mickey Mouse T-shirt a day off? Stop at this boutique to augment your Disney-oriented closet. Expect to find an assortment of merchandise featuring the nearby Haunted Mansion attraction: shirts, hats, coasters, and more. Also on hand: items with a *Tim Burton's The Nightmare Before Christmas* theme (coffee mugs, bags, dolls, dresses, pajamas, T-shirts, hats, etc.).

PORTRAIT ARTISTS: Sit for a portrait—done in pastel or watercolor—amidst the quaint charm of a New Orleans *rue* (street). Individual and group portraits are offered.

ROYAL STREET SWEETS: Satisfy your sweet tooth (or teeth) at this stand that specializes in sugary treats.

FRONTIERLAND

BONANZA OUTFITTERS: Oozing rustic ambience, this cozy yet quaint shop offers traditional frontier-wear with a trendy twist. Look for cowboy hats, plaid shirts, blankets, and coonskin caps. They sell pins and other Disney-themed merch, too.

PIONEER MERCANTILE: Inspired by the paraphernalia of the pioneer period in American history, this shop is home to a vast array of Disneyland paraphernalia. Expect to find plush toys, shirts, books, bags, towels, and more. There is a large selection of headwear, too—including cowboy hats. Got a quarter? Drop it in the shop's Ho-Down machine and watch Woody dance!

WESTWARD HO TRADING COMPANY: This rustic store stocks something for the whole pin-trading frontier family, including pins, lanyards, and other pin-collecting accoutrements.

CRITTER COUNTRY

BRIAR PATCH: Situated near Splash Mountain, this small shop offers hats, character merchandise, and other souvenirs.

POOH CORNER: This *hunny* of a spot is home to a candy kitchen filled with sweet treats. Lining its many shelves are other Disneyland logo merchandise and items with a Winnie the Pooh theme. Pooh's pals from the Hundred Acre Wood are also represented. All kinds of Pooh products await, including plush toys, watches, infants' apparel, and children's clothing, sleep shirts, and slippers. There is also a selection of freshly made cookies and chocolates.

STAR WARS: GALAXY'S EDGE

BINA'S CREATURE STALL: Stop here to adopt an other-worldly pet. Lifelike creatures from which to choose include tentacle-beast rathtars, cooing baby tauntauns, tongue-lashing worrt frogs, and growling pufferpigs.

BLACK SPIRE OUTFITTERS: Guests who wish to blend in on Batuu can suit up at this boutique. Costumes representing the light and dark side of the Force are available for guests of all ages.

DON-ONDAR'S DEN OF ANTIQUITIES: The mysterious Don-Ondar has stuffed this shop with everything from jewelry and ancient tools to rare kyber crystals, statues, and high-end lightsabers.

SAVI'S LIGHTSABERS: The First Order would not allow the manufacture of lightsabers—so Savi took that task underground. Head here to build your own, high-end lightsaber. Colors include Sith red, to Jedi blue and green, and Mace Windu purple. Choose wisely.

MUBO'S DROID DEPOT: If you've ever dreamed of owning your own droid, dream no more: Mubo has mini droids waiting for you to customize. There are two basic models: an R (like R2-D2 or R5-D4) or a BB unit (the ball-droid style similar to BB-8 and the evil BB-9E). Once you choose your droid pieces, you can piece them together in the assembly area. Then head to the chip station to select a personality circuit. Last but not least, bring your droid to life at the activation center.

TOYDARIAN TOY SHOP: Visit this street market to peruse a variety of hand-crafted toys and other play-things crafted by local artisans.

ADVENTURELAND

ADVENTURELAND BAZAAR: The plush and hand-carved jungle animals corralled here include lions, tigers, and hippos. You may also find rain sticks, drums, collector pins, *Indiana Jones*™ items, and California-themed apparel.

FANTASYLAND

BIBBIDI BOBBIDI BOUTIQUE: Nestled inside Sleeping Beauty Castle, this boutique offers young guests the chance to be transformed into "little princesses" and princely "cool knights." Makeovers are offered daily. Prices vary. Check-in is at Enchanted Chamber (see below for details).

Disney's PhotoPass & MaxPass

As you wander the theme parks, Disney Cast Members will be happy to snap your picture (with your camera and/or theirs). After mugging for their camera, you'll get a PhotoPass card. It'll link all such photos together for viewing on the Internet. You can ogle the low-res images for free (with watermarks) or purchase favorites for up to 45 days after they are taken. Disney's MaxPass includes unlimited downloads of photos taken on any given day (visit *www.disneyland.com* for details). Another option is a Photopass+ One Week Package: $78 for a week's worth of unlimited photo downloads. High-quality prints, plus mugs, shirts, and other items are for sale. To buy or just peruse, visit *disneyland.com*. Each theme park has a spot for photo-viewing and purchasing. Check a guidemap for locations. We think PhotoPass is a great way to get quality images of your whole party. It also includes photos taken on park attractions and "magic shots" (a nice bonus).

ENCHANTED CHAMBER: Sparkly crowns and regal costumes dazzle the eyes of every young princess who enters this shop tucked inside Sleeping Beauty Castle, to the left of the entrance to Fantasyland. It also serves as the medieval check-in spot for appointments at the nearby Bibbidi Bobbidi Boutique. For information and reservations, call 714-781-7895.

FAIRYTALE ARTS: Here guests of all ages are turned into princesses, among other things, via the magic of face painting (for a fee).

FANTASY FAIRE GIFTS: Found on Disneyland's parade route, near the entrance to the Fantasyland Theatre, this open-air stand stocks a selection of souvenirs and yummy treats spun from the colorful tales and sights in Fantasyland.

FAIRYTALE TREASURES: Conveniently situated next to the Royal Theater, this spot is all princesses all the time: Elena of Avalor, Elsa of Arendelle, and more.

IT'S A SMALL WORLD TOY SHOP: The whimsical open-air structure near It's a Small World stocks an assortment of Disney-themed toys, dolls, pins, and plush items featuring Disney characters and the It's a Small World attraction (of course!).

LE PETIT CHALET GIFTS: Designed to look like a little bit of Switzerland and as cozy as a warm cup of cocoa on a winter evening, this spot is the repository of traditional Disneyland gifts and souvenirs. Included in the wares are coloring books, autograph books, headbands, and a variety of hats—many of which can be personalized on the spot (for a fee). The small Swiss shop is nestled at the base of the Matterhorn, along the park's parade route. Handy!

MAD HATTER: Always a great place for hats and plush character caps—and Mouse ears, of course (they'll embroider them for you for a small fee). The selection of novelty headgear includes items such as Donald's sailor cap, a hat sporting Goofy's ears, and more.

STROMBOLI'S WAGON: Located near Red Rose Taverne, this stand offers a wagonful of wares—everything from plush toys to sunglasses. Some of the items available include key chains, pens, buttons, popcorn, and candy. The shop is named after one of the villains from Disney's 1940 classic, *Pinocchio*.

MICKEY'S TOONTOWN

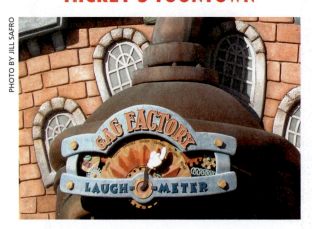

PHOTO BY JILL SAFRO

GAG FACTORY: A Laugh-O-Meter outside this shop (aka Toontown Five & Dime) gives some indication of the fun to be found inside, along with character merchandise—plush toys, stationery, souvenirs, T-shirts, novelty headwear, and candy. Take a moment to admire the toon architecture, especially the pillars at the back of the store. The Gag Factory will stitch your name on mouse ears for a small fee.

MICKEY & ME PHOTOS: Trying to get your photo taken with Mickey on busy days can be challenging, but if you follow this tip, it's a piece of cake: Mickey can often be found working in the Movie Barn behind his cottage in Toontown, and he's always happy to stop what he's doing to greet his guests and pose for

pictures. You can take as many photos as you like with your own camera (at no charge) or purchase any of the shots taken by a Disneyland photographer via Disney's PhotoPass program. (For details on PhotoPass, see page 85.) The line to meet the Mouse is often a long one—but to his legions of loyal fans, it's well worth the wait.

TOMORROWLAND

AUTOPIA WINNER'S CIRCLE: Racing enthusiasts will enjoy the Autopia-inspired souvenirs and toys offered at this small shop. Soft drinks are sold, too.

LITTLE GREEN MEN STORE COMMAND: Sharp traders know they can find an astronomical assortment of pins and collectibles at this spot. Disneyland's commanding pin destination, the store offers pins, lanyards, and pin-trading accessories, plus souvenirs and toys featuring Disney/Pixar characters.

THE STAR TRADER: The Star Trader is the repository of everything from T-shirts and jewelry to novelty headwear, mugs, key chains, candy, and more—many emblazoned with the likenesses of Disney pals and characters from the Star Wars universe.

TOMORROWLANDING: Whether it's the Jedi Force that draws you to Tomorrowland or simply your feet, what you'll find in this shop is a supersized selection of all things Star Wars.

Pin Trading, Disney Style

It's one of the biggest collectible crazes to sweep through Disney's land—pin trading. These small enamel pins (there are hundreds of different styles) can be purchased all over the property, but buying them is only half the fun. The real joy comes when you encounter another pin trader with a worthy swap. To get a head start, bring pins from home (Disney Stores carry pins, too). Once on-property, keep an eye out for Cast Members sporting a good selection of pins—they tend to be agreeable to almost any trade. And when negotiating a trade with a Disneyland Cast Member, always remember these rules: (1) Only Disney pins may be traded, and (2) Every trade must be an even pin-for-pin exchange.

Entertainment

Together with Walt Disney World, Disneyland presents more live entertainment than any other organization in the world. What follows is typical of the variety of what's offered. Check a complimentary Times Guide (available throughout the park) for specifics.

PERFORMERS & LIVE SHOWS

Performers stroll, march, croon, and pluck their way through Disneyland every day—so frequently that all you usually have to do to find them is follow your ears.

FANTASYLAND

MICKEY AND THE MAGICAL MAP: Mickey Mouse reprises his classic role of sorcerer's apprentice in this kid-pleasin', toe-tappin', and eye-poppin' performance. What's magic about the map? It transports dreamers to all the places they can imagine. But the massive map has an empty spot—and Mickey takes it upon himself to fill it. Dozens of singers and dancers join him, making this musical fun for all ages. For the best views, don't sit up front. The 22-minute show is usually presented several times a day.

MAIN STREET, U.S.A.

ATMOSPHERE BANDS: Look and listen for the musical groups that perform near the Fire House and Sleeping Beauty Castle on select days.

DAPPER DANS OF DISNEYLAND: The official greeters of Main Street, U.S.A., this classic barbershop quartet performs standards in perfect four-part harmony. The colorfully clad performers may be found strolling on the sidewalk, planted by a storefront, or whizzing by on a trolley or a bicycle built for four.

DISNEYLAND BAND: A presence in the park since opening day in 1955, Disneyland's signature musical group specializes in turn-of-the-century band music and Disney tunes, but it can play just about anything. The band performs inside the main entrance when the park opens, in Town Square (at the South end of Main Street), and at other locations.

The Disneyland Band's first performance of the day often takes place in front of the train station, just inside the turnstiles. It's an interactive and magical way to start the day. Kids of all ages simply love it.

FLAG RETREAT: The flag at Town Square is lowered just before sunset each day (times vary). The ceremony is often highlighted by a performance by the Disneyland Band or the Dapper Dans. The band has been known to perform several rousing marches per show. On the band's day off, the Dapper Dans perform a capella renditions of American classics. "The Star-Spangled Banner" makes for a stirring finale. (We always get choked up during this touching ceremony.) It is a rewarding experience that captures the essence of what Walt Disney hoped guests would feel as they experienced Main Street, U.S.A. It's usually presented daily.

MAIN STREET PIANO PLAYER: Piano players are often on hand to tickle the ivories on the snow-white upright piano at the Corner Café. Presented daily.

NEW ORLEANS SQUARE

THE BOOTSTRAPPERS: Yo, ho! Yo, ho! A Pirate Band for you! These musical buccaneers wander about New Orleans Square and perform on Tom Sawyer Island.

JAMBALAYA JAZZ: This group plays down-home New Orleans jazz with plenty of soul. Fetch yourself a mint julep (sans alcohol) or a bowl of gumbo, and let the music wash over you like the mighty Mississippi.

ROYAL STREET BACHELORS: Their style is early traditional jazz and blues, with a mellow four-beat sound similar to that once commonly heard in the Storyville section of the Crescent City. The Bachelors can be found performing throughout the Square.

FRONTIERLAND

THE GOLDEN HORSESHOE: Dishing up a "rootin', tootin' good time," this place never takes itself—or its guests—too seriously. The entertainment varies, but it always pairs nicely with the frontier-style grub offered at the counter for lunch and dinner (think wings, loaded potato skins, and more). Seating is available at the bar or at tables, on a first-come, first-served basis.

LAUGHING STOCK CO.: Sheriff Clem Clodhopper has no desire to marry Mayor McGillicuddy's daughter, Sally Mae, but neither of them will take no for an answer. An old-time serial in three parts is played out as the dysfunctional trio finagles to get Sally Mae hitched to someone (anyone), even an unsuspecting theme park guest. The show is presented at The Golden Horseshoe throughout the day.

PARADES

No Main Street is complete without a parade, and Disneyland's Main Street is no exception. The usual route runs between Town Square and the promenade in front of It's a Small World—or vice versa. The direction and route can vary, so it's wise to ask at the Information Center at City Hall or the Central Plaza Tip Board. The park traditionally offers an afternoon and an evening parade. For parade updates, visit *www.disneyland.com*. What follows is a description of the most recent evening parade presented at Disneyland Park (note that it spent some of 2019 in Disney California Adventure).

BIRNBAUM'S ★BEST **MICKEY'S SOUNDSATIONAL PARADE:** Meant to evoke happy, musical Disney memories, this processional showcases dozens of beloved Disney characters, including the Mouse himself. It is usually presented in the afternoon. Check a park Times Guide, a Tip Board, or the Disneyland Resort app for showtimes.

Where to Watch the Parade: Some of the best points from which to watch the parade are the platform of the Disneyland Railroad's Main Street depot, Town Square near the flagpole, and the curb on either side of Main Street, U.S.A. If you'd like to avoid crowds, any viewing location other than Main Street may be better for you.

Two other options are the terrace outside the Plaza Inn (but be aware that seating is limited) and the tables in the courtyard of the Carnation Cafe, where the view may be partially obstructed.

You can also stand on either side of the promenade area in front of It's a Small World whose facade provides a whimsical, only-at-Disneyland backdrop. Wherever you decide to station yourself for the running of the parade, plan to arrive about 30 to 45 minutes early to claim your piece of turf.

FIREWORKS

BIRNBAUM'S **★BEST★** **DISNEYLAND FIREWORKS SPECTACULAR:** Remember . . . Dreams Come True is an impressive, nostalgic fireworks show. The 16-minute spectacle dazzles guests with a combination of pyrotechnics, lights, a stirring soundtrack, and clever special effects projected onto and above Disneyland park icons.

First presented to mark Disneyland Park's fiftieth anniversary, the show takes guests on a wondrous journey through Walt Disney's original theme park. The popular fan favorite is presented on select nights throughout the year. It features Tinker Bell's flight and appearances by many Disney characters. Check a complimentary park Times Guide for the schedule.

A longtime Disneyland tradition, specially themed fireworks presentations take place throughout the year. Patriotic pyrotechnics fill the sky on the Fourth of July, while a spooky spectacular is presented during the Halloween season, and the December holidays feature Believe . . . in Holiday Magic.

Where to Watch: One of the best areas is about midway down Main Street, U.S.A., near the Main Street Photo Supply Company up to the Castle hub area. Another great spot is near It's a Small World.

Glow with the Show: "Made with Magic" accessories let guests be part of Disneyland Resort's nighttime spectaculars. The light-up accessories include glowing mouse ear hats, headbands, Mickey Mouse gloves, and magic wands. When the show is over, guests may switch the device to demo mode and enjoy their own personal light show. (Items range in price from about $25 to $30.)

Note: The fireworks spectacular is presented on select nights. It may be canceled due to inclement weather, including high winds. Details are subject to change.

SPECIAL OCCASIONS

Along with plenty of special events in the theme parks and hotels year-round (some require special admission tickets), Disneyland park celebrates three major seasons each year: summer (including the extremely popular Fourth of July holiday), Halloween (September through October), and the winter holidays (mid-November through early January).

SUMMER: While plenty of folks are on vacation, Disney offers a full slate of atmosphere entertainment and spectaculars from Memorial Day to Labor Day. Expect longer wait times at attractions, and plan to use Fastpass (see page 58) as often as possible. Past years have seen a patriotic, pyrotechnic tribute to the U.S.A. on Independence Day in a rousing celebration known as Disney's Celebrate America! A Fourth of July Concert in the Sky.

HALLOWEEN: Halloween at the Disneyland Resort brings a palette of fall colors, pumpkins, Disney characters dressed in Halloween costumes, and trick-or-treat touches, along with the extra-spooky Haunted Mansion transformation inspired by *Tim Burton's The Nightmare Before Christmas* (see page 10).

WINTER HOLIDAYS: This jolly period generally stretches from November through the first week of January, when the entire park glows with holiday themes. (We've witnessed Yuletide holiday decorations in place as early as October.) Expect the park to be festooned with holiday decor and perhaps even the occasional snow flurry (which is known to make Olaf very happy). The Disneyland Resort officially begins to celebrate the holidays in November, when the merriest attraction on Earth—It's a Small World Holiday—returns for the season.

It's a Small World Holiday celebrates Yuletide customs around the world. The singing Small World dolls add "Jingle Bells" to their repertoire in numerous languages, and the clock on the attraction's whimsical facade dons a Santa hat.

Main Street, U.S.A., is decked out in traditional red and green, including hundreds of poinsettias and a huge Christmas tree that's surrounded by oversize holiday packages. Highlights include the chance to meet the man in the red suit, Santa himself. Sleeping Beauty Castle gets in on the fun: Each evening during the holiday season, guests watch the castle transform into a shining, icicle-adorned spectacle. As the snow falls and music fills the air, Sleeping Beauty's Winter Castle glimmers with thousands of twinkling lights, illuminated in stages. On select December nights, a candlelight processional ending at Town Square takes place. Special music is provided by a large choir, and a holiday story is read by a well-known entertainer. (**A Christmas Fantasy Parade**, a Disney holiday favorite, takes place throughout the holiday season. The extra-merry, 40-minute processional traditionally includes favorite Disney pals, dancing gingerbread cookies, toy soldiers, colorful floats, and Santa Claus. Note that all parades at Disneyland Park are dependent on weather conditions and are subject to change or cancellation.)

Believe . . . In Holiday Magic is Disneyland's festive fireworks show. Set to seasonal music, the 15-minute pyrotechnic spectacular takes place above and around Sleeping Beauty Castle, with excellent vantage points on Main Street, U.S.A., and throughout the park.

Live entertainment and a truly dazzling fireworks show on **New Year's Eve** (no special ticket required) provide a grand finale for this happy holiday season.

For additional details about seasonal happenings in the park, use the Disneyland Resort mobile app or visit *www.disneyland.com*.

Where to Find the Characters

Look for Disney characters in Town Square on Main Street, U.S.A., as well as in Mickey's Toontown, where they live. Tinker Bell and fairy friends appear at Pixie Hollow. Princesses hold court at Fantasy Faire in Fantasyland, just off Main Street. Pooh and pals congregate in Critter Country. Tiana may appear on the *Mark Twain* riverboat. Aladdin and Jasmine mingle near Snow White's Wishing Well (by the castle) and the Fantasy Faire courtyard.

Cast Members at the park's Information Boards can help locate characters. Also refer to the *Good Meals, Great Times* chapter of this book and your park Entertainment Times Guide. Another good source for character appearance updates and schedules? The Disneyland Resort app.

Trip the Night, Fantasmic!

BIRNBAUM'S **BEST** FP A beloved Disneyland spectacular, Fantasmic! lights up the Rivers of America in dramatic, high-tech fashion. The classic show features cutting-edge projection technology and many character-laden scenes (including one where Aladdin and Jasmine float on a magic carpet during "A Whole New World").

An amalgam of music, magic, special effects, and live performances, Fantasmic! is a fan favorite. The show, which lasts about 20 minutes, lights up the Rivers of America on weekends, holidays, and throughout the summer. More than 50 performers put on an unforgettable show in a dazzling display of pyrotechnics, giant props, video, and light.

Fantasmic! is a good vs. evil tale, and it is up to Mickey Mouse to overcome a vast array of villains. Draped in his sorcerer's robe, Mickey first appears at the tip of Tom Sawyer Island and uses his imagination to make comets shoot across the sky while the river waters dance about. He materializes in a cone of light, and a shower of sparks dramatically shoots from his fingertips.

Top-notch technology makes Fantasmic! all the more impressive. Mickey works his magic and a film sequence appears in midair, above the Rivers of America. The effect is achieved by projecting state-of-the-art digital images onto giant screens of mist.

The illusions build toward a confrontation of good and evil in which Disney villains attempt to disrupt Mickey's wondrous fantasy. Fearsome creatures all have an opportunity, including an animated Maleficent, who morphs into a towering, animated, fire-breathing dragon.

Villains turn Mickey's dreams into nightmares, and he must overcome them with his own powers of goodness—with a little help from his friends. The Sailing Ship Columbia glides through the show with the swashbuckling cast of Peter Pan on board, and the Mark Twain riverboat brings along a host of Disney friends.

Where to Watch: The best spots are in front of the Pirates of the Caribbean (be sure you can see the water and have a view of Tom Sawyer Island). Get there early. (Late arrivals can sometimes find a place to watch by the Haunted Mansion, in New Orleans Square.) If possible, book a Fantasmic! show ticket via Disney's Fastpass system (see page 58).

If you decide to splurge, you can book a Fantasmic! Dining Package. It includes dinner at River Belle Terrace or Blue Bayou and premium seats for Fantasmic! The cost starts at about $45–$69 per adult, $25–$29 per kid (ages 3 to 9). Tax and gratuity are extra. Call 714-781-3463 for details and to make reservations (between 8 A.M. and 9 P.M. Pacific Standard Time). We recommend calling 60 days before your desired reservation date.

Note: Fantasmic! may be performed twice nightly during the summer, and there can be a crush of folks trying to leave post-show. The later presentation is usually less crowded. Some effects are quite realistic, and may be too intense for little ones.

Hot Tips

✳ Tuesday, Wednesday, and Thursday are the least crowded days to visit year-round. If you must come on a weekend, choose Sunday over Saturday.

✳ Measure your child before your visit so you will know ahead of time which attractions he or she may be too short to ride. This can help avoid disappointment later on.

✳ Wear comfortable shoes. Blisters are the most common malady reported to First Aid.

✳ Main Street, U.S.A., may open a bit before the rest of the park (usually when Disneyland opens at 9 or 10 A.M.). Take advantage of this to grab a quick snack, shop, or mingle with Disney characters.

✳ Avoid rides such as Star Tours, Splash Mountain, the Matterhorn Bobsleds, and the Mad Tea Party immediately after meals (for obvious reasons).

✳ Check the daily entertainment schedule in a current park Times Guide and plan your day accordingly.

✳ Wait times are posted at the attractions and on the Information Board at the north end of Main Street, U.S.A. (on the Adventureland side), and on the Disneyland app. The times are updated frequently.

✳ An attraction may reach its Fastpass limit before the end of the day, especially if the park is packed. Be sure to get yours early if you don't want to wait in the standby line.

✳ At press time, attractions in Star Wars: Galaxy's Edge did not offer Fastpass. However, that may change in 2020. Visit *disneyland.com* or check the Disneyland app for updates.

✳ During the busy afternoon hours, go to lower-key attractions, where the wait times are comparatively shorter. The afternoon is also prime time for shopping, enjoying an outdoor musical performance, watching a parade, taking in a show at the Golden Horseshoe Stage, or watching the daily Flag Retreat on Main Street, U.S.A.

✳ Try to eat lunch before 11:30 A.M. or after 2 P.M., and dinner before 5 P.M. or after 8 P.M. to avoid long register lines (which may be shorter toward the left of fast-food counters).

✳ If you're travelling alone or willing to split up your party, know that Indiana Jones Adventure, Space Mountain, Matterhorn Bobsleds, and Splash Mountain offer Single Rider lines—potentially much shorter than the standby lines.

✳ For a change of pace food-wise, head to Downtown Disney or to one of the three hotels on property. They have something for almost every budget and taste—from simple to sublime, ravioli to rack of lamb—as well as buffet meals with popular Disney characters (at the Disneyland resorts only).

✳ The monorail takes guests from Tomorrowland to the Disneyland Hotel end of Downtown Disney. All guests must disembark, but it's okay to reboard if you'd like to complete the round-trip journey. Keep your park ticket handy—you'll need it.

✳ Try to visit the major attractions—*Millennium Falcon: Smugglers Run, Star Wars: Rise of the Resistance,* Space Mountain, Star Tours, the Indiana Jones Adventure, Big Thunder Mountain Railroad, Finding Nemo Submarine Voyage, Haunted Mansion, the Matterhorn Bobsleds, and Splash Mountain—early or during parades. The lines are often shorter then.

✳ Main Street shops are a good place to escape the midday heat, but try to steer clear of them at the end of the park's operating hours, when they tend to be the most crowded.

✳ For most attractions, if you're in line up to one minute before the park's closing time, you'll be allowed on. It's a good tactic for popular attractions such as Space Mountain, Peter Pan's Flight, and the Indiana Jones Adventure.

✳ Avoid the crowds by returning your stroller (and getting your deposit back) before the evening's fireworks presentation comes to an end.

✳ Break up your time in the park (unless you have only one day). Arrive early, see major attractions until things get busy, return to your hotel for a swim or a nap, then go back to the park. Remember, you must present your valid ticket for re-entry.

DISNEY CALIFORNIA ADVENTURE

"The wonders of nature are endless." —Walt Disney

Fame, fortune, and fun in the sun have lured adventurous spirits to California for centuries. But now visitors have an alternative way to enjoy the glories of the Golden State: through Disney's eyes. In February 2001, The Walt Disney Company officially unveiled its California Adventure theme park—and it was a work in progress for quite some time. To that end, an amazing, billion-dollar expansion is complete. New themes and attractions have joined the landscape, while some veteran rides have been "re-imagined," and new attractions are constantly on the horizon. The result? An adventure to excite even the most devoted Disneyland Park devotees.

Disney California Adventure sits snugly in the heart of the Disneyland Resort, sharing an entrance esplanade with Disneyland, neighboring Downtown Disney District, and the Disney hotels. But once you set foot inside the park, you're in a world all its own. Regions blend into each other, and no matter where you stand, you're sure to see (or hear whoops and hollers coming from) one of the park's icons—Guardians of the Galaxy—Mission: BREAKOUT!, the Sierra-inspired Grizzly Peak mountain, Pixar Pier's Incredicoaster, Pixar Pal-A-Round, and the ever-popular Radiator Springs Racers.

With a small vineyard, upscale restaurants, scream-inducing thrill rides, and attractions tailored for everyone in the family, the 66-acre theme park has something for everyone to enjoy. California, here we come!

DISNEY CALIFORNIA ADVENTURE

PIXAR PIER

CARS LAND

PIXAR PIER

PACIFIC WHARF

GRIZZLY PEAK

BUENA VISTA STREET

HOLLYWOOD LAND

CARS LAND

PARADISE GARDENS PARK
10 The Little Mermaid—Ariel's Undersea Adventure
11 Golden Zephyr
12 Jumpin' Jellyfish
13 Goofy's Sky School
14 Silly Symphony Swings
15 World of Color

PIXAR PIER
16 Incredicoaster
17 Pixar Pal-A-Round
18 Toy Story Midway Mania!
19 Jessie's Critter Carousel
20 Inside Out Emotional Whirlwind

CARS LAND
21 Luigi's Rollickin' Roadsters
22 Mater's Junkyard Jamboree
23 Radiator Springs Racers

GRIZZLY PEAK
7 Soarin' Around the World
8 Grizzly River Run
9 Redwood Creek Challenge Trail

HOLLYWOOD LAND
1 Disney Animation
2 Guardians of the Galaxy—Mission: BREAKOUT!
3 Frozen—Live at the Hyperion
4 Monsters, Inc.—Mike and Sulley to the Rescue!
5 Disney Junior Dance Party!
6 Mickey's PhilharMagic

Getting Oriented

Disney California Adventure is a bit smaller than Disneyland Park, so guests should have no trouble covering all of it on foot—as long as they wear comfy walking shoes.

The main entrance area is known as Buena Vista Street. East of Buena Vista Street lies Hollywood Land. It's a mock studio backlot where guests can, among other things, meet Anna and Elsa (and see them in a lively stage show called Frozen—Live at the Hyperion), enjoy the lighthearted Monsters, Inc.—Mike and Sulley to the Rescue!, and see Mickey's PhilharMagic.

West of Buena Vista Street is Grizzly Peak, home of the popular Soarin' Around the World attraction and a drenching, white-water rapids ride known as Grizzly River Run. Pacific Wharf is a district dedicated to the cultures, industries, and natural beauty that shaped California, complete with a winery.

Pixar Pier (formerly known as Paradise Pier) and Paradise Gardens Park have nostalgic rides with a modern twist, located around a lagoon. (If you want to minimize the wait for Toy Story Midway Mania!, get there early.) The World of Color light show takes place right on the lagoon. The show is best viewed from the Paradise Gardens Park side of the water.

Finally, the impressively immersive Cars Land offers guests the opportunity to experience all the thrills of Radiator Springs. That's where to experience Mater's Junkyard Jamboree, Luigi's Rollickin' Roadsters, and the park's ever-popular Radiator Springs Racers.

Guests park in either the six-level Mickey & Friends parking structure or the Toy Story lot on Harbor Boulevard, which can be accessed from the I-5 freeway.

Parking Fees: Guests arriving in passenger vehicles pay about $25 to park. (The fee for vans and buses is $30; for trucks and buses with extended trailers, $35.) Preferred parking starts at $40. You may leave during the day and return later the same day at no extra fee. Hold on to your parking stub as proof of payment.

Lost Cars: Even if you take careful note of where you parked your car, you might have trouble remembering

or recognizing the exact spot when you return hours later. Hundreds more vehicles will likely be parked around yours. If this happens, tell a Cast Member approximately when you arrived. With that info, parking lot personnel can usually help narrow down your car's general location.

HOT TIP!

Radiator Springs Racers is still one of the hottest tickets in town—get a Fastpass as early as possible. Better yet, jump on the Single Riders line if you can!

GETTING AROUND

You'll have to depend a lot on your feet—other than the Red Car Trolley ride, there's no transportation in this theme park.

Guests staying at Disney's Grand Californian hotel have a private entrance into the Disney California Adventure park. (This entrance is exclusively reserved for guests of the Grand Californian. A valid hotel key card must be presented to use the private turnstiles.) All other visitors enter and exit Disney California Adventure through the park's main entrance, across the esplanade from Disneyland park. From here, trams transport guests to parking areas. Since the area is pedestrian-friendly, guests may walk from the park along the esplanade to the three Disneyland Resort hotels and the Downtown Disney dining, shopping, and entertainment district.

HOT TIP!

World of Color show tickets operate independently of the park's Fastpass system. You can get a W.O.C. show ticket even if you have a Fastpass assignment pending for another attraction.

Park Primer

BABY FACILITIES

Changing tables, baby-care products, and facilities for nursing can be found at the park's Baby Care Center. The center is next to Ghirardelli Soda Fountain and Chocolate Shop.

DISABILITY INFORMATION

Many park attractions and nearly all shops and restaurants are accessible to guests using wheelchairs. Services are also available for those with visual or hearing disabilities. Ask about these services at Guest Relations.

FIRST AID

Minor medical problems are handled at the First Aid Center, by the park's main entrance. In case of medical emergency, alert the nearest Cast Member and call 911.

GUIDED TOURS

Guided tours, which generally require park admission, may be offered throughout the year. For details or to book a tour, call 714-781-TOUR (8687), or stop by Disney California Adventure's Chamber of Commerce.

HOURS

Operating hours at Disney California Adventure park vary from about 10 A.M. until 8 P.M. to about 8 A.M. until 11 P.M., depending on the date and time of year. For the hours during your visit, use the Disneyland Resort app, visit *www.disneyland.com*, or call 714-781-4636.

INFORMATION

Chamber of Commerce (aka Guest Relations/Visitor's Center), located near the park's main entrance, is equipped with guidemaps, Entertainment Times Guides, and a helpful staff. Maps and Times Guides are also available at many of the park' shops. The Information Station, in Carthay Circle Plaza, is an excellent resource for attraction wait times and show schedules. Information is updated every hour.

LOCKERS

Lockers, available for unlimited use during the day, are near the park's main entrance. Fees range from $7 to $15 per day, depending on size.

LOST & FOUND

The Disneyland Resort's Lost & Found is on the left side of the Disneyland Park entrance. Report lost items there. If you find an item, kindly present it to the nearest Cast Member (a park worker wearing a name tag).

LOST CHILDREN

Report lost children at the Baby Care Center and alert the closest employee to the problem.

MONEY MATTERS

There are ATMs in the park. Currency may be exchanged at Guest Relations (aka Chamber of Commerce). Cash, credit cards, traveler's checks, Disney gift cards, and Disney Dollars are accepted for most purchases.

PARK RULES

To ensure a comfortable, safe, and enjoyable experience for all guests, visitors are asked to comply with all Park rules, signs, and instructions including:

- All bags are subject to inspection.
- Proper attire is required.
- Smoking—including e-cigarettes and all types of vaping—is prohibited. Disneyland Resort became an entirely smoke-free zone in 2019.
- Selfie sticks are not permitted in Disney parks.
- Weapons (including toys) are prohibited.
- Marijuana is prohibited.
- Guests under age 14 must be accompanied by a guest age 14 or older to enter the park.

For additional details and a complete listing of Disneyland Resort park Rules, visit Guest Relations or go to *www.disneyland.com/ParkRules*.

SAME-DAY RE-ENTRY

All guests have their picture taken upon initial entry to the park. The photos, which are linked to tickets, make for speedy and convenient re-entry, with the presentation of the respective park ticket. Note that hand stamps are no longer required for re-entry to the park.

SECURITY CHECK

All guests entering Disney parks are subject to a thorough security check, including a metal detector screening. Backpacks, parcels, purses, etc., will be searched by security personnel before guests may pass through the entrance.

STROLLERS & WHEELCHAIRS

Strollers, wheelchairs, and Electric Conveyance Vehicles (ECVs) can be rented outside the main entrance to Disneyland Park. If you need a replacement, just present a receipt. Strollers larger than 31 inches by 52 inches and wagons are not permitted.

PHOTO BY JILL SAFRO

BUENA VISTA STREET

When a young Walt Disney took the train from Kansas City to Los Angeles in 1923, he discovered a bustling metropolis teeming with pedestrian boulevards, shops, restaurants, and shiny red trolley cars. Buena Vista Street, inside the park's main entrance, sends guests back to this era—to an idealized version of a city beaming with optimism and opportunity.

Follow festive Buena Vista Street, which begins inside the turnstiles, to the Carthay Circle Restaurant—a replica of the theater where *Snow White and the Seven Dwarfs* premiered in 1937. (This version of the Carthay Circle houses a popular restaurant. For restaurant details, see page 117.) Or enjoy a trip back in time by hopping aboard a trolley.

PHOTO BY JILL SAFRO

RED CAR TROLLEY: The Red Car Trolley system revives the gone-but-not-forgotten Pacific Electric Railway right here in Disney California Adventure. This jolly trolley transports guests between Buena Vista Street and Guardians of the Galaxy—Mission: BREAKOUT! by way of Hollywood Land. It's also the backdrop for an entertaining musical show courtesy of the Red Car Trolley News Boys (see page 108).

HOLLYWOOD LAND

Lights! Camera! Action! The spotlight is on you in the glitzy Hollywood district of Disney California Adventure, where the action unfolds all around you. No movies are actually filmed here, so you'll have to keep waiting for your big break. You can think of this as the "Hollywood that never was and always will be."

Turn onto Hollywood Boulevard and enter Disney's version of the legendary street. And it all fits neatly into a two-block strip. Some of Disney California Adventure's most popular attractions lie within this zone, including Guardians of the Galaxy—Mission: BREAKOUT! and Frozen—Live at the Hyperion.

In contrast to the starstruck Hollywood Boulevard, the backlot area peels away the sparkly facade and takes a backstage look at Hollywood without its makeup. Alongside soundstage buildings,

Ticket Prices

Although prices[†] will likely increase, the following should give you an idea of what you will pay for tickets in 2020. Note that 1-Day tickets purchased in 2020 must be used by 12/31/20. The first day of use of multi-day tickets must be on or before 12/31/20. Multi-day tickets must be used within 13 days of first use or by January 13, 2021, whichever occurs first. For updates, call 714-781-4565, or visit *www.disneyland.com*. All details are subject to change at any time.

	ADULTS	CHILDREN*
1-Day Ticket (1 park)	$104/129/149	$98/122/141
1-Day Ticket (hopper)	$154/179/199	$148/172/191
2-Day Ticket	$225	$210
2-Day Ticket (hopper)	$280	$265
3-Day Ticket	$300	$280
3-Day Ticket (hopper)**	$355	$335
4-Day Ticket**	$325	$305
4-Day Ticket (hopper)**	$380	$360
5-Day Ticket**	$340	$320
5-Day Ticket (hopper)**	$395	$375
Deluxe Annual Passport		$799
Signature Annual Passport		$1,149
Signature Plus Annual Passport		$1,399
Premier Annual Passport		$1,949

[†] One-day prices are quoted in Value/Regular/Peak order. For dates, visit *www.disneyland.com*.
* 3 through 9 years of age; children under 3 free
** Includes one "Magic Morning" early Disneyland Park admission with select attractions on Tuesday, Thursday, or Saturday with advance purchase.
There is a single price (for adults and children) for annual passports.

behind-the-scenes support departments do their unseen, essential work: props are put into position, klieg lights are set to shine on the scene, and the crew is busy making sure every performer is on his or her mark before the director yells "Action!"

BIRNBAUM'S ★BEST★ MONSTERS, INC.— MIKE AND SULLEY TO THE RESCUE!: A monster's-eye spin through Monstropolis, this colorful, slow-moving attraction was inspired by the film *Monsters, Inc.* It invites guests to follow affable monsters Mike and Sulley as they valiantly attempt to deliver Boo safely back to her room—all while dodging trucks, helicopters, and the occasional yellow-suited representative of the Child Detection Agency.

PHOTO BY JILL SAFRO

DISNEY JUNIOR DANCE PARTY!: A joyful celebration of Disney Junior, this show is most popular with very young guests—who are the most enthusiastic members of the audience. The performance space holds large crowds (of mostly tiny) people at a time. All guests are invited to sing, dance, catch bubbles, and laugh themselves silly. Disney Junior favorites such as Vampirina, Doc McStuffins and Timon—and, of course, Mickey Mouse and Minnie Mouse—join the party, too. This show is presented daily. The park's Entertainment Times Guide lists the schedule.

MICKEY'S PHILHARMAGIC: Mickey Mouse and a panoply of his pals (including Donald Duck, Simba, and Ariel) strut their stuff in this snazzy new 3-D production.

The show is an amalgam of music, effects, and animation. Of course, this being Hollywood Land, the film is by no means ordinary. It's colorful, crisp, and to the delight of many a goggle-wearing guest, three-dimensional. The lively experience unfolds on a massive digital canvas. Special effects and surprises take place off the screen, too.

As with many Disney attractions, there are moments of darkness. If you are unsure as to whether your child

might find this (or any attractions) unsettling, express your concern to an attendant. They will help you make the right decision. Note that all guests must wear 3-D glasses to enjoy the show.

BIRNBAUM'S ★BEST★ DISNEY ANIMATION: When you look around at all the attractions, themed hotels, and dozens of familiar animated faces that Disney has become famous for, it's almost impossible to remember it all started with a simple sketch of a mouse. This behind-the-scenes exploration invites guests to step into Disney's wonderful world of animation. Here, visitors get an insider's look at the process, the heritage, and, above all, the artistry of this world-renowned art form, along with a possible preview of an animated feature that is currently in progress.

Disney Animation: This central area makes visitors feel as if they are stepping into an animated film. Sketches and artwork from Disney and Pixar film classics are projected onto giant screens that circle the colorful atrium as familiar tunes fill the air. From this hub, guests may progress to several interactive animation-inspired attractions.

Anna & Elsa's Royal Welcome: The royal siblings welcome visitors in the Disney Animation building in Hollywood Land. The colorful experience pays tribute to Arendelle and the revered characters from the beloved animated feature *Frozen*.

Anna and Elsa are popular, to say the least. Expect lengthy waits to meet the regal duo. Try to get there early, or late in the day (after most tykes have turned in for the night). And don't forget to have a camera or mobile device ready.

Animation Academy: Do you want to draw a snowman? Or perhaps a famous mouse? Inspired by the animation art in the courtyard, this attraction lets guests take a crack at drawing Disney characters. With step-by-step guidance provided by a Disney animator, you will use basic shapes and simple techniques to create your own sketch, suitable for framing. Check with a Cast Member or check the schedule out front to see which character is being drawn during your visit.

Sorcerer's Workshop: Budding animators and artists particularly get a kick out of these three rooms.

They are built around interactive exhibits featuring animation special effects. At Enchanted Books, for example, you can take a personality survey (hosted by *Beauty and the Beast*'s Lumiere and Cogsworth) to determine the Disney character or villain to which you are most similar.

Turtle Talk with Crush: If ever there were an attraction that left guests smiling and asking, "How do they do that?!"—this is it. The concept is simple enough: a 10-minute, animated show starring the surfer-dude sea turtle from *Finding Nemo*. The amazing part? The cartoon critter actually interacts with the audience. In doing so, he imparts turtle-y wisdom, answers questions, and cracks more than a few jokes. Dory and friends may join in the fun. You have to see it to believe it. To do that, you may have to wait a bit— the show is popular with guests of all ages. It's totally awesome, dude.

Little humans are encouraged to sit up front, on the floor by the big screen. That'll make it easier for Crush to see them. Grown-up humans can take a load off on the theater's bench-style seating (note that the benches do not have backs). You can collect the wee ones at the conclusion of the performance.

FROZEN—LIVE AT THE HYPERION: The Hyperion Theater is home to a rousing musical show inspired by the animated blockbuster hit *Frozen*. The dynamic production features favorite friends from the film, including Anna, Elsa, Olaf, Kristoff, and Sven. The peppy, popular production premiered in 2016. This fanciful re-telling of the *Frozen* tale is presented several times a day. Check a (complimentary) park Times Guide for the performance schedule and plan to arrive at least 20 minutes before showtime.

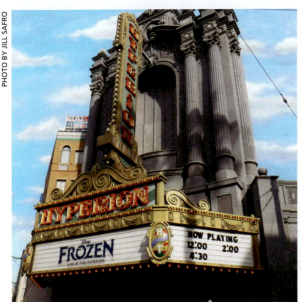
PHOTO BY JILL SAFRO

BIRNBAUM'S ★BEST★ GUARDIANS OF THE GALAXY— MISSION: BREAKOUT!: FP Inside this 183-foot, towering fortress is a collection of treasures, hoarded by one Taneleer Tivan, aka The Collector. Included in this trove are the Guardians of the Galaxy themselves. Your mission is to join forces with Rocket and attempt to break the superheroes out of their gilded cage.

The storytelling begins even before the ride does, with painted notes from Rocket scrawled throughout the queue area. (The attraction's story line expands on the film *Guardians of the Galaxy*—but even if you've never seen it, you'll have no trouble following along.)

The topsy-turvy ride experience is similar to this attraction's predecessor—The Tower of Terror. (If you have second thoughts about boarding the ride vehicle and following through with this daunting mission, simply ask the attendant to direct you toward the "chicken exit.") Once you take a seat in the gantry lift, the doors close and the room begins its ascent—and thus begins the chaotic and thrilling adventure.

Hang on—the gantry lift takes an immediate plunge (of about eight stories) before shooting up to the 13th floor. At the top (about 157 feet up), passengers can look out at the park below. Once the doors shut, you plummet 13 stories. The drop lasts about two seconds, but it seems a whole lot longer.

Just when you think it's over, the elevator launches skyward, barely stopping before it plunges again. And again. From the time you are seated, the mission takes about 5 minutes.

Note: You must be at least 40 inches tall to experience G.O.T.G.—Mission: BREAKOUT! The ride is not recommended for pregnant women, or people with heart conditions, back and neck problems, or other medical issues. Though thrilling (and rather scary), the drops are surprisingly smooth. Still, if you are susceptible to motion sickness, sit this one out.

GRIZZLY PEAK

The centerpiece of the Grizzly Peak recreation area (which includes the Grizzly Peak Airfield) is a bear-shaped mountain that juts 110 feet above the park floor. The eight-acre wilderness surrounding the Grizzly Peak mountain serves as a tribute to the Golden State's grandeur and natural beauty. The Grizzly Park Airfield area was inspired by California's aviation history. It pays tribute to famous flyers and their precious planes. A huge aircraft hangar, the focus of this section, houses the wildly popular Soarin' Around the World attraction.

BIRNBAUM'S ★BEST★ SOARIN' AROUND THE WORLD: FP Up, up, and away! On this smooth, high-flying attraction, you'll be suspended in a hang-glider–like ride vehicle 45 feet in the air, above a giant IMAX projection dome, and treated to an aerial tour of majestic landscapes and treasured landmarks. Soarin' has been delighting park guests with its wraparound glory since 2001—but these days, instead of hovering over one state (California), visitors experience a much broader tour.

Soarin' Around the World showcases some of the world's most compelling sights: The Great Wall of China, the plains of Africa, the oceans of Fiji, the Grand Canyon, Egyptian pyramids, and much more. With the wind in your hair and your legs dangling in the breeze, the hang glider feels so real that you may even be tempted to pull up your feet for fear of tapping the rooftops and landscapes below.

The flight takes about 5 minutes and employs synchronized wind currents, scent machines, and a musical score set to a film that wraps 180 degrees around you.

A Disney California Adventure original, there is now a version of this ride in several Disney theme parks around the world. The re-imagined version of this attraction touched down in 2016. It features a new digital screen and projection system and is a hit with all ages—get a Fastpass if you can.

Note: You must be 40 inches tall and free of back problems, heart conditions, motion sickness, and any other physical limitations to ride. Afraid of heights? Skip this flight.

GRIZZLY RIVER RUN: **FP** Disney legend says that Grizzly Peak was once chock-full of gold—which made it a magnet for miners in search of riches, as is evidenced by the mining relics scattered about the mountain. But the gold rush has come and gone, and the peak has since been taken over by another enterprising group—the Grizzly Peak Rafting Company. They converted the

area into a rafting expedition known as Grizzly River Run.

Each round raft whisks eight passengers on a drenching tour of Grizzly Peak. The trip begins with a 45-foot climb, and it's all gloriously downhill from there. Fast-moving currents send adventurers spinning and splashing along the river, bumping off boulders and rushing through an erupting geyser field. Because the raft is constantly spinning as it moves through the water, each rider's experience is slightly different, but one thing's for sure—everyone gets wet. During the expedition, rafters encounter two major drops. It's the 21-foot drop that earns Grizzly River the distinction of being the world's tallest, fastest raft ride.

Note: Passengers must be free of back and neck problems, heart conditions, motion sickness, and other physical limitations to ride. Pregnant women, guests not meeting the 42-inch height requirement, and children under age 3 will not be permitted to board. Finally, if you wish to stay dry, bypass this ride.

REDWOOD CREEK CHALLENGE TRAIL: Lace up your sneakers and test your skills on this rustic adventure zone near the eastern slope of Grizzly Peak. Highlights include the Cliff Hanger traverse rock climb, Boulder Bear rock formations, and a trio of wooden lookout towers featuring authentic ranger gear, rope bridges and hidden surprises to keep guests on their toes.

It's fun for guests of all ages.

Of course, even the most intrepid explorers need directions. Fortunately, there are maps at the trail's entrance—just ask a park ranger. Need a hand to assist you through the course? Just whistle for one of the workers outfitted in ranger gear. She or he will be happy to help.

There is a special cave hidden here, too. Find it and you will discover which noble creature—bear? salmon? skunk?—is your animal spirit.

Note: Redwood Creek Challenge Trail keeps shorter hours than the rest of the attractions in the park.

PACIFIC WHARF

Inspired by Monterey, California's Cannery Row, this industrial waterfront salutes the cultures, products, and industries that make the state of California so international in nature. Guests can tour a working bakery and watch local products such as fresh-baked San Francisco sourdough bread being prepared. There are also many tables scattered about, making this a good place to stop and enjoy a rest or a snack.

THE BAKERY TOUR: Soft sourdough bread is featured at this working bakery. While baking tips are shared in the walk-through corridor tour, the famous Boudin-family recipe remains a well-kept secret.

CARS LAND

Ladies and gentlemen, start your engines—there's a real-life Radiator Springs in this theme park! This 12-acre *Cars*-themed town invites guests to enjoy the following attractions:

LUIGI'S ROLLICKIN' ROADSTERS: Luigi's Flying Tires has, well, flown away. But Luigi fans, fear not! The mechanically inclined Radiator Springs resident has a fun-filled (or is that fun-fueled?) experience for guests to enjoy. The attraction, which sits behind Luigi's Casa Della Tires, takes guests for a wild ride as Luigi's cousins demonstrate dances from their native Italy. It's a "wheel" hoot! Guests must be at least 40 inches tall to ride. The experience involves quite a bit of motion, including a bit of spinning. Just a heads-up.

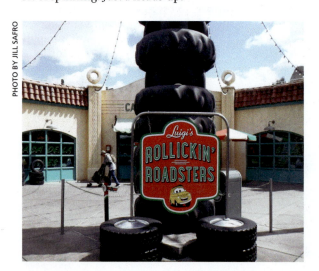

PHOTO BY JILL SAFRO

MATER'S JUNKYARD JAMBOREE: This attraction is a tractor-pulling square dance party hosted by everyone's favorite tow truck. As baby tractors pull the junkyard cart (with you in it), the cart gets whirled and twirled in time to tunes pumped through Mater's junkyard jukebox. Those tunes—all seven of 'em—are original songs performed by Disneyland Park legends, Billy Hill and the Hillbillies. To ride, guests must be at least 32 inches tall. Don't ride on a full stomach.

PHOTO BY MIKE CARROLL

BIRNBAUM'S ★BEST★ **RADIATOR SPRINGS RACERS:** FP Fasten your seat belts—this bona fide "E-Ticket" attraction will set your heart racing as you compete with other speed seekers. Using technology similar to that of Epcot's beloved Test Track attraction, Imagineers have devised a thrilling experience for guests: a high-speed tour of Ornament Valley, featuring hairpin turns, steep banks, and a head-to-head race to the finish. Sally, Luigi, Guido, Ramone, and other *Cars* friends zoom around this revved-up racetrack.

Notes: To ride, guests must be at least 32 inches tall and without health conditions. Expectant mothers must skip the race. Refer to a park guidemap for the location of the Fastpass distribution machines. And get there early!

FP = Fastpass attraction (see page 58)

PIXAR PIER

It's all about fun in the sun at Pixar Pier, a newly re-themed neighborhood featuring high-flying adventures with popular Pixar pals. Attractions here line a boardwalk amusement pier wrapped around a scenic lagoon.

At night, the district undergoes a dazzling transformation. Thousands of tiny lights illuminate the rides and building facades, creating a magical display—especially as you soar past them on one of Pixar Pier's most thrilling attractions: Incredicoaster. This area used to be known as Paradise Pier.

BIRNBAUM'S ★BEST **INCREDICOASTER:** FP Like many classic boardwalks, the centerpiece of Pixar Pier is a gleaming roller coaster. A steel structure, Incredicoaster is designed to look and sound like an old-fashioned wooden coaster, but the thrills are as modern as they get. The ride starts at lagoon level, where the long car bursts up the track as if catapulted up by a crashing wave. The car goes from zero to 55 miles per hour in 4.7 seconds—before reaching the first hill. Several long drops are combined with an upside-down loop, plus a blasting soundtrack. The result is the longest and fastest roller coaster ride in the Disneyland Resort.

Along the way, vehicles travel through bright red tubes that trap guests' yells as they test their vocal cords on the big drops, magnifying the hoots and hollers and adding to the excitement. Every time you approach a tube, you know you're in for a big thrill, so brace yourself and prepare to scream! (The previous version of this ride was called California Screamin'.)

Daredevils should be sure to enjoy this attraction after the sun goes down, when the night sky is speckled with the pier's glowing lights, and the topsy-turvy twists and turns on the roller coaster will prove even more disorientingly exciting—and scary!

Note: Passengers must be at least 48 inches tall and free of back problems, neck problems, heart conditions, motion sickness, pregnancy, and other physical limitations to ride.

INSIDE OUT EMOTIONAL WHIRLWIND: This attraction may trigger memories of the cherished Flik's Flyers from the now-defunct "A Bug's Land." If that's not enough to get your emotions churning, *Inside Out*'s Joy, Sadness, Disgust, Anger, and Fear will get the job done. This ride—which is big with fans of Disneyland's Dumbo the Flying Elephant—lasts about a minute and a half.

JESSIE'S CRITTER CAROUSEL: Yee-ha! Get ready to saddle up with one of the 56 cuddly critters on this carousel. Jessie's new ride was inspired by the *Woody's Roundup* TV show in *Toy Story 2*. It features a twirling herd of wilderness creatures such as bunnies, rams, armadillos, turtles, snakes, and one super silly skunk. There are two stationary logs in which guests may ride, too (both inhabited by owls). This attraction is fun for the young and the young at heart. On some nights, Jessie's Critter Carousel closes early to accommodate World of Color performances.

PIXAR PAL-A-ROUND: A modern loop-de-loop, this gleaming Ferris wheel, centered by a huge Mickey face, takes guests on a head-spinning trip. If you think this is a run-of-the-mill Ferris wheel, you're in for a surprise: While the wheel turns, most of its cabins rotate in and out along the interior edges of the wheel's colossal frame—which creates a dizzying effect. At 150 feet, this is one of the park's tallest attractions, and while it may wreak havoc on sensitive stomachs, thrill-seekers rave over its ride within a ride. For a tamer experience, request a non-rotating gondola.

Note: Passengers must be free of back problems, heart conditions, motion sickness, and other physical limitations to ride. Afraid of heights? Better skip this one!

BIRNBAUM'S ★BEST★ **TOY STORY MIDWAY MANIA!:** **FP** This beloved attraction is an energetic, interactive toy box tour with a twist: Guests wear 3-D glasses as they take aim at animated targets with spring-action shooters. The high-tech adventure is rooted in classic midway games of skill. As points are scored, expect effusive encouragement from a colorful cast of characters—*Toy Story*'s Jessie, Woody, Buzz, Hamm, Wheezy, Rex the Dinosaur, and, of course, the Little Green Men.

Fans of Disneyland Park's Buzz Lightyear Astro Blasters will no doubt delight in this adventure, which takes the experience of the interactive attraction into a new dimension. As far as skill level goes, there's something for everyone—from beginners to seasoned players alike. (Most folks up their score with practice.) And don't worry about your accuracy score—it's all about the point total.

Toy Story Midway Mania! is a very popular destination with guests of all ages—make a beeline for it when the park first opens. Better yet, get a Fastpass.

PARADISE GARDENS PARK

A colorful celebration of the Golden State, Paradise Gardens Park hugs the shores of Paradise Bay, a shimmering lagoon in the heart of the Disney California Adventure theme park. Here you'll find a dynamic lineup of shows and attractions:

SILLY SYMPHONY SWINGS: This attraction pays tribute to some of Walt Disney's earliest animated triumphs—the Silly Symphonies. The specific symphony highlighted here is the 1935 cartoon called *The Band Concert*. Riders take flight in swings, while Mickey and his barnyard band serenade them with a rousing rendition of the *William Tell Overture*.

As the attraction's momentum picks up, a cyclone reveals itself as guests swirl higher and higher. Avoid it if you fear heights.

Notes: Riders must meet the Silly Symphony Swings height requirement of 48 inches to ride solo. (Guests between 40 and 48 inches may ride in a double swing. Children under the age of 7 must be accompanied by a responsible person over age 14. Those under 40 inches are not permitted to take this flight.) All guests must be free of back problems, heart conditions, motion sickness, and other physical limitations to ride. Silly Symphony Swings closes early to accommodate World of Color performances.

GOOFY'S SKY SCHOOL: **FP** At this mini roller coaster, guests of most sizes climb into crop dusters and follow the same fluky flight path taken by the Goof himself. The planes zip through the farm and crash through a barn, causing quite a ruckus among the chickens. Don't let the size fool you. This roller coaster proves that big thrills come in small packages. Although guests as young as age 3 are allowed to ride, it may be too turbulent for some.

FP = Fastpass attraction (see page 58)

Note: Although it's small as roller coasters go, the ride's sudden stops and herky-jerky motion during turns may prove too scary for riders not used to more strenuous coasters. Riders must be at least 42 inches tall and free of back problems, neck problems, heart conditions, motion sickness, and any other physical limitations to take this jolting ride.

PHOTO BY JILL SAFRO

JUMPIN' JELLYFISH: A dense kelp bed tops this sea-themed attraction, from which riders sitting in brightly colored jellyfish seats are lifted about 40 feet straight up in the air. When you reach the top, hang on to your tentacles! A jellyfish acts as a parachute, and fish and friends float safely back down to the ground. While the trip is a rather gentle one with special appeal for younger riders, it might take a few minutes for guests with the most sensitive of stomachs to get their land legs back.

Notes: All guests must be at least 40 inches tall and free of back problems, heart conditions, motion sickness, and any other physical limitations to ride.

On nights when World of Color (see page 108) is presented, Jumpin' Jellyfish closes early to accommodate the evening's performances of the park's popular fountain and light show.

THE LITTLE MERMAID—ARIEL'S UNDERSEA ADVENTURE: In the first attraction ever to have featured everyone's favorite Disney mermaid, guests are invited to board (continuously moving) clam-mobiles and embark on a jolly journey above and below sea level. (Be sure to take in the 86-foot-long, hand-painted mural in the boarding area.) Along the way, they join Ariel, Flounder, Sebastian, and all of their aquatic acquaintances and enjoy major musical moments and pivotal plot points from the classic animated feature. It's fun for the whole family.

A wheelchair-access vehicle is available for this attraction. Ask a Cast Member for assistance.

GOLDEN ZEPHYR: Disney Imagineers took the rocket ride to new heights with the launch of Astro Orbitor in Disneyland. But long before those space-age ships took off, riders were taking flights in rocket-shaped swings on boardwalks and amusement piers across America. Disney pays homage to those old-fashioned attractions with rocket ships that take guests for a spin beneath the Golden Zephyr tower. As speed picks up, the rockets lift into the air and fly over the lagoon several times before touching down for a landing. The ride lasts approximately a minute and a half.

Note: Passengers must be free of back, neck, and heart problems, motion sickness, and other physical limitations to ride. This attraction closes for World of Color presentations (see page 108) and during inclement weather (including high winds). There is no height requirement, but youngsters must be able to ride without assistance. Have an unpleasant relationship with heights? Skip this attraction.

Shopping

BUENA VISTA STREET

ATWATER INK AND PAINT: Shoppers enjoy the quaint ambience of a 1930s Hollywood-style market house as they peruse collector pins, seasonal merchandise, kitchen gadgets, towels, mugs, dinner plates, flatware, and much more.

BIG TOP TOYS: Teeming with playthings, Big Top sells innovative and interactive toys and games, plus a plethora of plush character merchandise. You may also find Star Wars-themed toys and souvenirs (action figures, lightsabers, and other selections).

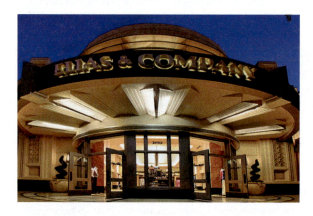

ELIAS & CO.: Paying tribute to the Art Deco–style buildings of yesteryear, this emporium features an array of fashion finery for the whole family—it rivals Disneyland Park's Emporium shop in size. It stocks clothing (hats, shirts, shoes, jackets, and more), snacks, accessories, and watches.

    F.Y.I.: Elias was Walt Disney's middle name and his dad's first name.

JULIUS KATZ & SONS: Adorned with old-timey clocks, radios, and assorted memorabilia, this cozy shop is a hotspot for Disney shoppers. Among its wares: kitchen items, mugs, frames, and Christmas ornaments. The store's name was inspired by Julius the Cat, a featured character in Walt Disney's classic Alice Comedies.

KINGSWELL CAMERA SHOP: Stop here to view and purchase photos taken by Disney's PhotoPass team of roving photographers. You'll also find frames, photo albums, and other souvenirs. The shop's name comes from Walt Disney's first California address. When he arrived in Los Angeles in 1923, he rented a room from his Uncle Robert on Kingswell Avenue. It's where the Walt Disney Company was born.

LOS FELIZ FIVE & DIME: In addition to attraction- and California-themed clothing and souvenirs, there is a selection of Disney character items. It's possible to have some items personalized (for a fee).

OSWALD'S: Stop here for autograph books, hats, bags, and souvenirs themed to the park, Oswald the Lucky Rabbit, and more. It's just inside the park entrance.

TROLLEY TREATS: If the thoughts of "mountains of candy" and "rivers of fudge" make you smile, this is the shop for you. Tasty temptations include caramel apples, toffee, chocolate-dipped cookies, fudge, and seasonal selections such as housemade marshmallows. Choose from packaged candy or items made fresh in the display kitchen. It's fun to watch the candy makers at work—and it's even more satisfying to gobble up their creative confections.

HOLLYWOOD LAND

THE COLLECTOR'S WAREHOUSE: The exit lobby of Guardians of the Galaxy—Mission: BREAKOUT! does double duty as a gift shop. It sells souvenirs themed to the attraction (pins, shirts, hats, comic books, backpacks, action figures, etc.). This is also the place to buy the photo that's taken on the attraction. The shot is snapped just before the ride's big drop, so that look of horror is captured forever!

GONE HOLLYWOOD: A cheerful boutique, Gone Hollywood celebrates Hollywood blockbusters. Here you will find apparel, books, toys, collectibles, and seasonal items—many with a Star Wars or Marvel twist.

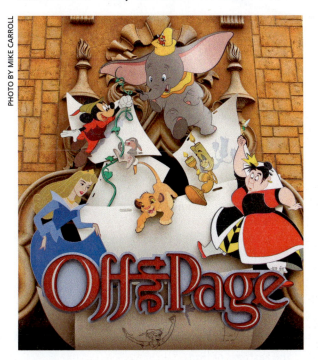

OFF THE PAGE: The magic of Disney animation leaps off the page at this shop that showcases collectible Disneyana pieces. Cels, limited-edition prints, books, and figurines are sold here, as are attraction-inspired items. Guests may interact with artists as they sketch classic Disney characters.

THE STUDIO STORE: This open-air shop puts the spotlight on current shows in Hollywood Land. The themes vary, but expect to find items such as T-shirts, hats, toys, snacks, and more. You'll find it across from Monsters, Inc.—Mike and Sulley to the Rescue!

GRIZZLY PEAK

HUMPHREY'S SERVICE & SUPPLIES: When you see the large selection here, you know this is a "beary" serious shopping spot. The grizzly-inspired merchandise includes hats, souvenirs, toys, pins, items with a Soarin' theme, and glow merchandise. This souvenir shop is across from the park's beloved Soarin' Around the World attraction.

RUSHIN' RIVER OUTFITTERS: This outpost is the perfect place to gear up for an outdoor adventure. Expect to find a variety of Rushin' River apparel, headwear, towels, ponchos, plush toys, and other items.

CARS LAND

RADIATOR SPRINGS CURIOS: Hit the brakes and make a quick stop at this country-style mercantile. You may be tempted to fill the trunk with the latest park logo merchandise, *Cars*-themed paraphernalia, and other accessories. There is also a substantial supply of items celebrating revered roadway Route 66.

RAMONE'S HOUSE OF BODY ART: Ramone stocks all manner of items with a *Cars* theme (hey, this *is* Cars Land). There are T-shirts, hats, Piston Cup trophy replicas, and Radiator Springs merchandise.

SARGE'S SURPLUS HUT: Young (and young-at-heart) racers, rejoice: Sarge has a super supply of clothes and toys that were designed with you in mind. Among the wares are costumes, hats, toys, and snacks. For many *Cars* fans, it's well worth making the pit stop—even if it is just to sneak a peek at the scale model of Radiator Springs. It's super cool.

PIXAR PIER

BING BONG'S SWEET STUFF: This sweet spot specializes in sugary treats and colorful merchandise celebrating friends from the film *Inside Out*. You'll find it on the boardwalk, across from Pixar Pal-A-Round.

KNICK'S KNACKS: The snow globe snowman stocks items themed to Disney•Pixar films. Look for items featuring *Finding Nemo*, *Up*, *Inside Out*, *Coco*, *WALL-E*, and more. The shop is across from Lamplight Lounge.

PARADISE GARDENS PARK

SEASIDE SOUVENIRS: A 1930s–style, open-air stand, Seaside Souvenirs offers character merchandise, hats, toys, sunglasses, and more.

Entertainment

Disney California Adventure boasts a lineup of live (and Audio-Animatronic) entertainment. For updates, go to *www.disneyland.com*. Check an Entertainment Times Guide for schedules.

FIVE & DIME: This singing group travels Buena Vista Street in their jalopy, hoping to get their big break in the music world. A fleet-footed Goofy joins in the jazzy fun. Details are subject to change in 2020.

MARIACHI DIVAS: Guests are invited to sing along as this talented, Grammy award-winning quintet performs pop music and traditional Mexican folk songs. This act performs during the holiday season.

OPERATION PLAYTIME: A rhythmic squad of *Toy Story*'s Green Army Men is on a mission to serve, protect, and entertain! The plastic platoon engages guests with games and percussive shenanigans.

THE PIXARMONIC ORCHESTRA: A bubbly band performs cheerful tunes from Disney•Pixar films at a spot known as Pixar Promenade—next to Bing Bong's Sweet Stuff on Pixar Pier. Seasonal. Details are subject to change.

RED CAR TROLLEY NEWS BOYS: Mickey joins in as the boys hawk papers and celebrate Hollywood in this 25-minute show on Buena Vista Street (near Carthay Circle Restaurant). They perform period tunes (and songs from Disney's *Newsies*) several times a day.

BIRNBAUM'S ★BEST★ WORLD OF COLOR: FP Arrive early and prepare to smile. This 25-minute spectacular, presented on select nights on Paradise Bay, is a kaleidoscopic journey of music, animation, water, special effects, and, of course, brilliant color. The show is best viewed from the esplanade near The Little Mermaid attraction. Get a show ticket via Disney's Fastpass or MaxPass if possible.

World of Color is intended for all audiences, but it does feature loud noises, fire, and other effects that may be too intense for some tykes. While not a drenching experience, guests closest to the water's edge will get spritzed.

A special, extra-festive version of this show—World of Color Season of Light—is presented during the holiday season.

HOT TIPS

❋ Disney characters (including Mickey Mouse) make appearances throughout the day. Refer to a park Times Guide for specifics.

❋ Take advantage of Disney's free, time-saving Fastpass system whenever possible.

❋ Curious about showtimes or wait times? Stop by the Information Station on Buena Vista Street or use the Disneyland mobile app. Guest Relations kiosks in Cars Land and Paradise Gardens Park serve as savvy resources, too.

❋ Many attractions have height restrictions—measure the kids before you leave home.

❋ Golden Vine Winery offers wine tastings (for a fee).

❋ The line for Soarin' Around the World may dwindle a bit by midday. Ride it then if you choose to forgo the Fastpass option.

❋ Shops on Buena Vista Street usually stay open about a half hour after the park closes.

❋ Ready for a break from the park? Head over to Downtown Disney to shop or grab a quick bite to eat. There are more than a few (relatively) cost-efficient snacking spots to consider (i.e., Wetzel's Pretzels, Diggety Dogs, Napolini Pizzeria, Tortilla Jo's, Jamba Juice, and La Brea Bakery).

❋ Radiator Springs Racers has maniacally devoted fans. To minimize your wait, get to the park as it opens, and head straight to this attraction after passing through the turnstile—or take advantage of the Single Rider line. Better yet? Get a Fastpass!

❋ Don't risk water-logging your valuables while riding Grizzly River Run. We recommend using zip-top bags to protect mobile phones and cameras while you ride. Better yet, use a complimentary locker (located near the ride's exit).

❋ If you want to see World of Color, pick up a (free) show ticket as you arrive. Tickets are dispensed from a machine near The Little Mermaid—Ariel's Undersea Adventure attraction.

FP = Fastpass attraction (see page 58)

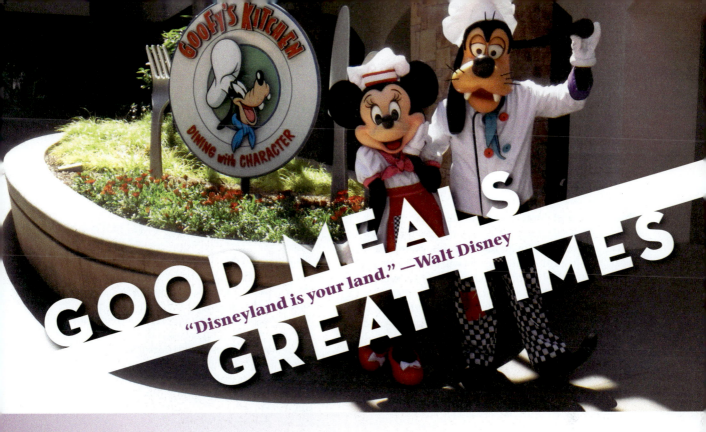

GOOD MEALS GREAT TIMES

"Disneyland is your land." —Walt Disney

Dining at the Disneyland Resort is definitely an adventure—and not just in Adventureland. There's more to any meal in a theme park, Downtown Disney, or a Disneyland Resort hotel than just food. Disney friends such as Mickey, Minnie, Goofy, Tigger, Pooh, Chip and Dale, or Donald Duck might drop by your table to say hello. A colorful parade or a romantic paddle wheeler could drift by. Or you might find yourself surrounded by twinkling stars (in the middle of the day!) as you savor Cajun cooking in a peaceful bayou setting.

In this chapter, the Disneyland Resort restaurant section is divided by location (Disneyland park, Disney California Adventure park, the three Disney hotels, and Downtown Disney). Within the theme parks, eateries are arranged by area, and then by category—table service or fast-food and snack facilities, including food courts; individual eateries are alphabetized within each respective category.

If you're hankering for something to do after dinner, or you just need to take a break from the theme parks, you'll find plenty of suggestions at the end of the chapter. Downtown Disney, the property's dining and entertainment district, is party central. Or for a more relaxed atmosphere, chill out in a lounge at one of the Disneyland Resort hotels.

Dining
In Disneyland Park

One of the most popular foods in Disneyland is the burger, followed closely by ice cream and churros (sticks of deep-fried dough rolled in cinnamon and sugar). But healthy-minded eaters will be happy to find fish, salads, grilled chicken, and vegetable gumbo, plus fresh fruit, smoothies, and juices. Disneyland's table-service restaurants (the Blue Bayou, Cafe Orleans, River Belle Terrace, and the Carnation Cafe) provide full-course meals and lighter fare, plus a welcome break from long lines and the California sun.

MAIN STREET, U.S.A.

TABLE SERVICE

CARNATION CAFE: On the west side of Main Street, near Town Square, this indoor/outdoor cafe is exceptionally pleasant, especially in springtime, when its planters are bursting with seasonal flowers. Stroll into the courtyard dining area that's filled with umbrella-shaded tables and surrounded by a cast-iron fence; from your table you'll hear the melodies from any passing parade. Breakfast choices include Mickey-shaped waffles; apple-granola pancakes; steel-cut oatmeal; eggs Benedict; ham and cheese omelet; country-fried steak and eggs, spinach, tomato, and egg white frittata; and fruit parfait, along with coffee, tea, and orange juice.

Lunch and dinner feature comfort foods, including some of Walt Disney's favorites—homemade meatloaf (with mashed potatoes and seasonal vegetables) and chicken-fried chicken. Popular menu items include fried pickles (with dipping sauce), salads, baked potato soup, penne pasta with shrimp, cheeseburgers, and

Restaurant Primer

The eateries in this chapter have been designated inexpensive (lunch or dinner under $15), moderate ($15 to $29), expensive ($30 to $50), and very expensive ($51 and up). Prices are for an entrée, a soft drink, and either soup, salad, or dessert for one person, excluding tax and tip. Note that some prices may be higher during peak-attendance times throughout the year.

The letters at the end of each entry refer to the meals offered: breakfast (B), lunch (L), dinner (D), and snacks (S).

Cash, credit cards, traveler's checks, and Disney gift cards can be used as payment at all of the following full-service restaurants and fast-food spots. Disneyland Resort hotel guests can charge meals from most theme park eateries to their rooms.

While only a few park restaurants (Blue Bayou, River Belle Terrace, Cafe Orleans, Carnation Cafe, and Plaza Inn [breakfast only] in Disneyland, plus Lamplight Lounge, Wine Country Trattoria, and Carthay Circle Restaurant in California Adventure) take reservations, you can book a table at most Downtown Disney spots and at the Disney hotels. Unless otherwise noted, make reservations up to 60 days in advance by calling 714-781-3463, or by using the Disneyland Resort app.

vegan burgers. There are special selections just for kids, too. Finish off the meal with a housemade dessert (a chocolate malt, perhaps?) and specialty coffees. This cafe is one of four restaurants at Disneyland park that offers table service for lunch and dinner. (River Belle Terrace, Blue Bayou, and Cafe Orleans are the others.) **B L D** $-$$

FAST FOOD & SNACKS

JOLLY HOLIDAY BAKERY CAFE: A festive tribute to Disney's *Mary Poppins*, the Jolly Holiday is at the far end of Main Street. There is always a steady supply of pastries here, including cookies, cupcakes, and Mickey macarons. Specialty coffee drinks are available all day (hot and iced). Also on the seasonal menu (after 10:30 A.M.): soups, salads,

> ## HOT TIP!
> For a jolt of java, head to the Market House (aka Starbucks) or Jolly Holiday Bakery Cafe on Main Street, or Cafe Orleans in New Orleans Square. The iced and hot specialty coffees are sure to please.

B breakfast **L** lunch **D** dinner **S** snacks   **$** *under $15* **$$** *$15–$29* **$$$** *$30–$50* **$$$$** *$51 and up*

and sandwiches. Wash it down with a soft drink—Practically Perfect Punch, anyone? Children's meals are available as well. **B** **L** **D** **S** **$**

GIBSON GIRL ICE CREAM PARLOR: A perennially popular place, with a polished-wood soda fountain, the parlor serves up a delightful array of scoops and toppings in paper cups, handmade waffle cups, and plain or chocolate-dipped cones. Choose from 9 flavors, including no-sugar-added butter pecan. We are big fans of the "firehouse Dalmatian mint sundae" (hold the cherry). Don't be daunted by the long line; it moves rather quickly. **S** **$**

LITTLE RED WAGON: This wagon, near the Plaza Inn, is a throwback to the delivery trucks of the early 1900s, with ornate beveled and gilded glass panels. Step right up and order your hand-dipped corn dogs, the specialty of the wagon. A selection of soft drinks and chips is also served. **L** **D** **S** **$**

MAIN STREET FRUIT CART: Parked between Disney Clothiers Ltd. and Market House, this old-fashioned

HOT TIP!

Do you spend a lot of time visiting the Disneyland Resort each year? If so, we highly recommend the purchase of an Annual Pass. It could net you a 10 to 15 percent discount (depending on the type of pass) at many eateries and shops property-wide. It practically pays for itself.

cart is stocked with fresh fruit, chilled juices, bottled water, and other soft drinks. Other snack options include pickles, hummus, and fresh veggies. It's the perfect pit stop for a (relatively) healthy snack. **S** **$**

MARKET HOUSE: Visit this Victorian-style market for a fresh-baked or brewed treat. It sells sweet and savory snacks and a cornucopia of tea and coffee concoctions, courtesy of Starbucks. Breakfast items, fresh fruit, and pastries are served all day. **B** **S** **$**

Where to Dine with the Characters

Meals with Disney characters take place daily at Disneyland Park's Plaza Inn (breakfast with Minnie and friends) on Main Street; Paradise Pier Hotel (breakfast with Donald Duck and friends); Storytellers Cafe (breakfast with Mickey Mouse) in the Grand Californian Hotel; and Goofy's Kitchen in the Disneyland Hotel (breakfast and dinner with Goofy and friends). For updates, visit *disneyland.com* or use the Disneyland Resort app.

PLAZA INN: On the east side of Central Plaza, this eatery is the one Walt Disney was most proud of, and with good reason. Tufted velvet upholstery, gleaming mirrors, and a fine, ornate floral carpet elevate this cafeteria above similar eateries. Two ceilings are stained glass framed by elaborate painted moldings. Sconces of Parisian bronze and Baccarat crystal are mounted on the walls, and two dozen basket chandeliers hang from the ceiling.

The setting, including front-porch and terrace dining (with heat lamps to keep guests toasty at night), creates a lovely backdrop for the food—pasta; seasonal fish; fried chicken served with mashed potatoes and mixed vegetables; pot roast served with fresh veggies and mashed potatoes; salads; and desserts.

A popular character breakfast is held here daily, from park opening until 11 A.M. Minnie and her pals make the rounds. A fixed-price buffet features omelets, eggs, French toast, Mickey waffles, sausage, bacon, yogurt, fresh fruit, pastries, cereal, and more. **B** **L** **D** **S** **$–$$**

REFRESHMENT CORNER: Better known as Coke Corner, this eatery at the northern end of Main Street is presided over by a ragtime pianist who tickles the ivories periodically throughout the day while visitors nibble hot dogs, chili cheese dogs, turkey dogs, or chili in a bread bowl. Mickey pretzels (stuffed with cream cheese), chips, soft drinks, lemonade, hot cocoa, and coffee are sold, too. **L D S $**

ADVENTURELAND

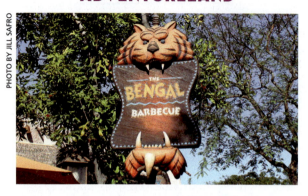

PHOTO BY JILL SAFRO

FAST FOOD & SNACKS

BENGAL BARBECUE: Opposite the entrance to Tarzan's Treehouse, this is a great place to munch on a skewered snack of bacon-wrapped asparagus (a local favorite), or chicken, beef, or veggies. It's possible to have skewers served on a bed of rice with citrus slaw. Other choices include tiger tails (bread sticks), shrimp spring rolls, and a trio of housemade seasonal hummus served with fresh vegetables. The "Thirst Aid" menu includes fountain drinks, bottled water, coffee, tea, specialty beverages,

---

Dining Packages

Disneyland may offer a "meal and a show" experience in 2020—possibly pairing a meal with preferred viewing for Fantasmic! Here's a sample of previous offerings:

   1. Blue Bayou Restaurant and **River Belle Terrace:** A three-course, table-service meal (including a starter, entrée, and dessert).

   2. Hungry Bear On-the-Go: One grab-and-go meal (which can be picked up between 3 P.M. and 8:30 P.M.).

   Space is limited for these special experiences, so reservations are recommended. For updates, pricing, and reservations, visit *www.disneyland.com*, or call 714-781-3463. Reservations require a credit card guarantee. Cancellations must be made at least 24 hours ahead to avoid a $10 per-person fee.

---

and more. There is a large indoor seating area in which to savor your skewers. **L D S $**

TIKI JUICE BAR: Located at the entrance to Walt Disney's Enchanted Tiki Room, this thatched-roof kiosk sells fresh Hawaiian pineapple spears and juice, but the biggest draw here is the Dole Whip soft-serve—a frozen, non-dairy, pineapple treat. **S $**

TROPICAL HIDEAWAY: An alfresco courtyard behind the Tiki Room, this enchanting hideaway has two counters from which to order sweet and savory treats. The menu features steamed bao buns (lime chicken, beef, and spicy veggie), fruit, chips, and (frozen non-dairy) Dole Whip desserts. (In addition to the traditional pineapple, this spot sells raspberry- and orange-flavored Dole Whip confections.) Diners are entertained by talented Tiki Bird, Rosita—who tells tales and cracks one-liners worthy of the nearby Jungle Cruise attraction. **L D S $**

TROPICAL IMPORTS: A close neighbor of Bengal Barbecue, this stand offers whole fresh fruit, hummus and vegetable cups, pickles, assorted chips, bottled water, and soft drinks. This is also the place to get your fortune told by Shrunken Ned (for 50 cents). **S $**

CRITTER COUNTRY

FAST FOOD & SNACKS

CRITTER COUNTRY FRUIT CART: This modest peddler's cart is filled with refreshing selections, including fresh fruit, dill pickles, chilled bottled water, and soft drinks. It's handy if you need some fortification after taking the big Splash Mountain plunge. **S $**

HARBOUR GALLEY: This tiny place, tucked into the shanties that line the docking area for the *Columbia*, offers bread bowls with New England clam chowder, broccoli and cheddar cheese soup, and seasonal soup of the day; shrimp salad; lobster rolls; lobster mac and cheese dogs, "power packs" (snack packs with mini yogurt smoothie, sliced apples, carrots, petite banana, and crackers); soft drinks; and fresh cut fruit. **L D S $**

HUNGRY BEAR RESTAURANT: A rustic, waterside classic, this eatery serves cheeseburgers, vegan burgers, crispy chicken sandwiches, fish sandwiches, french fries, and onion rings. For kids, there are chicken breast nuggets, burgers, or mac and cheese (kids' meals come with applesauce, fruit, and a choice of milk or bottled water). Dessert options include strawberry fruit bars, ice cream sandwiches, and funnel cakes. **L D S $**

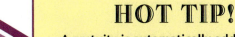

HOT TIP!

A gratuity is automatically added to the bill at some Disney restaurants. Examine your tab and tip accordingly.

NEW ORLEANS SQUARE

TABLE SERVICE

BLUE BAYOU: The lure of this popular dining spot is as much the enchanting atmosphere as it is the menu. Occupying a terrace alongside the bayou in the Pirates of the Caribbean attraction, the restaurant appears perpetually moonlit—stars shine through Spanish moss draped languidly over the big, old live oaks. Off in the distance, an old settler rocks away on the porch of a tumbledown shack.

The menu features starters such as fried calamari, golden beet salad, crab hush puppies, house salad, and N'awlins gumbo. Entrée options may include catch of the day, bone-in rib eye, roasted chicken maison, herb-crusted rack of lamb, bone-in pork loin, seafood pasta, vegetarian pasta, plus a surf & turf combo—split lobster tail paired with a petite filet mignon. A sweet finish to the meal may come in the form of 8-layer chocolate hazelnut cake. Specialty beverages include (non-alcoholic) Louisiana lemonade and mint juleps. Children's menu selections include a "beefy specialty," chicken breast with pasta topped with marinara, sustainable fish with pasta, and Mickey's cheesy macaroni. All kids' meals are served with vegetables and fresh fruit with a choice of low-fat milk or bottled water.

The busiest periods are from about noon to around 2 P.M. and from about 5 P.M. until 9 P.M. Reservations are recommended. **L D** **$$–$$$**

CAFE ORLEANS: An authentic Cajun-Creole spot, the cafe offers starters such as seafood gratin, seasonal soup, salad, and pomme frites. Among the entrées, look for muffuletta chopped salad; steak and potatoes; vegetable Bolognese; Bourbon Street chicken; two versions of the venerable Monte Cristo sandwich; and shrimp and grits. For dessert, there's Mickey-shaped beignets. There is a special section of the menu for little ones. Guests may dine inside or outside overlooking a gristmill on Tom Sawyer Island and the *Columbia* and the *Mark Twain* resting on the Rivers of America. Reservations are suggested. **L D S** **$$–$$$**

FAST FOOD & SNACKS

FRENCH MARKET: Situated beside the old-time train depot in New Orleans Square, this eatery is a destination in its own right. On a pleasant day, nothing beats sitting on the open-air terrace, savoring a Cajun breakfast croissant (while supplies last), oven-roasted chicken, creamy corn chowder, slow-roasted Louisiana beef stew (both served in a bowl fashioned from a hollowed-out loaf of bread), a variety of sandwiches (including French dip, pulled pork, and shrimp po' boys), New Orleans salad, chicken Caesar salad, or jambalaya (the house specialty). Coffee, tea, and soft drinks are served. Kids' selections such as baked chicken, macaroni and cheese, and pasta with marinara sauce are available. Dixieland jazz music is played periodically throughout the evening; the Royal Street Bachelors hold forth with such spirit that you could listen for hours. **L D S** **$–$$**

MINT JULEP BAR: Beside the New Orleans Square train station, this window-service bar serves Mickey-shaped beignets (topped with powdered sugar), hot cocoa, hot tea, and coffee (regular and decaf). The alcohol-free mint juleps taste a bit like lemonade

Happy Birthday, Disney Style

For starters, it is always a good idea to inform Disney Cast Members when you are celebrating a special occasion, no matter where you are at the Disneyland Resort. But it also helps to plan ahead. Birthday cakes can be delivered to any full-service restaurant. The cakes range in price from about $60 to $300 and can be ordered from 3 to 60 days in advance. For more information or to order a cake, call 714-781-3463.

Finally, be sure to pick up (and wear!) a special Happy Birthday button. The buttons are complimentary and available at City Hall in Disneyland Park, at the Chamber of Commerce in Disney California Adventure, and at some shops throughout the theme parks.

spiked with mint syrup (definitely an acquired taste); regular lemonade is also on tap. Seasonal specials are often on the menu. Enjoy your snack at one of the tables on the French Market's terrace. **B** **S** **$**

ROYAL STREET VERANDA: Situated opposite Cafe Orleans, this snack stand has bread bowls overflowing with creamy clam chowder, steak or veggie gumbo (each with a bit of a slightly spicy kick); fritters that come with a dipping sauce; and a variety of beverages. Check out the wrought-iron balustrade above the Royal Street Veranda's small patio. The initials at the center are those of Roy and Walt Disney (this balcony belonged to an apartment that was being constructed for Walt himself). **L** **D** **S** **$**

FRONTIERLAND

TABLE SERVICE

RIVER BELLE TERRACE: The terrace, between the Golden Horseshoe Saloon and the Pirates of the Caribbean, offers one of the best views of the Rivers of America and of the passing throng—and the food is wholesome and hearty. Walt Disney himself used to dine here most Sundays. Start your meal with grilled and chilled shrimp, creamy pimento cheese dip, or a house salad. Choose from entrées such as beef short ribs,

HOT TIP!

If you plan to celebrate a special event while at Disneyland (anniversary, birthday, honeymoon, engagement, etc.), tell reservationists ahead of time. They can help you make the occasion even more special. Call Disney Dining at 714-781-3463 for additional information and to make reservations.

pork spare ribs, sustainable catch of the day, sandwiches (pulled pork, fried chicken, or beef brisket), citrus herb-crusted Cornish game hen, and BBQ tofu. The dessert menu tempts with maple bacon parfait (salted cookie crumble, chantilly cream, candied bacon, and bacon pepita brittle) and seasonal parfait. Children's meals are available. Lunch and dinner may include a ticket for same-day, premium viewing of Fantasmic!—as part of a Dining Package (see page 112). With a lovely interior, it's just as pleasant to dine inside as it is out. Menu items are subject to change during 2020. **L** **D** **$–$$**

FAST FOOD & SNACKS

RANCHO DEL ZOCALO: Big Thunder Mountain Railroad's neighbor, this Frontierland eatery features south-of-the-border specialties. Several of the usual

PHOTO BY JILL SAFRO

Mexican dishes, including soft tacos and burritos, along with selections such as fire-grilled citrus chicken, carne asada, nachos topped with beef or chicken, chile relleno, tostada salad, and Mexican-inspired Caesar salad, are sure to hit the spot. For dessert, there's flan, cinnamon crisps, and fresh fruit. **L D S** **$**

PHOTO BY JILL SAFRO

GOLDEN HORSESHOE: Head to this (dry) saloon for chicken tenders, fish and chips, loaded potato skins, and salad with grilled chicken. Wash it down with a refreshing soft drink. The kids' menu offers chicken sliders. Cap off the meal with an ice cream sundae. Seating is on a first-come, first-served basis. Disneyland purists may remember that the Golden Horseshoe Revue was one of Disneyland's original 18 attractions and was the world's longest-running stage show (July 17, 1955–October 12, 1986). **L D S** **$**

SHIP TO SHORE MARKETPLACE: Nestled near the shores of the Rivers of America, this satisfying snack stand sells turkey legs, fresh fruit, buttered corn on the cob, chimichangas, frozen lemonade, soft drinks, and hot cocoa. **S** **$**

Sweet Treats

Sweet teeth may be satisfied at a plethora of places in Disneyland Park. After passing through the turnstiles, make a beeline for Main Street, U.S.A., and the Jolly Holiday Bakery Cafe, the Gibson Girl Ice Cream Parlor, or the Candy Palace, which has tasty salt-water taffy. And by all means, sample a churro (fried dough rolled in cinnamon and sugar) from a food cart—it's quite popular. Finally, no trip to the "happiest place on earth" is complete without savoring the classic frozen pineapple treat known simply as the Dole Whip. The line at the Tiki Juice Bar is often long, but for many a Dole Whip fan, it's well worth the wait.

STAGE DOOR CAFE: In the mood for one of Disneyland's famous hand-dipped corn dogs? Head here. This small stand, which adjoins the Golden Horseshoe Stage, also serves fish and chips, chicken nuggets, funnel cakes, and soft drinks. Grab a seat at an outdoor table. **L D S** **$**

FANTASYLAND

FAST FOOD & SNACKS

EDELWEISS SNACKS: Next door to the Matterhorn, this chalet-style kiosk can supply a quick post-ride pick-me-up in the form of jumbo turkey legs, chimichangas, buttered or chili-lime corn on the cob, chips, and soft drinks (including frozen beverages). **S** **$**

TROUBADOUR TAVERN: Located within the Fantasyland Theatre (home of the Mickey and the Magical Map stage show), this spot dispenses bratwurst in a garlic-and-herb brioche bun with hickory smoked sauerkraut, stuffed baked potatoes, jumbo pretzel with cheese sauce, turkey legs, frozen treats, and soft drinks. **B L S** **$**

RED ROSE TAVERNE: This eatery, with its gables, pointy roof, and wavy-glass windows, could easily have been relocated to Fantasyland from that small provincial town in Disney's *Beauty and the Beast*. Breakfast items include breakfast burgers, egg platters, pancakes, and French toast. The lunch/dinner menu offers cheeseburgers, chicken sandwiches, veggie sandwiches, flatbreads, chopped salad with grilled chicken, crispie treats, "grey stuff" mousse, and soft drinks. We dig Gaston's Famous Brew—a refreshing apple-mango punch topped with passion fruit foam. Kids' meals are available. This eatery replaced Village Haus. **B L D S** **$**

MICKEY'S TOONTOWN

FAST FOOD & SNACKS

CLARABELLE'S: On Toon Square, adjacent to Pluto's Dog House, Clarabelle's specializes in "udderly" sweet treats, such as ice cream and frozen yogurt, plus sandwiches and salads. Wet your whistle with lemonade, root beer, milk, or other soft drinks. **S** **$**

DAISY'S DINER: This walk-up window serves up individual cheese and pepperoni pizzas. Assorted snacks, milk (plain and chocolate), juice, sodas, and lemonade round out the menu. **L D S** $

GOOFY'S FREEZE: The vacation trailer parked by Goofy's House is a dispenser of large frozen slurpy drinks. **S** $ (Seasonal)

PLUTO'S DOG HOUSE: Nestled between Clarabelle's and Daisy's Diner, this is the place to find a hot dog served with chips or fresh fruit. Extras include sweet treats and soft drinks. The kids' meal consists of a turkey hot dog or turkey sandwich, served with a small yogurt smoothie, seasonal fruit, and low-fat milk or bottled water. **L D S** $

TOON UP TREATS: Make a pit stop near Goofy's Gas for a quick snack: whole fruit, sliced fruit, pickles, chips, juice, and bottled water, and more. **S** $

TOMORROWLAND

FAST FOOD & SNACKS

GALACTIC GRILL: This is one of the park's largest dining areas. For breakfast there's a choice of breakfast burritos, sandwiches, and French toast sticks. At lunch and dinner, choose from burgers, cheeseburgers, fried chicken sandwiches, veggie wraps, and chopped salads. Kids' selections include hamburgers and chicken nuggets. For dessert, there are ice cream sandwiches, strawberry fruit bars, and seasonal parfaits. Coffee, tea, milk, juice, and other soft drinks are served. Menu items are subject to change. **B L D** $–$$

HOT TIP!

Well-balanced options are available throughout Disneyland—and children's meals are no exception. Kids' meals generally include a small entrée, side dish, and beverage, and are served in kid-pleasing shapes and sizes. All meals come with a healthy side and a choice of low-fat milk, or water. Toddler meals are available in some spots, too. If you don't see a kids' menu, just ask—they are offered at many eateries.

REDD ROCKETT'S PIZZA PORT: Situated near the Space Mountain entrance, this food court overlooks the Moonliner and Cosmic Waves. Separate stations serve pizza, pasta, or salads, all prepared in a display kitchen.

Menu choices have included pizzas (cheese, veggie, pepperoni, and a daily special, by the slice or pie), antipasto salad, chicken Caesar salad, edamame noodle salad, chicken fusilli, and green miso pesto pasta. Soft drinks, milk, coffee, and cocoa are served. **L D S** $$

TOMORROWLAND FRUIT CART: Fruit may not sound very futuristic, but it's a healthy way to snack today *and* tomorrow. Stop here for fresh fruit, pickles, soft drinks, and more. **S** $

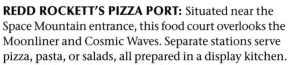

FAST FOOD & SNACKS

DOCKING BAY 7 FOOD AND CARGO: Chef Strono "Cookie" Tuggs has docked a food freighter loaded with fresh supplies and he appeases appetites with an array of exotic offerings. His flavors, while unusual, are palate-pleasing. Kids' selections are available. **B L D S** $$

MILK STAND: Vendors at this stall offer travelers a drink that's a favorite among the locals—and Luke Skywalker himself. The plant-based (non-dairy) frosty beverage comes in blue or green. Cheers! **S** $$

RONTO ROASTERS: To find this stand, just follow your nose—the tantalizing aromas of spit-roasted specialties fill the air. The menu features the Ronto Wrap (grilled sausage and roasted pork), turkey jerky (sweet or spicy) and Meiloorun Juice. The aforementioned spit, incidentally, is operated by a pit-master droid. **B L D S** $$

KAT SAKA'S KETTLE: Pop over to this snack stand for a serving of Outpost Mix—a sweet and savory popcorn-based treat. **S** $

OGA'S CANTINA: Come to the cantina to quench your thirst and rub elbows (or not!) with bounty hunters, smugglers, and travelers of all ages. As guests quaff spirited beverages such as the Jedi Mind Trick, Bad Motivator IPA, or Toniray wine, they're treated to bold musical entertainment courtesy of droid DJ R-3X, a former Starspeeder 3000 pilot. Non-alcoholic specialty drinks are served, too. Guests of all ages are welcome to enjoy Oga's hospitality, but valid ID is required for alcohol. **S** $–$$$

In Disney California Adventure

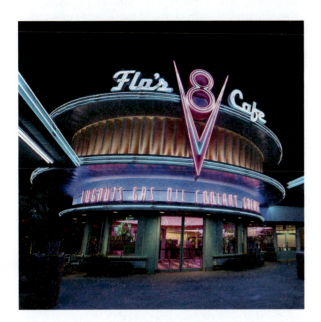

With a winery and an elegant bay-side eatery, the tastes at Disney California Adventure are clearly grown-up. But several fast-food spots and snack stands supply theme park fare with an entertaining flair—retro Hollywood decor or a seaside boardwalk setting. Just don't gorge before experiencing thrill rides.

Full-service eateries—including Lamplight Lounge, Carthay Circle Restaurant, and Wine Country Trattoria—accept reservations. Use the Disneyland mobile app or call 714-781-3463 to book a table. Details are subject to change. For updates, visit *www.disneyland.com*.

BUENA VISTA STREET

TABLE SERVICE

CARTHAY CIRCLE RESTAURANT: The original Carthay Circle Theatre was one of the best known and revered movie palaces in Hollywood history. It also happens to be where Walt Disney's *Snow White and the Seven Dwarfs* made its dazzling debut. The theatre has been re-created here at Disney California Adventure. But don't go expecting to catch a flick—this version of Carthay Circle Restaurant is actually a popular signature restaurant. Menu items such as fried cheddar-stuffed biscuits, firecracker duck wings, ceviche of citrus-marinated cobia, seasonal soup, and sustainable fish earn rave reviews. Reservations are recommended. Walk-ins may be accommodated in the lounge. **L D $$$-$$$$**

FAST FOOD & SNACKS

CLARABELLE'S HAND-SCOOPED ICE CREAM: Cones, shakes, and sundaes are the frosty treats served here. The specialty of the house is hand-dipped ice cream bars. Simply choose your bar flavor, milk or dark chocolate for dipping, and a topping (Mickey-shaped candy confetti, chocolate chips, blue raspberry bursts, and more). Sweet! **S $**

FIDDLER, FIFER & PRACTICAL CAFE: Named for everyone's favorite trio of house-building pigs, this is a great spot to quell hunger pangs and enjoy your favorite Starbucks beverage. Breakfast items, fresh-baked pastries, salads, sandwiches, yogurt, and snacks are served all day. **L D S $**

MORTIMER'S MARKET: Stop here for "the freshest fruit in town." In addition to produce, there are other healthy snacks and soft drinks from which to choose.

F.Y.I.: The Mouse was almost named Mortimer. Fortunately, Lillian Disney talked her husband into naming him Mickey! **S $**

HOLLYWOOD LAND

FAST FOOD & SNACKS

AWARD WIENERS: Hot and heaping cheese, barbecue, bacon, and chili dogs are the specialties here. Sausages and a vegetarian option round out the menu. A kids "power pack" meal may be ordered for little ones. A nearby seating area provides plenty of shaded tables (across from Disney Junior Dance Party!). **S $**

FAIRFAX MARKET: Inspired by the historic Farmers Market in Los Angeles, this alfresco stand serves whole fresh fruits, sliced mango, pineapple, and watermelon. Also gracing the menu: fresh vegetables with ranch dip, hummus, dill pickles, chips, and soft drinks. **L D S $**

SCHMOOZIES: Yogurt-and-fruit smoothies such as Mango Madness are the specialty of the house. For some, these chilly drinks are a meal unto themselves. Lemonade (served with or without a scoop of vanilla ice cream), hot tea, latte, cafe mocha, cappuccino, and ice cream topped with espresso are also available. **S** **$**

GRIZZLY PEAK

FAST FOOD & SNACKS

SMOKEJUMPERS GRILL: Paying tribute to the brave souls who parachute into forest fires, this spot serves items such as cheeseburgers, bacon cheeseburgers, spicy buffalo chicken sandwiches, BBQ jackfruit sandwiches, grilled chicken salad, chili cheese fries, and campfire chili for lunch and dinner. For dessert, there are s'mores and chocolate and vanilla shakes topped with whipped cream. **L D S** **$**

PACIFIC WHARF

TABLE SERVICE

GHIRARDELLI SODA FOUNTAIN: San Francisco's famous sweet-maker also calls Disney California Adventure home. Stop by this soda fountain for a chocolaty treat, root beer float, or a malt. There's no better place to please a sweet tooth. (And there's always the possibility of a free sample.) The coffee is tops, too—both the hot and iced varieties. **S** **$-$$**

PHOTO BY JILL SAFRO

WINE COUNTRY TRATTORIA: Located on the lower level of the mission house at the Golden Vine Winery, this bright spot offers Mediterranean fare that blends nicely with the wine list. Favorites include Caprese salad, lasagna, fettuccine shrimp Alfredo, salmon, steak, and osso bucco. There is a children's menu, too. Wines are available by the glass or the bottle.

Outdoor dining in the plaza features a fountain surrounded by herbs and flowers, conjuring images of Napa Valley. Inside, the dining room is reminiscent of an Italian villa, with plastered walls, terra-cotta tiles, and arched doorways. Reservations are recommended. **L D S** **$-$$$**

FAST FOOD & SNACKS

ALFRESCO TASTING TERRACE: One flight up from Wine Country Trattoria is an inviting lounge with a full bar and appetizers. On the menu: meatballs marinara, flatbreads, classic bruschetta, and a charcuterie and cheese board. Nibbles may be paired with wine from "Disney's Family of Wines" (available by the glass or the bottle). There is a full bar at the ready. The terrace offers guests a great view of Cars Land. **L S** **$$-$$$**

COCINA CUCAMONGA MEXICAN GRILL: Come here for authentic street-style Mexican cuisine, inspired by family favorites of Mexico and Southern California. Among the taco selections are steak, chicken, and pork. Non-taco selections include bowls filled with marinated steak, chicken, or pork with rice, black beans, queso fresco, and roasted corn, cucumber-tomato slaw. Augment your entrée with house-made tortilla chips with guacamole or salsa. Seasonal fruit is offered. Kid-friendly tacos, bowls, and quesadillas are offered. Toddlers may enjoy the arroz con pollo (chicken and rice) meal, which was crafted with their palates in mind. Details are subject to change. **L D** **$-$$**

LUCKY FORTUNE COOKERY: This walk-up eatery serves beef, chicken, or tofu with vegetables, rice, and a choice of four sauces (Mandarin orange, spicy Korean, Thai coconut curry, or teriyaki). Sides include chicken or vegetable pot stickers, mango slices, and edamame. There's a special selection for kids, too: chicken and brown rice. Menu items are subject to change. **L D** **$-$$**

MENDOCINO TERRACE WINE TASTING: Take a break beside a hand-carved stone fountain and sip local varietals in this alfresco lounge at the Golden Vine Winery. Cheese platters and cold cut plates complement the vino nicely. The extensive sipping menu includes reds, whites, rosés, ports, and sparkling wines from around the world. Sparkling apple cider and other soft drinks round out the menu. **S** **$$-$$$**

PACIFIC WHARF CAFE: Guests at this extension of Boudin's display bakery have the chance to sample some of the country's finest sourdough bread (from a secret family recipe dating back to 1850). Hearty soups such as New England clam chowder or broccoli and cheese, plus salads, are served up in thick bread bowls for lunch and dinner. Pastries are offered throughout the day. `B L D S` `$–$$`

PIXAR PIER

TABLE SERVICE

LAMPLIGHT LOUNGE: A two-story waterside retreat, the lounge is a breezy celebration of storytelling—with the spotlight on the creativity and inspirations of the folks who bring Pixar stories to life. The California casual gastro-pub offers a panoramic perspective of Pixar Pier's amusements and the Paradise Bay lagoon. The area is especially festive in the evening hours, when the boardwalk is aglow with twinkling lights. Lamplight serves small and large bites (the latter is available downstairs only). Menu items of note include (very popular) lobster nachos, tuna poke, deviled eggs and toast, crab and tuna rolls, crispy pork drumettes, along with soft drinks, beer, wine, and a slew of signature cocktails. Downstairs, diners may chow down on burgers, sandwiches, salads, ratatouille, and more—plus a dessert of warm fluffy doughnuts with chocolate dipping sauces. Reservations are highly recommended. `B L D` `$$$`

FAST FOOD & SNACKS

ADORABLE SNOWMAN FROSTED TREATS: Frozen treats are ostensibly doled out by the not-so-abominable snowman from *Monsters, Inc.* Soft-serve offerings (lemon, chocolate, and vanilla) come in cones, cups, and a specialty treat known as the Snowcapped Lemon. Helping guests cool off during a day of fun in the sun makes the snowman feel warm and fuzzy. `S` `$`

ANGRY DOGS: It seems Anger, from *Inside Out*, is channeling his rage into cooking. Head to his snack stand for hot dogs and other blazing bites. `L D S` `$`

JACK–JACK COOKIE NUM NUMS: Among the num nums that Jack-Jack is willing to share (for a price) are warm chocolate chip, shortbread, and gluten-free blackberry-jam-filled cookies—which may be washed down with milk or bottled water. `S` `$`

POULTRY PALACE: Chicken drumsticks, turkey legs, corn-on-the-cob (buttered or chili-lime), and chips are served at this waterside walk-up window. `L D S` `$–$$`

SEÑOR BUZZ CHURROS: Stop at this window for Caliente Churros (spicy), Super Galaxy Churros (with cinnamon and sugar), and soft drinks. `L D S` `$`

PARADISE GARDENS PARK

FAST FOOD & SNACKS

BOARDWALK PIZZA AND PASTA: Near the Jumpin' Jellyfish attraction, this eatery serves Italian dishes, including pizzas, pastas, and tossed salads. For dessert, choose from tiramisu, chocolate cake, and more. Meals may be enjoyed alfresco, on the shaded patio. Live entertainment provided at the Paradise Garden Bandstand is an added treat. `L D S` `$`

CORN DOG CASTLE: Juicy corn dogs, deep-fried to a golden brown and served on a handy stick, reign supreme. `L D S` `$`

PARADISE GARDEN GRILL: Despite its name, this spot offers nothing from the grill. Though the menu changes seasonally, it has been known to serve beer-battered cod, pork tacos, turkey legs, and large soft pretzels with cheese dipping sauce. Beer, wine, and soft drinks are served year-round. `L D S` `$`

CARS LAND

FAST FOOD & SNACKS

COZY CONE MOTEL: Sally's cozy motel has been converted to a colorful eatery in Radiator Springs. Here guests may find items such as bacon mac and cheese cones, soft-serve ice cream cones, pop "cone," and chili "cone" queso. Soft drinks of note include Ramone's Pear of Dice Soda and Red's Apple Freeze. `L D S` `$`

FILLMORE'S TASTE-IN: Guests here fuel up on healthy snacks like fresh fruit and crunchy vegetables, chips, and soft drinks. It's the perfect place for a speedy and refreshing pit stop. `S` `$`

FLO'S V8 CAFE: Inspired by classic roadside diners, Flo serves comfort food along the lines of fried chicken, sandwiches (turkey club or tuna), Cobb salad, cheeseburgers, and shakes (vanilla, chocolate, or strawberry). There's indoor and outdoor seating. `L D S` `$–$$`

DISNEYLAND HOTEL

The diverse dining possibilities here range from grand to Goofy. For reservations up to 60 days in advance, visit *www.disneyland.com*, use the Disneyland Resort app, or call 714-781-3463.

THE COFFEE HOUSE: Order bagels, muffins, pastries, fruit, yogurt, cold cereal, and coffee in this small but busy shop. Sandwiches are added to the menu at lunchtime. As the name indicates, this place specializes in fresh-brewed coffee—with everything from a simple cup of decaf to a cafe mocha and ice-blended latte. Outside seating only. Expect long lines in the morning hours. **B L S $**

GOOFY'S KITCHEN: This whimsical dining room features popular meals and personal encounters with Goofy and other Disney characters. Service here is buffet style, so fill your plate as high and as often as you please. Just be sure to clean that plate!

Highlights at brunch include Mickey Mouse–shaped waffles, made-to-order omelets, and Goofy's famous peanut-butter-and-jelly pizza (a favorite with youngsters and Birnbaum editors alike). Dinner offers a carving

station, catch of the day, macaroni and cheese, pizzas, salads, breads, fruit, and desserts. Don't forget a camera—Disney characters provide prime photo opps. Reservations are required. (Same-day reservations may be secured via *www.disneyland.com* up to 20 minutes in advance, based on availability.) **Brunch D $$–$$$**

STEAKHOUSE 55: An upscale dining establishment, Steakhouse 55 is decorated with oak paneling and etched glass and has a nostalgic Hollywood motif featuring pictures of the matinee idols of yesteryear. But the real stars here are the steaks, all cooked to perfection. The menu also boasts lamb, chicken, and seafood selections. Specialties of the house include a bone-in rib eye with the signature Steakhouse 55 rub, and Maryland crab cakes. The impressive wine list touts several fine California vintages. Breakfast selections include steak and eggs, German apple pancake, chicken and waffles, and pork belly chilaquiles. Traditional afternoon tea service is offered on Friday, Saturday, and Sunday from noon to 3 P.M. Reservations are recommended. Menu specifics are subject to change. **B D $$$$**

TANGAROA TERRACE TROPICAL BAR & GRILL: Visit this eatery and travel back in time. The retro-tiki design was inspired by the Tahitian Terrace restaurant—a longtime Adventureland staple. The fare at this casual counter-service restaurant, however, is decidedly modern. The breakfast menu includes French toast topped with warm banana-caramel sauce, pineapple pancakes, a scrambled egg breakfast platter; and a breakfast sandwich with pulled-pork, fried egg, brown gravy, and chives served with fruit. All-day items include Hawaiian cheeseburgers (with teriyaki sauce, bacon, and grilled pineapple), salad with sautéed shrimp, and Kalua-style

HOT TIP!

You may encounter a very long line at The Coffee House in the morning. If so, head to Downtown Disney's Earl of Sandwich, La Brea Bakery, or Starbucks for breakfast and/or a cup of coffee.

poutine with pork, cheese curds, and brown gravy. For dinner, choose from chili garlic edamame, pu pu platter, sweet-and-spicy chicken wings, pork gyoza, nachos with pulled pork, and more. The kids' menu includes chicken breast nuggets, grilled salmon, and burgers. There is a small grab-and-go selection, too (mostly fruit and pastries). **B L D S** **$–$$**

DISNEY'S PARADISE PIER HOTEL

The eatery here has all the bases covered—from beer-battered fish or zucchini tacos to dry-rubbed smoked steak. And wait till you see what Donald has cooked up for breakfast! For reservations at the PCH Grill, call 714-781-3463.

DISNEY'S PCH GRILL: Disney's PCH Grill—the initials stand for Pacific Coast Highway—reflects classic California tastes. The morning meal is known as Donald Duck's Seaside Breakfast. It offers a bountiful buffet and the chance to mingle with Donald, Daisy, and Stitch. Diners nosh on breakfast flatbreads, egg white frittatas, smoked salmon, smoothies, made-to-order omelets, and more. Dinner—a character-free, buffet affair—offers a California/Italian menu featuring

HOT TIP!

Any full-service dining location at a Disneyland Resort hotel will validate your parking at that hotel; remember to get your parking pass stamped before you leave.

HOT TIP!

Napa Rose's adjoining lounge offers the restaurant's full menu, as well as its impressive wine list. It's an excellent option for diners without reservations.

build-your-own pasta dishes, sustainable fish, create-your-own salads, and pizzas. The kids' section has mac and cheese, chicken nuggets, corn on the cob, and hot dogs. For dessert, consider tiramasu, cannolis, panna cotta, mini pastries, and Italian rum cake. Reservations are suggested. **B D** **$$**

SURFSIDE LOUNGE: A lobby lounge, Surfside serves hearty fare throughout the day. This spot covers all the bases, serving breakfast burritos, buffalo wings, chicken and waffles, seared salmon burgers, steak, soup, salads, sundaes and more. **B L D S** **$–$$**

THE SAND BAR: This rooftop stop offers a full bar, plus hot dogs, sandwiches, soft drinks, and snacks. **S** **$**

DISNEY'S GRAND CALIFORNIAN HOTEL & SPA

The restaurants at this resort offer a taste of (and a bit of a twist on) California cuisine. To make reservations, visit *www.disneyland.com*, or call 714-781-3463.

NAPA ROSE: This popular, nationally recognized, award-winning restaurant features a creative menu of market-fresh, wine country-inspired dishes flavored by fruits of the sea and vine (the eatery is named after California's most famous valley of vineyards). A striking, 20-foot, stained-glass window offers views of Disney California Adventure, while the open kitchen gives insight into California cooking.

The offerings evolve as new items are introduced, but favorites include grilled diver scallops with porcini butter bacon whipped potatoes and English pea coulis; roasted Colorado lamb rack chops, heirloom Berkshire pork loin, filet mignon, and market fish of the day. The dessert menu offers delectable creations: artisanal ice cream, pumpkin custard bar, warm California fig crumble bar, and honey crisp apple confit. Kid-friendly entrées and desserts are served. The California wine list is one of the most extensive on-property.

A character breakfast is presented Thursday through Monday from 8 A.M. until noon. The three-course "Princess Fairytale Breakfast Adventures" cost about $125 (plus tax and gratuity) for all guests age 3 and older. The breakfast adventure includes a personal princess portrait moment and a special keepsake. Reservations are suggested. **B D** **$$$$**

HEARTHSTONE LOUNGE: Though primarily a drinking spot, this lounge offers appetizers and is open in the morning for early risers in search of a fresh-brewed cup of joe. Continental breakfast items—including specialty coffees—are also available. **B S** **$**

STORYTELLERS CAFE: It's hard to imagine a time before computers and smartphones (especially for the youngest members of the group), when children were exposed to new cultures and histories only through the stories of others. This restaurant salutes tales set in the state of California, like "The Celebrated Jumping Frog of Calaveras County" and *Island of the Blue Dolphins*, through murals that act as backdrops to the chefs at work in the exhibition kitchen. In the morning, the stage is set for a festive, character-hosted buffet known as Mickey's Tales of Adventure Breakfast. Mickey Mouse and other Disney characters engage guests throughout the meal. The buffet offers a feast of breakfast options, with oatmeal, bagels with lox, eggs (including made-to-order omelets), sausage, and a selection of fresh fruit. The brunch buffet includes all breakfast offerings, plus pancakes, waffles, a carving station and more. The

dinner menu features artisanal pizzas, pastas, steak, salads, seafood, and chicken.

Mickey's Tales of Adventure Character Breakfast is offered daily from 7 A.M until 2 P.M. Reservations are recommended for all meals. **B D** **$$-$$$**

WHITE WATER SNACKS: The splish-splash of the waterfall and kids soaring down the slide at the Redwood pool set the mood for this elegant casual dining spot. Recently refurbished, White Water is open for all meals (though hours vary). The snack bar serves fresh-brewed coffee, muffins, and made-to-order breakfast selections in the morning. Housemade sandwiches, poke bowls, skewers, burgers, avocado toast, soup, hot dogs, artisanal pizzas, and chicken-fried brisket and waffle are lunch and dinner options. Other items that may be offered: candy, fruit, yogurt, cereal, soft drinks, beer, and wine. Details subject to change. **B L D S** **$**

POOL BAR: The Grand Californian Resort's Arts and Crafts theme extends to this new watering hole, located near the Redwood Pool. Beer, wine, cocktails, soft drinks, and appetizers are served. **S** **$-$$**

In Downtown Disney District

TABLE SERVICE

BALLAST POINT: Complete with an on-site brewery, Ballast Point pairs its award-winning beers with an extensive menu of Southern California cuisine—salads, small plates, flatbreads, and entrées featuring local, sustainable, and seasonal ingredients. In addition to the aforementioned brewery, this sleek space houses a tasting room, kitchen, and outdoor beer garden. You can save money at Ballast Point by using the coupon at the back of this book. **L D S** **$$–$$$**

BLACK TAP CRAFT BURGERS & SHAKES: A casual burger and shake destination, Black Tap has a casual atmosphere that's a bit reminiscent of an old-time American luncheonette. Guests may dine in- or outdoors, enjoying burgers, chicken wings, sandwiches, salads, fried pickles, and crispy Brussels sprouts. Shakes (of the classic and "crazy" varieties), beer, wine, and soft drinks round out the menu. The new eatery is across from Catal Restaurant & Uva Bar. **B L D S** **$$**

CATAL RESTAURANT & UVA BAR: A sun-kissed balcony, outdoor tapas bar, and villa-style dining room set the Mediterranean mood at this restaurant. The menu focuses on grilled seafood, chicken, and vegetables, infused with olive oil and citrus accents. With pastas and salads available, vegetarians have much to choose from here. Reservations are suggested; 714-774-4442. **B L D** **$$$**

LA BREA BAKERY: Many offerings at this destination—breakfast treats and classic sandwiches—are built on La Brea's legendary, freshly made bread. Also available are salads (with organic greens), soups, and coffees. There is counter service and a covered patio with table service. **B L D S** **$–$$**

NAPLES RISTORANTE E BAR: Dine inside or alfresco at this contemporary Italian trattoria. A large outdoor terrace provides perfect views of the Disney landscape, plus a peaceful and romantic setting for lunch or dinner. Pizzas are served in individual portions or al metro (one meter long and perfect for a hungry family to share). The menu includes piccoli piatti (small plates), pastas, and seafood. There's a new outdoor bar, too. For reservations, call 714-776-6200. **L D** **$$$**

RALPH BRENNAN'S JAZZ KITCHEN: Sample some home-style New Orleans specialties at this comfy cafe while listening to jazz. Gumbo, jambalaya, chicken, and fresh pasta dishes are house favorites. Reservations are suggested; 714-776-5200. **L D S** **$$–$$$**

SPLITSVILLE LUXURY LANES™: Some go expecting just to bowl, not realizing that Splitsville's kitchen turns out impressive casual fare such as freshly rolled sushi, grilled salmon, smokehouse chicken, seared ahi tuna, and sliders. They've also got taco bowls, pizzas, cheeseburgers, fish 'n' chips, sandwiches, and salads. Many menu items are gluten free. Super-sized desserts include sundaes, brownies, "giant cake," and root beer floats. There is a full bar. Reservations are suggested, but walk-ins may be accommodated. **L D S** **$$–$$$**

TORTILLA JO'S: A table-service Mexican restaurant and open-air cantina, this spot offers culinary traditions including freshly prepared tamales, carnitas, and fajitas, made-to-order guacamole, and lime-marinated ceviche. Reservations are recommended; 714-535-5000. The adjacent Taqueria serves classic Mexican quick-service selections. **L D S** **$$–$$$**

FAST FOOD & SNACKS

DIGGITY DOGS: A handy spot for a portable bite, Diggity Dogs may be found near the World of Disney shop. Do you like the idea of buying a hot dog and getting one for free? Use the coupon at the back of this book! **L D S** **$**

JAMBA JUICE: In the mood for a tropical smoothie? Perhaps one with protein or a berry blast? They've got that and more. **S** **$**

KAYLA'S CAKE: Come to this kiosk for homemade premium macarons—and save some money on your purchase by using the coupon at the end of this book. Sweet! **S** **$**

SALT & STRAW: All of the ice cream at Salt & Straw is handmade with local, organic, and sustainable ingredients. It's all super yummy, too. **S** **$**

LA BREA BAKERY EXPRESS: Nestled within La Brea Bakery, this convenient counter also offers freshly prepared breakfast selections including steel-cut oatmeal, brioche French toast, and bacon-and-egg paninis. The lunch and dinner menu features personal pizzas, paninis, salads, and soups served in bread bowls. Sweet treats include gelato and sorbet. Kids' meals are available, as is a selection of grab-and-go items. Specialty coffee drinks are brewed all day long. **B L D S** **$–$$**

NAPOLINI PIZZERIA: Adjacent to the popular Naples Ristorante e Bar, this newly renovated quick-service eatery specializes in customized "build-your own" pizzas, hearty sandwiches, fresh salads, and traditional desserts. **L D** **$$**

RALPH BRENNAN'S JAZZ KITCHEN EXPRESS: A good venue for a quick breakfast, this counter spot offers breakfast platters, burritos, and sandwiches, plus cereal and cinnamon "French toast" dippers (sticks cut from classic beignets). Lunch and dinner bring more N'awlin's favorites to the table: popcorn shrimp, red beans and rice, gumbo ya ya, and jambalaya. Burgers, po' boy sandwiches, and kids' meals are also served (popcorn chicken and corn dog nuggets), as is housemade bread pudding. Deliciously decadent beignets topped with powdered sugar are available throughout the day. **B L D S** **$–$$**

STARBUCKS: The familiar coffeehouse has two Downtown Disney locations: next to the World of

HOT TIP!

Want to save a little money at Downtown Disney? Visit *www.disneyland.com* to see if there are any special offers available for the day you plan to visit—and use the coupons at the back of this book!

Disney store and near the LEGO store. In addition to a full menu of coffee drinks, there are teas, smoothies, pastries, breakfast sandwiches, snacks, packaged coffee, and more. Both spots are popular—build in a little extra time to get that java jolt. **B L D S** **$**

PHOTO BY JILL SAFRO

TAQUERIA AT TORTILLA JO'S: Are you craving tacos y cerveza? Get your fill at this festive courtyard adjacent (logically) to Tortilla Jo's. In addition to tacos and Mexican beer (served at lunch and dinner), Taqueria invites you to indulge in breakfast selections along the lines of burritos, huevos rancheros, and chilaquiles (tortilla chips cooked with salsa and topped with cheese, scrambled eggs and sour cream). Later in the day, look for customizable burritos, nachos, bowls, and tacos. Wash it down with a margarita, beer, or soft drink. *Salúd!* For dessert, consider cookies, brownies, fresh fruit, or a Mexican ice pop (aka paleta). Kids' meals are offered at lunch and dinner. **B L D S** **$–$$**

WETZEL'S PRETZELS: Whether you prefer pretzels salty or sweet, Wetzel's can satisfy. Ambitious snackers enjoy the Sinful Cinnamon and the Cheese Meltdown. Buy one, get one free with the coupon at the back of this book. **S** **$**

RESTAURANT ROUNDUP

There are more dining choices than ever before at the Disneyland Resort. We've picked some favorites, based on food quality, restaurant atmosphere, and overall value. Use these Birnbaum's Bests to help you decide where to grab a quick bite or have a hearty meal.

BEST RESTAURANTS FOR FAMILIES

TABLE SERVICE

Goofy's Kitchen .... Disneyland Hotel (p. 120)
Blue Bayou .... Disneyland Park (p. 113)
Storytellers Cafe .... Grand Californian Hotel (p. 122)
Plaza Inn .... Disneyland Park (p. 111)

QUICK SERVICE

Royal Street Veranda .... Disneyland Park (p. 114)
Rancho del Zocalo .... Disneyland Park (p. 114)
Refreshment Corner Cafe .... Disneyland Park (p. 112)
Pacific Wharf Cafe .... Disney California Adventure (p. 118)
Flo's V8 Cafe .... Disney California Adventure (p. 119)

BEST RESTAURANTS FOR ADULTS

Napa Rose .... Grand Californian Hotel (p. 121)
Steakhouse 55 .... Disneyland Hotel (p. 120)

RUNNERS-UP

Carthay Circle .... Disney California Adventure (p. 117)
Lamplight Lounge .... Disney California Adventure (p. 119)
Wine Country Trattoria .... Disney California Adventure (p. 118)

BEST CHARACTER MEAL

Goofy's Kitchen .... Disneyland Hotel (p. 120)

RUNNERS-UP

Disney's PCH Grill .... Paradise Pier Hotel (p. 121)
Plaza Inn .... Disneyland Park (p. 111)
Storytellers Cafe .... Grand Californian Hotel (p. 122)

BEST SNACKS

Jolly Holiday Bakery Cafe .... Disneyland Park (p. 110)
Tropical Hideaway .... Disneyland Park (p. 112)

BEST LOUNGE

Trader Sam's Enchanted Tiki Bar ....
     Disneyland Hotel (p. 126)

RUNNERS-UP

Lamplight Lounge ....
     Disney California Adventure (p. 119)
Tangaroa Terrace Tropical Bar & Grill ....
     Disneyland Hotel (p. 120)

BEST QUICK SERVICE

Flo's V8 Cafe ....
     Disney California Adventure (p. 119)

BEST SANDWICHES

La Brea Bakery ....
     Downtown Disney (p. 123)

BEST PIZZA

Naples Ristorante e Bar ....
     Downtown Disney (p. 123)

Entertainment
Disney Hotels

The Disneyland Resort has more to offer than theme park attractions. There's plenty to do at Disney's three hotels and in the Downtown Disney dining, shopping, and entertainment district. Whether you're seeking a break from the parks or a place to party the night away, the following options are sure to please.

Note: For additional information on theme park entertainment, refer to the *Disneyland Park* and *Disney California Adventure* chapters of this book.

LOUNGES

DISNEYLAND HOTEL: The **Lounge at Steakhouse 55**, with its comfortable leather sofas, convenient conversation areas, and sophisticated decor, provides an intimate meeting place. It features a full bar, plus appetizer menu (for guests seated in the lounge area). Those seated at the bar may order from the full Steakhouse 55 menu—a bonus for those caught without reservations to the popular, neighboring eatery. The boisterous **Trader Sam's Enchanted Tiki Bar**, named for the infamous "head" salesman at the Jungle Cruise (he'll gladly trade you two of his heads for one of yours), mixes drinks and light bites with a bit of Disney magic.

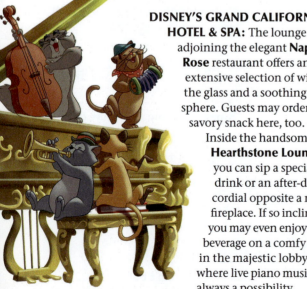

DISNEY'S GRAND CALIFORNIAN HOTEL & SPA: The lounge adjoining the elegant **Napa Rose** restaurant offers an extensive selection of wines by the glass and a soothing atmosphere. Guests may order a savory snack here, too. Inside the handsome **Hearthstone Lounge**, you can sip a specialty drink or an after-dinner cordial opposite a roaring fireplace. If so inclined, you may even enjoy your beverage on a comfy couch in the majestic lobby, where live piano music is always a possibility.

HOT TIP!
Trader Sam's Enchanted Tiki Bar usually hosts brave adventurers daily from about 11:30 A.M. until 1 A.M. (or later). Young explorers are welcome to enjoy nibbles and "no booze brews" until 8 P.M.—after that, this lounge is strictly available to guests over the age of 21 (with valid government-issued photo ID to prove it).

Guests staying at Disney's Grand Californian may also relax and unwind at a new lounge near the resort's Redwood Pool.

DISNEY'S PARADISE PIER HOTEL: The Surfside Lounge in the resort's lobby serves hot breakfast items in the morning and light fare (burgers, salads, sandwiches, snacks, and more) throughout the day. Out by the pool, you'll find The Sandbar. This rooftop spot serves beer, wine, cocktails, soft drinks, and snacks.

LIVE ENTERTAINMENT

DISNEY'S GRAND CALIFORNIAN HOTEL & SPA: As a tribute to the early 1900s storytelling tradition, entertainers tell tall tales in the hotel's main lobby during the evening hours. A piano player adds to the ambience. The Grand Quest, recommended for guests with kids ages 3 to 12, invites explorers to search for clues in a scavenger hunt through the hotel. Visit the Guest Services desk for details.

SPA SERVICES

DISNEY'S GRAND CALIFORNIAN HOTEL & SPA: A spa escape is as welcome a diversion as they come—especially when it's a visit to the world-class pampering palace known as **Mandara Spa**. Treatments include all manner of massage, facials, body wraps, manicures, pedicures, and more. There are services specially tailored for couples and teens. For a complete list of services, go to *MandaraSpa.com*. To make an appointment, call 714-300-7350.

Downtown Disney

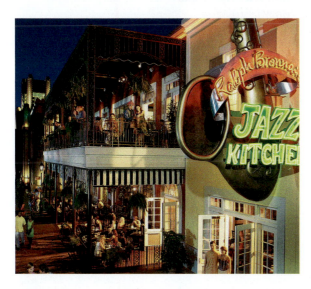

Easily accessed by foot (from the Disneyland Resort hotels or theme parks) or monorail (from Disneyland Park's Tomorrowland), this entertainment district offers a break from the theme park hustle and bustle during the day and a busy place to mix and mingle in the evening. Many Downtown Disney venues serve double (sometimes triple!) duty as dining, playing, and shopping spots.

Shops open early and don't close until late in the evening. Performers generally hit the stage post-dinner and wrap by midnight.

LOUNGES & ENTERTAINMENT

BALLAST POINT: Featuring a modern, on-site brewery, Ballast Point pairs its award-winning beers with a lineup of Southern California cuisine—salads, small plates, flatbreads, and entrées featuring local, sustainable and seasonal ingredients. In addition to the aforementioned brewery, this sleek venue houses a tasting room, kitchen, and outdoor beer garden. Ballast Point is located across from Catal Restaurant and Uva Bar. **L D S $$–$$$**

BLACK TAP CRAFT BURGERS & SHAKES: A colorful burger and beer joint, Black Tap has a casual atmosphere reminiscent of a classic American luncheonette, with a distinctly New York vibe. Guests may sit in- or outdoors, enjoying burgers, chicken wings, sandwiches, salads, fried pickles, crispy Brussels sprouts, and more. Shakes (classic and "crazy"), beer, wine, and soft drinks round out the menu. **B L D S $**

CATAL RESTAURANT & UVA BAR: Meant to resemble the Art Nouveau style of a Paris metro station, this large wine and tapas bar tempts guests with the fruits of the vine and sea. Guests can drink under the stars at the outdoor bar or mingle indoors, and can select from the extensive wine list.

OUTDOOR PERFORMERS: Downtown Disney boasts an eclectic lineup of free, live musical entertainment. From calming classical to rousing rhythm and blues, professional musicians create a party-like atmosphere every day. For updated entertainment schedules, follow @Disneylandtoday on Twitter. Text DTDNOW to DPARK (37275) to receive up to three updates via text per week, or visit *www.disneyland.disney.go.com/downtown-disney/*.

RALPH BRENNAN'S JAZZ KITCHEN—FLAMBEUX'S JAZZ CLUB: The sounds of jazz set the tone for the relaxed atmosphere at this restaurant's lounge. Bands and singers entertain with live jazz every evening. A smooth soundtrack provides music when the stage is dark. Special tickets may be required for certain performances. Call 714-776-5200 to inquire about ticket prices and reservations.

SHOPPING

CURL SURF: You have to figure that anybody who spent not one but 17 years as a champion water-skier has to know quite a bit about trends in beachwear and water-sport equipment. See for yourself at this high-end surf shop by Sammy Duvall. Among the wares you will discover are sunglasses, jewelry, earphones, watches, activewear, and shoes.

THE DISNEY DRESS SHOP: Get dolled up, Disney style! The shop carries an assortment of detailed dresses and accessories with a decidedly Disney design. Each item pays homage to a beloved character or attraction: Alice in Wonderland, Minnie Mouse, Snow White, the Haunted Mansion, It's a Small World, and more. Such fetching, fashion-forward accessories as handbags, hats, and jewelry are available, too. This spot is sure to please your inner Dapper Dana.

DISNEY HOME: If you're like the merry multitudes who would happily call Disneyland home, you're in luck: This new shop lets Disney devotees add pixie-dusted touches to their actual homes. Many items vary seasonally, but D.H. always offers fans a variety of Disney-themed treasures: glasswear, linens, kitchen goods, and more. Here's to the happiest home on earth!

DISNEY PIN TRADERS: Do we really need to spell out what this spot specializes in? Didn't think so.

THE LEGO STORE: Hundreds of the world's most famous building brick sets and products are for sale here. There's a play area, too. The shop hosts workshops and LEGO Club meetings for LEGO enthusiasts of all ages. It's across from Disney Pin Traders.

PHOTO BY JILL SAFRO

MARCELINE'S CONFECTIONERY: Named for Walt Disney's boyhood hometown in Missouri, Marceline's offers candies, pastries, and other sweet treats. It's fun to watch the candymakers at work.

PANDORA JEWELRY: Known for its customizable bracelets, PANDORA also offers gold and silver necklaces, rings, earrings, and charms—many featuring accents like gemstones, cultured pearls, Murano glass, and cubic zirconia.

SANUK: Retire those pinchy old shoes and replace them with comfy footwear at Sanuk. In addition to "sidewalk surfers" for kids and grown-ups, this shop sells hats, hoodies, T-shirts, and more.

   F.Y.I.: *Sanuk* is the Thai word for fun. Note that the shoes stretch a bit with wear—so don't worry if they are a tad snug when you first put them on.

SEPHORA: A black-and-white motif provides the backdrop for the colorful palette of products in this cosmetics mecca. Sephora's own line of makeup is complemented by a selection of beauty products and designer fragrances.

SPRINKLES: "The world's first cupcake bakery," as dubbed by Food Network, the Beverly Hills–based Sprinkles now serves said signature cakes, slow-churned ice cream, and cookies at the Downtown Disney District.

SUGARBOO & COMPANY: Sugarboo is out to make the world a better place through uplifting art prints, charming home goods, and fanciful paper products. This "dealer in whimsy" is next to Starbucks, near the monorail station.

SUNGLASS ICON: Custom-fit shades are the stock-in-trade at this shop. All the big-name designers are represented here.

WORLD OF DISNEY: The shelves are stacked sky-high at this newly refurbished, souvenir seeker's go-to. With areas dedicated to plush toys, dolls, home decor, clothing, and collectibles, everyone is bound to find something here. The place is busy most evenings and weekends—especially after the parks close for the day.

WONDERGROUND GALLERY: Notably distinctive and eclectic, Wonderground is a work of art in and of itself. The contemporary venue showcases unique art collections and works from a new generation of artists, interpreted through various mediums, styles, and forms.

FUN & GAMES

SPLITSVILLE LUXURY LANES™: Boasting bowling, bars, finger food, upscale menu offerings, and more, Splitsville offers something for just about everyone—however, some areas are zoned exclusively for folks over age 21 (with valid government-issued photo ID to prove it). The venue features 30 bowling lanes, a high-end kitchen, specialty drinks, live music—and billiards! For details, visit *www.splitsvillelanes.com*.

STAR WARS: SECRETS OF THE EMPIRE: Here's a chance to join the Rebellion! A "hyper-reality" experience, from ILMxLab and The VOID, this adventure immerses Jedi wannabes in the Star Wars universe. Surrounded by 3-D imagery and sound, guests move about freely while virtually interacting with Star Wars characters—as well as each other—in a multi-sensory environment.

   A second VR experience, based on the Disney film *Ralph Breaks the Internet*, may also be available.

   Guests must be at least 48 inches tall and 10 years old to participate. Those under age 18 must have a parent or guardian's signature. Tickets start at about $30 (plus tax) and may be pre-ordered at *thevoid.com*. This attraction is not operated by The Walt Disney Company. Pricing and details are subject to change without notice.

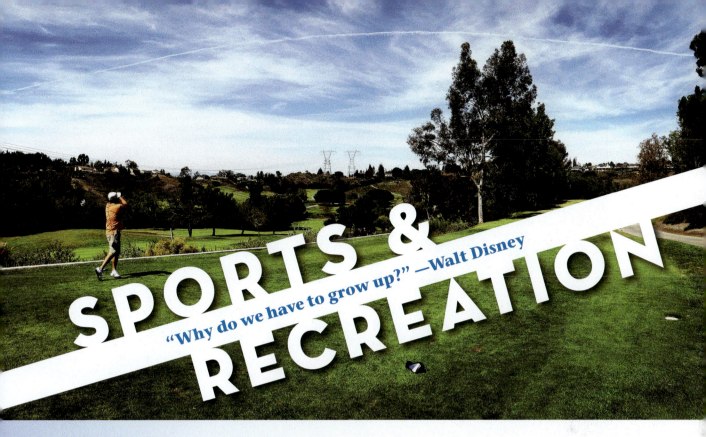

SPORTS & RECREATION

"Why do we have to grow up?" —Walt Disney

Southern California's combination of warm, sunny weather and invigorating ocean breezes has created a population of outdoors and exercise enthusiasts. Athletes flex their muscles on golf courses and tennis courts; atop surfboards, bikes, and in-line skates; on hiking and jogging trails; or 15 feet underwater, mingling with shimmering schools of fish.

As part of Orange County, California, Anaheim is within easy distance of the county's 35,000-plus acres of parkland and several hundred miles of bike trails. Hiking paths and fishing streams crisscross 460,000 acres of mountain terrain in Cleveland National Forest. Just 15 miles south of Anaheim, prime Pacific Ocean beaches—perfect for basking in the sun or catching the ultimate wave—await the wayfarer. In fact, 42 miles of glistening sand and sleepy seaside communities are within an hour's drive of Anaheim.

Those who delight in spying on Mother Nature can catch glimpses of California's gray whales as they migrate to Mexico for the winter, or ospreys, blue herons, and swallows returning to the area in the spring. A team of Orange County's most entertaining creatures, hockey-playing Ducks, can be spotted from September through April (and later, if they make a run for the Stanley Cup). Even Angels have been sighted, gracing the bases at Angel Stadium, April through September (and possibly October).

No doubt about it, the sporting opportunities in and around the city of Anaheim, California, are quite bountiful indeed.

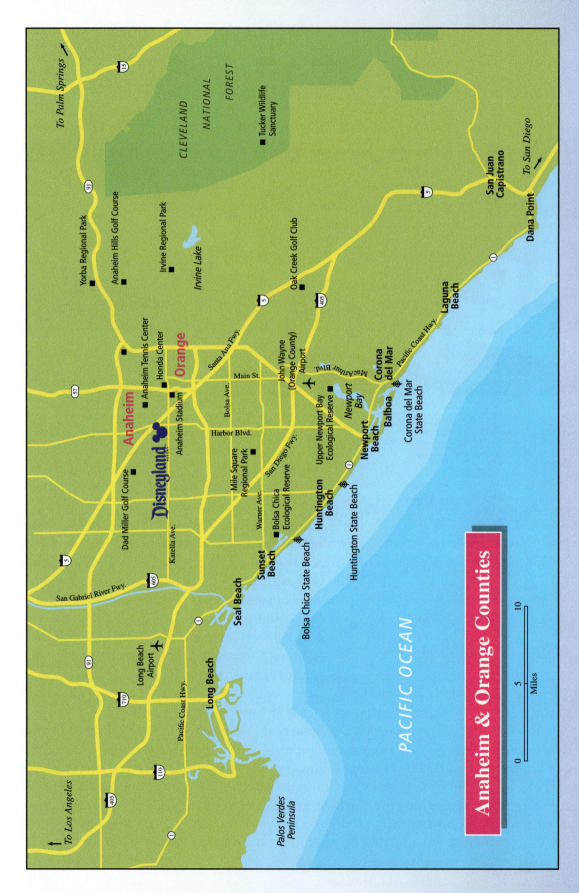

Anaheim & Orange Counties

To Palm Springs

CLEVELAND NATIONAL FOREST

Tucker Wildlife Sanctuary

To San Diego

San Juan Capistrano

Dana Point

Yorba Regional Park

Anaheim Hills Golf Course

Irvine Regional Park

Irvine Lake

Oak Creek Golf Club

Laguna Beach

Pacific Coast Hwy.

Anaheim Tennis Center

Honda Center

Orange

Santa Ana Fwy.

John Wayne (Orange County) Airport

MacArthur Blvd.

Corona del Mar

Main St.

Anaheim

Anaheim Stadium

Bolsa Ave.

Newport Bay

Balboa

Corona del Mar State Beach

Disneyland RESORT

Harbor Blvd.

Upper Newport Bay Ecological Reserve

Newport Beach

Dad Miller Golf Course

Mile Square Regional Park

San Diego Fwy.

Huntington Beach

Katella Ave.

Warner Ave.

Bolsa Chica Ecological Reserve

Huntington State Beach

Sunset Beach

San Gabriel River Fwy.

Seal Beach

Bolsa Chica State Beach

PACIFIC OCEAN

Long Beach Airport

Pacific Coast Hwy.

Long Beach

To Los Angeles

Palos Verdes Peninsula

0   5   10
Miles

Eye on the Ball

GOLF

ANAHEIM HILLS GOLF COURSE: This challenging championship course is a hilly, par-71, 6,245-yard layout nestled in the valleys and slopes of the scenic Anaheim Hills. Greens fees (cart included) are $54 Monday through Thursday, $61 on Friday, and $72 on weekends and holidays. Guests age 55 and older can play Monday through Friday for $44. Clubs can be rented for $30. Reservations are recommended (call seven days ahead for both weekend and weekday play). The Anaheim Hills Golf Course is open 365 days a year, from 6 or 6:30 A.M. till sunset. 6501 Nohl Ranch Rd., Anaheim; *www.anaheimhillsgc.com*; 714-998-3041.

DAD MILLER GOLF COURSE: "Dad" Miller made a historic hole in one on this course (on the 116-yard 11th hole) when he was 93 years old, and it's still a favorite with older guests, who appreciate the flat, walkable terrain and park-like setting. But if you're a tad on the younger side, don't let that keep you from playing here. This par-71, 5,892-yard golf course is one of the busiest in California—partly because of its convenient location in the northwest corner of the city, but also because it's just right for the strictly recreational golfer. The cost to play changes daily, based on demand. Guests 60 and older can play standby for $20 Monday through Friday. Golf carts cost about $13 for 18 holes, $8.50 for nine holes.

Reservations are suggested and may be made up to a week in advance. The course is open 365 days each year, from 6 A.M. till 8 P.M. 430 N. Gilbert St., Anaheim; *www.dadmillergc.com*; 714-765-3481 (pro shop and reservations).

TENNIS

ANAHEIM TENNIS CENTER: This public facility has all the perks of a private tennis club—an inviting clubhouse, a well-stocked pro shop, computerized practice machines, lockers, and showers. The staff will make an effort to pair you with a suitable partner, as long as you make your request in advance.

There are 12 fast, hard-surface courts, all lighted for night play. Singles rates range from about $10 to $16 per hour (depending on the time of day); doubles rates are about $15 to $24 per hour, depending on time of day. Use of a ball machine is about $25 per hour; they are separated from the courts, but this area is still a good place to practice forehand and backhand strokes.

Playing hours begin at 7 A.M. and end at 10 P.M. Monday through Friday, and start at 7 A.M. and end at 6 P.M. weekends and holidays. Racquets are free for those taking lessons. Locker and shower facilities are free of charge (if you want towels, you must supply them yourself). A half-hour private lesson with the resident pro costs about $45; call for rates for semiprivate or group lessons. Reservations (which are bookable up to three days in advance for nonmembers) are suggested, especially for court times after 5 P.M. It's approximately three miles from the Disneyland Resort. 975 S. State College Boulevard, Anaheim; 714-991-9090; *www.anaheimtenniscenter.com*.

> **HOT TIP!**
> To get additional information about these and other Orange County area golf courses and tournaments, visit *www.playocgolf.com*.

POWER WALKING

DISNEY'S GRAND CALIFORNIAN HOTEL: Rise and shine! Guests staying at one of the three Disneyland Resort hotels (The Disneyland Hotel, Paradise Pier, and Disney's Grand Californian) can enjoy an early, fast-paced two-mile power walk through Disney California Adventure Park before it comes to life—or opens to the public.

The group power walk begins promptly at 6 A.M. at the Grand Californian's private entrance to the park. Participants (ages 14 and older) must maintain a 15-minute-mile pace. Guests under age 17 must be accompanied by an adult. Strollers and cameras are not permitted. (Park admission is not required, as the walk ends before the park opens.) Athletic shoes are required. The walk is not recommended for those with knee, hip, joint, or other physical limitations.

To reserve your space (a requirement), sign up at the Guest Services desk in the main lobby of any of the three Disneyland Resort hotels. There is no fee to participate. Activity time and availability are subject to change without notice. "Get Up and Go" walks may be cancelled due to inclement weather.

YOGA

THE YOGA MAT: At this yoga studio's two convenient locations, visitors can sign up for a single class ($20) or a set of five classes ($85) during their stay. Types of classes include vinyasa, blended yoga, and meditation, as well as those held by candlelight. The Anaheim location is found at 209 W. Center St. Promenade, 714-313-1614; the Orange location is at 1315-G North Tustin St., 714-403-1550. For class schedules and parking information, visit *www.theyogamatoc.com.*

YOGA AT THE HILTON ANAHEIM: Located in the lower lobby, the Health Club at Hilton Anaheim offers a yoga stretch class three days a week. A one-day pass is $16 for visitors and $14 for guests. To make a reservation, call 714-740-4431; *www.hiltonanaheimhotel.com.*

Spectator Sports

BASEBALL

Los Angeles Angels of Anaheim (April–September): Angel Stadium of Anaheim, 2000 E. Gene Autry Way, Anaheim; 714-634-2000 (info) or 714-663-9000 (tickets); *www.angelsbaseball.com*

Los Angeles Dodgers (April–September): Dodger Stadium, 1000 Elysian Park Ave., Los Angeles; call 866-363-4377; or visit *www.dodgers.com*

BASKETBALL

Los Angeles Clippers (September–April): Staples Center, 1111 S. Figueroa St., Los Angeles; 800-462-2849; *www.nba.com/clippers*

Los Angeles Lakers (October–April): Staples Center, 1111 S. Figueroa St., Los Angeles; 800-462-2849; *www.nba.com/lakers*

Los Angeles Sparks (May–September): Staples Center, 1111 S. Figueroa St., Los Angeles; 877-447-7275; *www.wnba.com/sparks*

HOCKEY

Los Angeles Kings (September–April): Staples Center, 1111 S. Figueroa St., Los Angeles; 800-745-3000 (Ticketmaster); *www.lakings.com*

Anaheim Ducks (September–April): Honda Center, 2695 E. Katella Ave., Anaheim; 877-945-3946 (information) or 800-745-3000 (Ticketmaster); *www.anaheimducks.com*

Surf & Sun

BEACHES

Orange County's public beaches cover 42 miles of coastline—some dramatic, with high cliffs and crashing waves; others tranquil, with sheltered coves and tide pools. In summer, the water temperature averages 64 degrees but can get as high as 70; in winter, it's a nippy 57 to 60 degrees.

Beaches are usually open from around 6 A.M. to 10 P.M., with lifeguards on duty in the summer. Bicycles, in-line skates, and roller skates are available for rent in some locations. Access is free, but there is usually a fee to park. For additional beach information, go to the Surf and Sand section of *www.orangecounty.net.*

BALBOA/NEWPORT BEACH: The Balboa Peninsula juts into the Pacific Ocean, creating beaches—Newport on the mainland, Balboa on the peninsula—that are long and horseshoe-shaped, pleasant and sandy, and popular with families, surfers, and sightseers alike. Visit *www.ocbeachinfo.com* for water quality and environmental information.

The largest small-craft harbor in the world, Newport Harbor shelters more than 9,000 boats. For the best view, drive south along the peninsula on Newport Boulevard to Balboa Boulevard; turn right on Palm Street, and you'll find parking for the Balboa Pier and Fun Zone; *www.balboaferriswheel.com.*

HOT TIP!

For a scenic 45-minute walk, follow the harbor-hugging pathway around Balboa Island. For a mini-expedition, head to Little Balboa Island—it can be easily circumnavigated in about 20 minutes.

Throughout the fall and winter, the 1,000-acre Upper Newport Bay Nature Preserve and Ecological Reserve teems with great blue herons, ospreys, and many other winged creatures. The park's partially subterranean Peter and Mary Muth Interpretive Center, at 2301 University Drive (at Irvine Avenue), has exhibits on bird life, the watershed, and the history of Newport Bay (closed Mondays).

During migratory season (October through March), the Newport Bay Conservancy leads several free walking tours, pointing out birds, as well as fossils, marsh plants, and fish. Every Saturday and Sunday morning, year-round, the conservancy also offers a 2-hour guided kayak tour of the Back Bay for $25 per person, ages 8 and up.

The reserve is open daily 7 A.M. to sunset. To obtain updated information about guided tours and various special events year-round, as well as directions to specific parts of the reserve, contact Newport Bay Conservancy: 949-923-2269 or *www.newportbay.org.*

CORONA DEL MAR STATE BEACH: Secluded Corona del Mar State Beach is a favorite for swimming and snorkeling; and the lookout point above the beach is a great place to watch the sun set. There are picnic tables, grills, fire rings, a snack bar, and showers. For information, visit *www.orangecounty.net* (Surf and Sand section) or call 949-644-3151.

HUNTINGTON BEACH: The self-proclaimed "Surf City, U.S.A." (and home to the International Surfing Museum) hosts competitions year-round (winter is best for wave height). Surfboards and wet suits may be rented or purchased; *www.surfcityusa.com.*

Huntington City Beach is a 3.5-mile stretch of sand fronting the town and is a popular place for swimming, bodysurfing, and beach volleyball. The pier provides an ideal spot for fishing and a good vantage point for observing the passing scene. For surf information, call 714-536-9303; *www.hbonline.com.*

Bolsa Chica Wetlands, 1,449 acres of Pacific Ocean marshland a mile north of Huntington Beach pier on Pacific Coast Highway, harbors fish and wetland birds. To get there, cross the bridge from the beach parking lot and follow a trail through the marsh; 714-846-1114; *www.bolsachica.org.*

LAGUNA BEACH: More than 20 different beaches and coves line this seven-mile coastline, popular

with surfers, kayakers, body boarders, and snorkelers. Laguna is one of the best spots in Orange County to scuba dive, though you need a wet suit year-round.

Laguna Sea Sports (925 N. Coast Hwy.; 949-494-6965; *www.beachcitiesscuba.com*) offers full rentals, guided beach dives, classes, general information, and more; there's a pool on the premises, and it's only two blocks from the beach. Main Beach (which is located in the middle of town) offers basketball and volleyball.

A short walk away, Heisler Park has picnic areas, beaches, cliff-top lookout points, benches, and charcoal grills; stairs lead to tide pools. Serious hikers like to head for the Aliso and Wood Canyons Wilderness Park (*www.ocparks.com*), the Crystal Cove State Park (*www.crystalcovestatepark.org*), or the Laguna Coast Wilderness Park. Watch the sun set from Laguna Art Museum or Laguna Village; *www.lagunabeach.com*.

FISHING

In Orange County, you can cast for bass, catfish, and trout in tranquil lakes; troll the Pacific for bonitos, barracuda, halibut, and more; and hand-scoop grunions (license required) off the beach.

GRUNION ALERT: One scenic place to try your hand—literally—at catching grunion (provided that you have a license) is at Cabrillo Beach in March, June, July, and August, when the tiny fish come ashore to lay eggs in the sand and then head back out to sea on outgoing waves. (Grunion catching is illegal—even if you have a fishing license—in April and May.)

Know that grunion are notoriously slippery, and you are required to catch them exclusively with your hands; fortunately, they also shimmer in the moonlight, so they're fairly easy to spot. The best time to go grunion fishing is about an hour or two after high tide on the second through fifth nights after a new or full moon. The park closes at 10 P.M.; gates close at 9 P.M. For additional information, visit *www.wildlife.ca.gov*, or call 831-649-2870.

SPORTFISHING: Fishing boats set out from Davey's Locker at Balboa Pavilion in Newport Beach (949-673-1434; *www.daveyslocker.com*) and from Dana Wharf Sportfishing at Dana Point Harbor (888-224-0603). Reservations are suggested. Licenses, which are legally necessary for deep-sea sportfishing, must be purchased

in advance via *https://www.wildlife.ca.gov/Licensing/Online-Sales*. Fishing licenses cost about $16 per day.

PARKS

IRVINE REGIONAL PARK: Located in Santiago Canyon, near Irvine Lake, this peaceful place has hiking and equestrian trails that wind through 491 hilly acres and centuries-old sycamores and oaks. The oldest county park in California, it offers bike trails, the Orange County Zoo, playgrounds, a small waterfall, creek, and picnic facilities. Zoo admission is $2 for guests age 3 and up. There is a $3 to $5 parking fee per vehicle year-round (the parking fee is usually $7 to $10 on major holidays). 1 Irvine Park Rd., Orange; 714-973-6835; *www.ocparks.com*.

MILE SQUARE REGIONAL PARK: It's one square mile in area—hence the name. Besides five miles of winding bike trails, the park has a walking course, a nature area, and picnic areas and shelters. Bicycles may be rented here on weekends and holidays. 16801 Euclid Street, Fountain Valley; *www.ocparks.com*; 714-973-6600.

TUCKER WILDLIFE SANCTUARY: This 12-acre sanctuary in the Santa Ana Mountains' Modjeska Canyon is an oasis of flora and fauna. Naturalists are there to answer questions, and there are hiking trails, a small natural history museum, and a sensory garden. A donation is suggested. 29322 Modjeska Canyon Rd., Modjeska Canyon; *www.tuckerwildlife.org*; 714-649-2760.

YORBA REGIONAL PARK: These 140 acres in the Santa Ana Canyon cradle four lakes (with connecting streams), picnic areas, playgrounds, hiking trails, equestrian activities, horseshoe pits, model sailboating, volleyball courts, baseball fields, and biking trails (bike rentals on weekends). Visitors can walk or ride a bicycle into the park without charge; parking costs $3 to $5 ($7 to $10 on holidays). 7600 E. La Palma Ave., Anaheim; *www.ocparks.com*; 714-973-6615.

WHALE WATCHING & DOLPHIN CRUISES

Whale watching and dolphin cruises leave from Newport Beach daily throughout the year. You may see giant blue whales, finback whales, gray whales, humpback whales, minke whales, and even several species of dolphins. Birnbaum's readers net a discount on weekday ($14 per person) and weekend ($22 per person) cruises with promo code disney18. Other types of cruises available as well. Call 949-673-1434 or visit *www.daveyslocker.com*.

Index

COUPONS

arribas brothers

10% OFF

ENTIRE PURCHASE

Offering authentic Disney collectibles, exquisite crystal mementos, and sparkling hand-blown glass gifts.

Subject to terms and conditions on reverse side.

BREWERY AND KITCHEN

10% OFF FOOD

(Excludes alcohol)

Subject to terms and conditions on reverse side.

10% OFF

ENTIRE PURCHASE

Premium brand surf apparel, women's fashion, swimwear, accessories, and goods for the entire family!

Subject to terms and conditions on reverse side.

BUY ONE DOG, GET SECOND DOG FREE

Subject to terms and conditions on reverse side.

15% OFF

ENTIRE PURCHASE

Subject to terms and conditions on reverse side.

KAYLA'S CAKE

Inspired Artisan Delicacies

10% OFF

ENTIRE PURCHASE

Delectable French macarons and cake in a jar. Visit our kiosk in the *Downtown Disney*® District near the World of Disney store.

Subject to terms and conditions on reverse side.

TERMS AND CONDITIONS

Offer valid at *Downtown Disney*® District Anaheim location only.

Does not include Pura Vida Jewelry.

Cannot be combined with other offers or discounts.

Not valid on sale items or gift cards.

Reproductions of coupon not accepted.

Must surrender coupon at time of purchase.

No cash value in whole or in part.

Offer subject to change without notice.

(714) 635-8400

Offer valid through 12/31/20

TERMS AND CONDITIONS

Valid on full-price merchandise in the *Downtown Disney*® District Anaheim store only and excludes alcohol.

Coupon must be surrendered at time of purchase.

Not valid with any other offers, discounts, or promotions.

Coupon has no cash value.

Photocopies will not be accepted.

Non-transferable, non-negotiable.

Limit one coupon per transaction.

Offer subject to change without notice.

For information, call (714) 490-0233.

Offer valid through 12/31/20

TERMS AND CONDITIONS

Offer valid at *Downtown Disney*® District Anaheim location only.

Cannot be combined with other offers or discounts.

Not valid on sale items or gift cards.

Reproductions of coupon not accepted.

Must surrender coupon at time of purchase.

No cash value in whole or in part.

Offer subject to change without notice.

www.sugarbooandco.com

Expires 12/31/20

This offer is valid on Compact through Midsize size vehicles reserved in advance for travel 10/1/2019 through 12/31/2020 at participating locations in the U.S. and Canada. Vehicle must be returned by 01/31/2021. Reservations must be made at least 24 hours in advance of scheduled pick-up time. A minimum one-day rental is required, and a 27-day maximum applies. For more information, including an estimate of your total rental cost, visit our Internet website at *www.alamo.com* or *www.alamo.ca*. This offer cannot be combined with any other discount and cannot be applied to a previous or existing reservation or rental. Alamo reserves the right to terminate the offer or change the terms at any time. Offer is subject to vehicle availability at the time of booking. Renter and additional driver(s) must meet standard age, driver and credit requirements. Please check your auto insurance policy and/or credit card agreement for rental vehicle coverage. Other restrictions, including holiday and blackout dates, may apply. Non-transferable. Void where prohibited.

TERMS AND CONDITIONS

Redeemable at *Downtown Disney*® District in Anaheim, California.

Coupon must be surrendered at time of purchase.

Not valid with any other offers or discounts.

Offer subject to change without notice.

Limit one per coupon.

For information, call (714) 535-5994.

Photocopies will not be accepted.

Non-transferable, non-negotiable.

Offer valid through 12/31/20

Say *"VOID FAN"* at check-in to receive 10% off your ticket purchase and a free digital photo of your experience.
1 photo per party. Valid only at the *Downtown Disney*® District Anaheim location.

One photo per coupon per party with ticket purchase.

All guests must be 48" (122 cm) or taller and age 10 or older.

Guests are required to sign a liability waiver. Parent or guardian's signature required if 18 or under.

Advance reservations recommended.

Coupon cannot be combined with any other offers.

Reproduction of coupon not accepted.

Must surrender coupon at time of purchase.

Coupon not redeemable for cash in whole or in part.

Other restrictions may apply.
Offer subject to change without notice.

Book Tickets Now!
www.thevoid.com
Expires 12/31/20